MY TRIAL
A Star Special

In itself a unique event, the publication of John Stone-house's MY TRIAL marks the conclusion of a remarkable story which began more than a year and a half ago, with the author's disappearance from a Miami beach. His subsequent arrest in Australia, the extradition proceedings, his frustrated attempts to make a personal statement in the House of Commons, the monumental difficulties in obtaining bail, the committal proceedings, and the historic trial at the Old Bailey – all have involved John Stonehouse at the very heart of a world from which he took such pains to escape. The modus operandi of the police and our political machine, the power of the media, the stringent system of law, have served to underline his conviction that for him idealism is dead.

His recent single-minded commitment to writing MY TRIAL, despite imprisonment in Brixton Prison since the case for the defence began, is a mark of Stonehouse's total dedication to expose the predicament as he sees it, of the Individual struggling for survival against the establishment.

A remarkable achievement, MY TRIAL stands alone in publishing history. It does not purport to be a transcript of the trial, although the reader is taken through the scene as it happened. That one is biased to one's cause is tautological; that MY TRIAL is John Stonehouse's *own* book is the substance of its impact.

The very fast publication of MY TRIAL would not have been possible without the kind co-operation and efficiency of the printers.

MY TRIAL

John Stonehouse

A STAR BOOK

Published by
WYNDHAM PUBLICATIONS

A Star Book
Published in 1976
by Wyndham Publications Ltd.
A Howard and Wyndham Company
123, King Street, London W6 9JG

Copyright © John Stonehouse, 1976

Printed in Great Britain by
The Anchor Press Ltd, Tiptree, Essex

ISBN 0 352 39749 7

MY TRIAL

My early life was rich in experiences: assistant in a Probation office at sixteen, forming an organisation called 'Citizens of Tomorrow' at seventeen, enlisting in the Royal Air Force and training as a pilot during the Second World War and, as an ex-serviceman, joining the throng of students from all over the world at the London School of Economics and Political Science. By the time I was twenty-five I had fought three elections – one for the London County Council and two for Parliament. It was a time of hope and idealism and after missing election as MP for the Burton constituency by a mere 700 votes, I was soon enmeshed in a new interest and one of deep concern: the emergence of the repressed colonies in Africa.

With my young family I went to Uganda to work for the African Co-operative Movement. It was the start of an association with the cause of the newly-developing countries which was to absorb much of my energies during my subsequent political career. After my return to England I was elected for the Wednesbury constituency at a by-election in 1957 and soon was busy in the Movement for Colonial Freedom. Within two years I had been expelled from Rhodesia for advocating democratic partnership between blacks and whites and wrote a book on the experience called *Prohibited Immigrant* (Bodley Head, 1960). I also took an active interest in developing the Co-operative Movement in Britain and became a director and then president of the largest retail co-op in the world: the London Co-operative Society. But I fell foul of Communist opponents and spent all my resources on co-op campaigning. I was glad to get out of Co-op politics to become a Minister in the first Labour Government of Harold Wilson, which had been elected with a wafer-thin majority in 1964.

For six years I was promoted through a series of posts:

Junior Minister of Aviation under Roy Jenkins, to Under-Secretary of State for the Colonies and then Minister of Aviation, Minister of State for Technology, Postmaster General and finally Minister of Posts and Telecommunications, after I had guided the Act through Parliament to set up the Post Office Corporation. My work as a Minister had been completely absorbing: responsibility for the negotiations on Concorde, organising sales of aircraft and electronics worth hundreds of millions to Saudi Arabia and other countries, leading missions to the U.S.S.R. and U.S.A., and signing technological agreements in Czechoslovakia and Australia.

After Labour's defeat I felt dispirited by the humbug of political life and decided to re-charge my batteries – and repair my financial position, which was badly depleted – by setting up an export consultancy. I thought it would be patriotic to use my skills in promoting British exports. I kept up my political work and my seat in Parliament, moving after small boundary changes to the constituency of Walsall North.

Then a dramatic event broke on the international scene. West Pakistan started a brutal military action against the Bengalees in East Pakistan. The killings and the rapings were ghastly and ten million people fled for their lives as refugees to India. I was asked to go out on a fact finding mission for War on Want and Oxfam. As a result of numerous visits I became totally wedded to the cause of an independent Bangladesh. In the House of Commons I recruited much support; I spoke in Trafalgar Square and on American Television for the campaign. Eventually after international pressure had made its mark, India intervened to help the Bengali guerrillas defeat the Pakistani army. Bangladesh emerged as a nation and, uniquely, made me a citizen in recognition of my work.

When soon afterwards, a group of Bengalis in England approached me to help them set up a Bank to create a bridge between Britain and Bangladesh, I responded by becoming the unpaid Chairman. It was part of my continuing mission. But a series of attacks – partly from hostile Pakistani elements – undermined the project and I found myself engaged in the hideous task of trying to save the Institution against attempts to destroy it. To make matters much worse the secondary banking system collapsed and we had to contend with those general economic problems as well as everything else.

I threw all my personal resources into the enterprise to try to save it but in the process broke myself. And by this time – 1974 – my disillusionment with British politics had grown more intense. As far as politics was concerned I was a sensitive idealist increasingly engaged in a game of sham.

The pressures became too great and, after a series of minor breakdowns, I eventually broke completely away from the Stonehouse burdens on 20th November, 1974 at Miami Beach. I was reborn as a simple, uncluttered Joe Markham, able to live and breathe again as an ordinary person. Markham went to Hawaii and, in a confused telephone call, contacted the one person in Stonehouse's world who could instinctively understand his breakdown and help him. Suicide was ever near if Markham was forced, too soon, to return to the tortured Stonehouse shell and this, Sheila Buckley, his lover and secretary, could grasp as she more than anyone could understand his deep anguish. It was a terrible burden on her as the man telephoning from across the world was clearly disembodied and obviously unwilling to acknowledge that Stonehouse was alive. Her love was the one and only link with the past.

Markham wandered in a daze to Australia, to Copenhagen and back to Melbourne via Moscow and Singapore; then into another personality – Clive Mildoon – whilst still retaining the links with Markham. It was a journey into schizophrenia. His conduct was erratic and foolish and before long the Victoria State police put him under surveillance, thinking he might be the missing Lord Lucan. On Christmas Eve, 1974, Markham/ Mildoon was arrested as an illegal immigrant and the world of Stonehouse was thrust back into the reluctant shell of my body.

Then followed an even worse torture. The media, oppressive and bullying in their gross insensitivity, pursued me everywhere, as well as my wife who had come to join me in Melbourne. Likewise Sheila Buckley had no respite and also escaped from the rigours of the media to Australia where she went to stay with old friends in Sydney. I wanted peace and tranquillity to complete a recovery but that was not to be.

Moves were made to expel me from the House of Commons and when these failed, authority was given for charges to be laid against me.

From Christmas Eve, when I had sent a telegram to the Prime Minister explaining I had suffered a breakdown, no one in Parliament or the British Government attempted to help me. I was condemned in the media and in most people's minds on a one-sided and jaundiced account of what had happened to me.

The writing of *Death of a Idealist* (W. H. Allen, London 1975), completed in April, helped me greatly to re-emerge from my traumas. But then a new pressure was being applied; my long trial on criminal charges – of which this book is my account – began on 21st March 1975. I have no idea when it will end; my only wish in writing this volume is to record the facts of the case and my feelings as the story develops. And writing might help me to survive the ordeal, although nothing could be as bad as the experiences I have already suffered.

Having felt the anguish of involvement in the problems of others I make only one request of the reader. Do not suffer with me, please just read this book out of interest in a real life adventure story.

JOHN STONEHOUSE

PART ONE

The Arrest

CHAPTER ONE

On a typically Australian autumnal day in March, I was sitting alone in the lounge of a small rented 'unit' on the Toorak Road in the Melbourne suburb of Hawthorne, reading a copy of *Time* magazine. My wife, Barbara, and son, Mathew – nearly fifteen years old – were out at the shops. For a few days I had felt some respite from the pressures of the previous year. Although I had not achieved the peace and tranquillity which were essential to my full recovery from a traumatic breakdown, the daily harassment had – at least – appeared to cease. The situation, it seemed, could only get better. The events of the previous few months had been truly awful.

In November: complete breakdown after the years of increasingly harrowing tension had finally claimed their victim. In December: apprehension as an illegal immigrant by the Australian authorities. In January: the constant pressure from reporters, who attempted to follow me and harass me everywhere, and the pouring out by the 'popular' media of a stream of distorted stories, designed by the editors to confirm the readers' impression that I was an ogre of the Western World. In February: the official Department of Trade Inquiry which had me under intense grilling for over a week, although I was obviously still a sick man.

But then things began to improve. The Australian Minister for Immigration announced in the Australian House of Representatives that he had been told by the British High Commissioner that no charges were contemplated by the U.K. authorities. That had been no more than I had expected as it seemed to me there were no criminal acts for which I had been responsible and I believed that proceedings against me would not be justified. That clamour in the press had certainly built up a climate of opinion against me: many of the articles had blatantly condemned me for crimes which the journalists, for the sake of exciting copy, had written into their lurid stories. However, I had remained confident that – in England at any rate –

3

trial by media was not a feature of justice. The British authorities, after all, had full access to the facts. They would, I thought, have realised that I had been terribly ill and that there was no rational – nor criminal – explanation for my bizarre action in adopting another personality and 'freaking out'. The Australian Department of Health had, indeed, reported to Australian Ministers that I had suffered a breakdown and it had been on these grounds of my ill-health – and no other – that Ministers had then denied me permission to remain as an immigrant.

Agitation against me in the House of Commons was influenced by three main factors: firstly, outraged indignation that a person who had held high office should suffer a breakdown as a result of his disillusionment with the political system which most others accepted; secondly, that this breakdown should take the form it did which, they felt, would bring them into disrepute if they did not roundly and publicly condemn it; and thirdly, the wish to cast out the heretic with all possible speed so the complex and disturbing issues raised by his experience would not have to be faced. Some Members wanted me expelled without any more ado.

In reply to such reckless attacks on the independence of a Member of Parliament, I had written a long article for the *Daily Telegraph* spelling out the consequences to Parliamentary democracy of hasty action. For an MP to be expelled simply because he had suffered adverse press publicity would be a most damaging precedent, I argued. Also for a Member to be expelled because he was sick would be as ludicrous and unjust. After all, many sick Members had been absent for far longer periods than I had been and none of them had been expelled.

The *Daily Telegraph* had given the article front-page prominence, which was most unusual – if not unique – for an outside contributor. Predictably its arguments had a profound effect on the Select Committee which decided it would not do what the Chief Whip had requested and it could not recommend that I should be expelled. Instead it proposed to mark time on the issue and not rush into any conclusions.

I heard of the Select Committee's decision on Monday, 17 March. It was a great relief. I was fully intending to return to Westminster as soon as I was fit enough – and had in fact told the Select Committee just that. An expulsion without my case being heard would have been the height of injustice and an unhealthy precedent. But any relief was short-lived; for as soon as the fact became known that I was staying on as a Member of Parliament, moves were made by the British authorities to get rid of me by other means. The blow hit me on 21st March with a knock at the door of the unit. Later at the Extradition Proceedings in the Melbourne Magistrates' Court, Detective Inspector Robert Gillespie of the Australian Commonwealth police gave his account of what happened:

'Mr. Stonehouse said, "Hello, Bob, come on in." We walked into his unit and I said, "You know me, I am Detective Inspector Gillespie, this is Detective Inspector Craig, and you know Detective Senior Sergeant Coffey?" He said, "Yes." I said, "I have here with me a warrant for the arrest of John Thomson Stonehouse." I then read the contents of the warrant to Mr. Stonehouse and I said, "Are you the person, John Thomson Stonehouse, mentioned in this warrant?" He said, "Yes." I said, "I am now arresting you by virtue of this warrant." I said, "I now warn you that you are not obliged to answer any questions or make any statement, as anything you say or any statement you may make may be used in evidence. Do you clearly understand that?" He said, "Yes. I don't wish to make a statement. Can I ring my solicitor?" I said, "Yes, by all means." Mr. Stonehouse then telephoned Mr. Patterson, his solicitor, and I also spoke to Mr. Patterson and arranged to meet him at the Commonwealth Police Headquarters a short time later. I then said to Mr. Stonehouse, "Do you have any documents which may be relevant to the charges mentioned in this warrant?" He said, "No." I said, "Do you mind if we search your premises?" Mr. Stonehouse said, "No, not until I have seen my solicitor, or unless you have a search warrant." Shortly after this time Mrs. Stonehouse and Mr. Stonehouse's son Mathew arrived back at the unit and Mr. Stonehouse said, "Is it all right if I speak with my wife?" I said, "Yes, but I will have to accompany you as you are in custody." I then accompanied he and Mrs. Stonehouse to the bedroom where they had a whispered conversation, and he later had a shave and went to a drawer in the bedroom near the bed, and I there noticed documents in his drawer in the name of Markham. I said, "I deem that those documents would be relevant to the subject matter of the charges mentioned in this warrant. Would you like to examine them with me?" He said, "No, I do not intend to examine anything unless my solicitor is present." I said, "By virtue of this warrant I intend to seize these documents".'

The police officers seized every piece of paper they could lay their hands on. Mathew, who was in the lounge, even saw Inspector Craig looking behind pictures on the wall in the vain search for hidden material.

In cross-examination by the defence lawyer Mr. James Patterson, Detective Inspector Gillespie revealed that he had received a telephone call from Chief Superintendent Etheridge of Scotland Yard at 5.20 a.m. on the morning of the arrest and that two hours later a telex message arrived. It included the instruction to seize all property belonging to me. There was no reference in the telex to the necessity to ensure the relevance of the property to the charges. It was all to go.

Protests were made that the officers were taking all the copies of chapters of a book I was writing, but to no avail. They were still seized. Gillespie acknowledged that copies were made and passed to Etheridge of the Yard. It is not without significance that one of the chapters concerned detailed allegations against Scotland Yard from over a year before and which events had contributed heavily to my eventual breakdown.

The telex message was also revealing in another aspect. It gave instructions that bail was to be refused. But at the hearing in the Melbourne Court my solicitor made great play with this advice from twelve thousand miles away. 'The Bow Street Magistrate and Scotland Yard don't seem to be aware that Australia is now an independent country and cannot be instructed on the matter of bail,' he said. It raised a titter in court – not least with the magistrate who commented that I had been in the country three months and had been no threat to Australia.

Bail was granted but from that time I was effectively locked into the processes of law. It is, as I was to discover, a lengthy and constricting process.

CHAPTER TWO

Within a few days of my own arrest, a reporter rang me from Adelaide to say his London office had telephoned the news that a warrant had been issued in Bow Street for the arrest of Sheila Buckley. I was thunderstruck. It was – in a way – understandable for Scotland Yard to go to whatever lengths were necessary to pursue charges against me. But to prosecute Mrs. Buckley struck me as impossibly vindictive.

Since her arrival in Australia in February, Mrs. Buckley had stayed with friends in Sydney. Her wish in leaving England was to escape the harassments from reporters to which she had been subject for nearly three months. Apart from some disagreeable incidents just after her arrival in Australia, she had succeeded in staying well away from the press. They had tried to track her down but had completely failed. In fact she had been living quietly in Cronulla, just outside Sydney, first with the family of a long-standing boyfriend, who had met her years before when staying in London, and latterly with a girlfriend in a lovely house overlooking a tranquil bay. It must have been idyllic while it lasted.

Whilst I tried to make more enquiries, I got my daughter Jane to ring Sheila to tell her what was coming. She could apparently hardly believe her ears and was even more thunderstruck than I was. When, in January, she had been staying in a Cornish farmhouse with her aunt to escape the attentions of the British press, the police arranged a special meeting at an Exeter motel bedroom so they could interview her. Around that time they had, in fact, seen most of my previous associates. They did not give her warning that charges might be laid and she therefore had no fears of any prosecution. It was quite unthinkable. Her visit to Australia was coming to an end within a few days as she had decided to return to London before the air fares were increased. Apart from what she regarded as the likelihood of any prosecution in itself, she could not fathom why Scotland Yard should want tedious extradition proceedings when she was returning anyway to London under her own steam. Sheila was learning, as so many had before her, that when the long arm of the police is stretching out to claim a victim, there is little commonsense or rationality about its grabbing.

We realised that if the police contacted her in New South Wales she would be subject to the extradition proceedings in that State. We therefore decided that she should travel to Melbourne so my solicitor, Jim Patterson, could represent her at joint proceedings within the State of Victoria. I checked with Jim and he agreed. As soon as she arrived he would take her to the local police station to report. It would avoid a lot of agitation to do that.

Sheila, who had been due to go to a play at the Royal Shakespearean Theatre that evening, dropped the bombshell on her friends that she had to make a personal appearance at another but totally unexpected show. Her boyfriend immediately left work to drive her in his Volkswagen the six hundred miles to Melbourne. To attempt to fly would be risky as the ever-persistent press hounds could have seen her at the airport and blown up an erroneous story that she was trying to flee.

By dusk they had reached a small town near the State border and they decided to stay overnight. They were not to know that all Australia's police forces had been alerted to look out for them. Fortunately, they were not located and crossed the border next day into Victoria. It would take them most of the day to drive to Melbourne and the plan was agreed that as soon as they were near enough they would telephone Jim Patterson with the news of their arrival and he would guide them from there.

We knew it would be lunacy for Sheila to telephone the 'unit' where I was staying as the line was certainly bugged. All my calls to Sydney had been made from a call-box to avoid detection. For some reason the Australian police were obsessed with keeping me under surveillance. No doubt it was under pressure from Scotland Yard who, by this time, were again represented in Australia by two senior officers. They had been thwarted in their attempts to put me immediately into

9

gaol by denying bail and tried to justify their stance on that issue by having me followed everywhere. Even when I was driving my son Mathew to the local grammar school, the plain-clothes agents would follow. Sheila and I had agreed therefore, we would not attempt to meet before she had herself reported to the police in Melbourne.

That night my family had a date with Peter Game's family to go together to see the Agatha Christie film *Murder on the Orient Express.* Peter was – and is – the most eminent reporter on the *Melbourne Herald* and had been extremely kind to Mathew. We had discussed the arrangements for the evening on the telephone and what happened later was to confirm the existence of bugging.

As soon as my wife, Mathew and Jane drove out of the driveway to our little 'unit', the police car pulled in behind and kept the regulation distance on the trip into town. Just to be awkward I decided to lose the 'tail' by getting into a traffic jam and suddenly doubling back along the clear roads before the other car could follow. It necessitated a long diversion but we made it on time to the cinema. To our amazement the policeman who had been following us was waiting in the foyer, having driven straight to the rendezvous point he had overhead on my telephone.

For me the real-life drama going on outside somewhere in New South Wales or the lower reaches of Victoria, was more dramatic than the adventures portrayed by Albert Finney and Ingrid Bergman. I skipped the film several times to telephone Jim to try to get news. He had none. I also telephoned a sympathetic police officer, and discovered that his evening plans to celebrate his daughter's birthday were being dislocated. Let me give you some advice, he said surprisingly, she should not come in by the Princes Highway route – the usual and most direct from Sydney – as the road was being watched. By this time the police had been told by Jim Patterson that he would be bringing Sheila in to see them on the following day. Why they had gone to elaborate lengths to intercept her was puzzling, unless it was the old story that the force does not like to appear to be outwitted.

Later that evening Sheila and her friend were apprehended

in a little town on the southern route to Melbourne – the Volkswagen had been followed soon after Sheila had put a telephone call through to Jim Patterson. It seemed that in their efforts to intercept the vehicle, even the solicitor's telephone was tapped. Clearly the Victoria State police took the whole challenge more seriously than the Ronald Biggs episode. They let the Great Train robber get away, but no expense or effort was spared in arresting Sheila Buckley, although the authorities were well aware that she was on her way to report.

The State police put out a press statement claiming credit for her arrest and added that they had information that I was planning to meet her secretly on the outskirts of Melbourne. That was plain peppycock and the police knew it as they had me under close surveillance at the cinema and at a Chinese meal afterwards. Peter Game, as an experienced journalist, had been amused to pick out the plain-clothes detectives at the adjoining table.

This press statement was not the first or last experience of the sinister liaison between police and press to print stories damaging to the defendants so as to put them in a bad light with the public – and magistrates.

Sheila was subjected to the indignity of spending a sleepless night in a filthy cell at the old decrepit Melbourne Watchhouse, but not before the press had been enabled to take their prized photographs of the hunted girl, under guard, just in time for the last editions of the morning papers. The so called processes of justice had already shown themselves to be a circus.

We heard later that the two Scotland Yard officers had flown from Melbourne to Sydney to arrest Sheila there. As the airline stewards were on strike they could not go by regular service and had to hire a light aircraft. This delayed their arrival and enabled Sheila and her friend to get away. The police turned the two houses where she had stayed upside down in a vain search for 'evidence'. Even the barbecue ashes were raked over.

The legal machine grinds very slowly. It was not until 5th May – weeks after the arrest – that the prosecution opened the case for extradition. On that day they proposed an adjournment for another three weeks. We would be well into the Australian winter before the hearing was underway.

It should be emphasised at this point that there is no way a defendant can speed up extradition proceedings, or indeed any other case, unless he makes a deal with the prosecution which often undermines his defence. Deals are often made between opposing counsel without any proper reference to the defendant himself. Such arrangements are to be avoided like the plague. Defendants should always be aware of professional advisers who claim to be acting 'in the client's best interests'. Fortunately, my solicitor, who was also a qualified barrister would never have entertained any proposal for a deal. He was adamant that the charges and the extradition proceedings should be opposed in the strongest possible way. As an ex-policeman, who had taken up a defence practice after years on 'the other side', he knew the tricks of prosecuting authorities better than most.

We had agreed that if, as he hoped, the extradition attempt could be thrown out, I should travel to England as a free man. Sheila would also return to England if her case was thrown out. It would demonstrate that we had nothing to fear from the charges and, indeed, would have already travelled to London if Scotland Yard had quietly informed us that charges were in any way contemplated.

The first day of the hearing opened in a tiny courtroom with the British and Australian press corps spilling onto the front benches, supposedly reserved for the accused. The senior magistrate, Mr. C. J. Thompson, presided; he was apprehensive, for never had a case in his court attracted so much world publicity. We were to discover to our surprise that Australian (or at least Victorian State) stipendiary magistrates are not legally qualified. They are appointed from the ranks of court clerks and have to depend on prosecuting counsel to guide them on legal matters. It is no wonder that over the years they become imbued in the ways – and attitudes – of the police and seldom show the independence of which the English stipendiaries are capable from time to time.

The first day was taken up with legal points which the magistrate could not properly follow. Jim Patterson and George Hampel, representing Sheila Buckley, both argued that under Victoria State law, a separate warrant had to accompany each indictment or 'information'. There were twenty-one charges against me and under Section 18 (3) of the Justices Act, it was wrong to include them under one warrant. The provision was designed by the State legislators as a protection against the prosecution pushing in unauthorised charges.

To this the magistrate said: 'Surely what should govern here is what the procedure is which can be adopted – surely in England, not the procedures here. If they have a number of informations here on a warrant, surely that is what it should be judged by, not what can be done here.'

If the reader should think that the most convoluted and confusing statement ever made in a court of law, he is wrong. Mr. Thompson surpassed himself that afternoon in his summing up, as we shall soon see. Jim Patterson, an Englishman turned patriotic Australian, responded with a phrase which put the matter in a nutshell and with contrasting clarity:

'With respect, sir, in our submission this is not the true situation. What we say is this, that it is not for these courts to comply with the courts of England, it is for England to comply with our courts.'

His Worship, taken aback: 'Perhaps we can discuss this later.'

After a great deal of argument and quotation of cases by defence counsel, and after the adjournment for lunch, the magistrate made his ruling on the disputed point of law. It bears repeating in full as a triumph in obfuscation:

'It is a matter, perhaps not an easy matter to decide. I think at this stage I say that in my opinion there are more offences – do not invalidate the proceedings here. I think it would be open to me of the procedure in the case to say what cases there were sufficient evidence to justify the extradition of either of the defendants here.'

The learned magistrate wagged his head gravely as he gave the ruling, thus indicating in gestures if not in words, that the defence lawyers had lost. At this point most of the reporters had given up for the day and gone home or on to more rewarding – and understandable – stories.

13

CHAPTER THREE

In legal proceedings it has become the technique of any prosecution to spin a spider's web with the evidence and then to try to enmesh the defendant securely in that web. The defence, in its turn, must try to knock holes in the evidence so a way out appears for the defendant. It is a game for professionals in which ploy is followed by counter-ploy. My lawyers in Melbourne had a well-nigh impossible task to break the web as the stacks of depositions, brought out in heavy bundles from London, could not be questioned in any way. None of the witnesses in Britain could be brought to Melbourne for cross-examination and the British authorities had refused my solicitor's request to be allowed to travel to London to question them there. Furthermore, Australian witnesses heard in Melbourne could not be compelled to travel to Britain to appear in the eventual proceedings, if the extradition application succeeded.

The defence is put at a decided disadvantage by this situation and the two defending counsel decided to pursue that very valid legal point in an attempt to strengthen their position.

The prosecution counsel, a portly Australian barrister by the name of Mr. James, would not concede an inch in these arguments; the magistrate ruled in his favour. Defence lawyers then indicated that they would contest the ruling by presenting a 'writ of prohibition' so the point could be contested at the High Court for the State of Victoria.

Sitting on the front seats of that tiny court, listening to the lawyers during the development of these extraordinarily complex proceedings, I felt as if I was slowly sinking into a legal bog. From my own point of view I wanted a speedy end to the court hearings so I could fly back to Westminster. Naturally I hoped to win the case against extradition and then return to London as a free man, and with dignity. For five weeks I had been under restraint in the State of Victoria, forbidden, under the bail conditions, from venturing one foot out of the State. But the lengthy delays in proceedings irked me; I could see my hopes of throwing out the case within a few days, as I had hoped, becoming extremely remote.

I therefore instructed my lawyer to propose to the prosecution that the extradition case against me should be withdrawn so I could fly forthwith to London. Such an arrangement would be tantamount to extradition, as the Scotland Yard officers could fly with me all the way. As I would be without a passport I could not possibly leave the plane en route. The world's press would ensure I was kept under close surveillance even if the escorting policemen did not. It seemed a sensible suggestion. The expense of the extradition hearings would be saved and the Director of Public Prosecutions would have achieved his purpose of getting me back to England, where, of course, I could be charged with whatever offences he chose as soon as the plane landed.

During the adjournment there were discussions in the corridors whilst everyone else, particularly the press, who never realised what was going on, waited in the courtroom, getting increasingly perplexed. Finally the answer came back: the prosecution would agree to my proposal provided Mrs. Buckley also agreed to return. But her counsel was adamant that she should not do this; I agreed that his advice, which she accepted, was sound. She was just as anxious to get back to England as I was and would do so just as soon as she had won her case against extradition. Her counsel was convinced that she would win her case as the evidence against her was threadbare.

The prosecution had thrown in the sinister 'conspiracy' charge against us – an offence which still carries the possible sentence of life imprisonment; it was done, as in so many other conspiracy cases, to enable them to bring in extraneous detail which has nothing to do with the real charges. It was essential for their purposes that the cases against Sheila Buckley and John Stonehouse were run parallel at all stages. The prosecution knew that the defence had a powerful legal point to argue and that, in some circumstances, it could take a year or more to resolve in the Australian courts. Mrs. Buckley had no personal wish to remain in Australia for that long but the prosecution feared she might, and that would undermine their 'conspiracy' strategy. The Bonnie had to go with the Clyde; otherwise they might lose their best ploy in the campaign, which had been building up with the ready and willing co-operation of the British press.

I was learning fast that the processes of justice are labyrinthine: what appears simple to a layman becomes as tortuous as a three-dimensional chess game in the hands of counsel. The wisdom of Solomon cannot be applied because it might cut a way through the maze; the functions of lawyers as guides would then be rendered as superfluous as those of medieval alchemists. It is no wonder that most defendants in complex cases give up and leave it to the professionals. In my case I could not afford to. Another spider's web was being spun in another place twelve thousand miles away and it threatened to entrap me before I could even move to protect myself.

The 'Select Committee on the Right Honourable Member for Walsall North' had issued its second report just after the opening of the extradition proceedings on 5th May. The contents of the report were probably known to the prosecution at that time and may explain why they proposed an adjournment for three weeks. The report, in fact, recommended that a motion to expel me from the House of Commons would now be justified but that it should not be moved earlier than one month after publication of the report, to give me an opportunity to attend the House. The report was published on 6th May; I had until 6th June to get back to Westminster and the legal proceedings were adjourned until 26th May. Time was running out. I was caught in a *Catch 22* situation which might have been devised by Joseph Heller himself, for whatever I did would be wrong. If I left the jurisdiction of the Victoria Courts while the extradition proceedings were on, I would be arrested, but if I did not go to England within ten days I would be expelled as an MP. The situation was made all the more crazy by the fact that the extradition case had one object – and ostensibly one object only – which was to get me to England where I desperately wanted to go. It might be asked why had I not just accepted the prosecution case on the first day. That course was strenuously resisted by Jim Patterson, who was convinced of my innocence and wanted me to avoid any plea of guilty, however technical. He advised – and how right he was – that technical pleas have a habit of rebounding, particularly when they used by the prosecution to their advantage in other courts in other countries, far removed from the original circumstances of the plea.

Sitting in the court on 26th May, I could hardly believe my ears when I heard the prosecution counsel, Mr. James, proposing another adjournment of fourteen days. His proposal would take us to 9th June, well beyond the House of Commons deadline date.

My solicitor patiently explained that his client was anxious to return to England at short notice and suggested a delay of only three or four days; the magistrate was confused and could not understand why the prosecution was deliberately delaying the case, whilst the defence were trying to speed it up. It was a reversal of the usual roles. In retrospect it is clear to me that the prosecution may have been spinning out the adjournments so I would be expelled from the House of Commons in my absence. It seems to me that the issue raises the question of whether the Executive was using the power of Government to get rid of an awkward and embarrassing Member of Parliament. It was a desperate situation for me and called for desperate action. I appealed to Harold Wilson, the Prime Minister, but only received an innocuous 'Dear John' in reply, avoiding the real issue.

As there was now no alternative, I had to petition Her Majesty the Queen. My submission, regrettably, ran to four thousand five hundred words; such inordinate length was demanded by the necessity of explaining the incredible series of spider's webs in which her Privy Councillor was caught. No court had found him guilty of any offence but for almost ten weeks he had been prevented – by court procedures – from attending Parliament. Now his nonattendance was being used as the excuse for his expulsion. It needed royal wisdom, or prerogative, to break that Gordian knot. If the Queen could not act, perhaps my very action would shock my fellow Parliamentarians into coming to their senses. The Government was anxious to get rid of me – of that there was no doubt – but the backbenchers should, I thought, have been jealous of the rights of Members against such cavalier – and totally illogical – treatment.

I had written to the Chairman of the Select Committee setting out my situation clearly and the petition, which I released, gave the date and time of a flight I would take to fly back to London if no action was taken to delay the moves in the House of Commons. Mr. Ted Short, the Lord President of the Council, meanwhile had announced that the debate on my expulsion would be held on 12th June.

Before attempting to catch the plane I attended the Melbourne Magistrates' Court to request a hearing on my extradition case so I could be allowed to leave Victoria. No leave was so given; the prosecution deliberately keeping away from the front of the court, so they would not be involved. The Scotland Yard officers were in the rear of the court as observers, but they made no move to help. One word from them could have stopped the extradition proceedings and enabled us all to fly to London without delay. But that simple course cannot have suited their purposes or presumably those of the British Government.

I made the appeal personally to avoid implicating my solicitor in my announced decision of taking the drastic step of removing myself from the jurisdiction of the court. The magistrate, who must have felt events were well out of his control, heard me frankly admit to an intention to desert the court and break my bail, as I was constrained to do by the higher duty I owed to Parliament.

When I arrived at Melbourne Tullamarine International Airport with my daughter Jane and son Mathew, who were also booked to fly, the press were there in force. Over a hundred were milling around, including the television crews, photographers and the microphone-clutching reporters from the numerous commercial radio stations. It was like something approaching bedlam but I managed to collect my boarding pass along with the several journalists who were hoping to travel with me. As no obstacles were put in my way by customs or immigration officials, I felt I had an even chance of getting away. Perhaps, I surmised, the British and Australian authorities had decided, in all the extraordinary circumstances, which were recently of their own creation, to allow the Gordian knot to be cut in this inspired way.

I was allowed to walk along, with Jane and Mathew, those last steps towards the British Airways' plane. But it was only a shortlived delight. Inspector Gillespie appeared, clutching a warrant for my arrest. My offence, as he read it out, was, 'Attempting to obstruct the course of justice', which was not a little odd as I was doing exactly what the prosecution were attempting to achieve: going back to England.

The authorities clearly could not allow anything so simple. It could only be done their way after still more tedious proceedings. Accordingly the police took me to the cells at the Watchtower to await a brief appearance in court – this time, as I was in custody, without my tie or comb, always removed from prisoners. The press were thus able to write a little colour into their despatches; I was said to look dishevelled. As I remained mute and did not request bail, the magistrate remanded me to Pentridge Prison.

My first taste of prison lasted four days. On the third day of the stay, during which time I had refused food and remained mute as a protest against the British Government's actions in forcing my expulsion, I heard the glad and surprising news that Ted Short had suddenly cancelled the debate on the proposal to expel me. At last I had gained one trick in the game.

CHAPTER FOUR

Early on the morning of Friday 13th June, I was escorted from Pentridge Prison to attend the resumed hearing of the extradition proceedings. I did not know whether I would be returning to prison that night; that would depend on the magistrate. Mr. James, for the prosecution, made his position clear at the opening of the court: 'My instructions are to oppose bail', he said. Those instructions could only have come from the British Attorney General as the Scotland Yard officers on the spot would hardly have taken responsibility for locking up a Privy Councillor, simply because he had petitioned the Queen and then tried to attend Parliament. As was to become clear later in the evolvement of the story, the prosecution's use of the bail weapon was ample confirmation to me of the political overtones in the case.

Jim Patterson briefly indicated that he would apply for bail at the appropriate time. To everyone's surprise the magistrate, at the end of the day's proceedings, granted it without any more ado. It was given on my own recognizance for $500 and a surety of $500. These were low figures and demonstrated that, however limited was the magistrate's legal training, he had firmly grasped the point that, whatever the prosecution might say, I had not really tried to 'obstruct the course of justice'.

During the adjournment both defence counsel had consulted leading lawyers about the complex jurisdictional points raised earlier. Legal aid was obtained for Mrs. Buckley on this aspect of the case, as the authorities recognised that it was a matter of wider political interest. No individual could, in the circumstances, be expected to bear the massive legal fees involved. As the dispute concerned relations between the States and the Commonwealth of Australia, the matter would have to be transferred from the Supreme Court of Victoria to the Supreme Court of Australia. It would take at least six months and possibly a year to resolve. The constitutional experts were already wetting their legal lips at the prospect.

However, their hopes were soon dashed; no such dispute can be argued unless the corpus is willing to be submitted to the ordeal. Sheila Buckley was most unhappy at the prospect of a long delay in Victoria and as I wanted to get back to the House of Commons as soon as possible, we both instructed counsel to drop the constitutional points. Jim Patterson was upset about our decision; he was convinced the prosecution would have lost the legal argument and that extradition would have been rejected. For me it would have been a hollow victory if I had been expelled as an MP in the meantime.

The court then turned to the hearing of witnesses. The prosecution had more than a dozen of them and the ritual took several days. First on the list was Detective Inspector John Sullivan of the Commonwealth police, a kindly and sympathetic man who had done his best to show humanity to the defendants, despite the rigours of the official machine which he served. He described the events of Christmas Eve 1974, when a man living in Melbourne under the names of Joseph Arthur Markham and Donald Clive Mildoon had been apprehended by the Victoria State police, and then passed to the custody of the Commonwealth police as a suspected illegal immigrant. Mr. James, for the prosecution, handed Inspector Sullivan a passport in the name of Markham, a birth certificate in the name of Mildoon and an international vaccination certificate in the name of Markham, and went on with his examination:

'After the recovery of those items, did you have a conversation with Mr. Stonehouse, Mr. Sullivan?'

'Yes, sir.'

'With the aid of your notes, would you tell His Worship what was said?'

'Yes, sir. I said, "What is your name?" He said, "John Thomson Stonehouse." I said, "What is your date of birth?" He said, "28th July, 1925, at Southampton, England." I said, "What is your occupation?" He said, "Member of Parliament, United Kingdom." I said, "What constituency do you represent?" He said, "Walsall North." I said, "When did you first enter Australia and where?" He said, "27th of November at Melbourne." I said, "How did you obtain entry to Australia?" He said, "I used a passport in the name of Markham." I then produced the British Passport number . . .'

Mr. James: 'That is the one you referred to?'

'That's the one I referred to. He appeared to examine it and I said, "How did you obtain this passport? Was that the one you used?" He said, "Yes. I obtained it by presenting a birth certificate in that name to the Passports Office in London." I said, "Was Markham a relation?" He said, "No relation, the man is deceased." I said, "How did you obtain the birth certificate?" He said, "By making an application for one at Somerset House, London."

'I said, "How did you know he was dead?" He said, "Through making enquiries at hospitals; I asked about persons who may have died who were in my age group." I said, "Is this the copy of the certificate you obtained?" I then produced the certified copy of an entry of birth already produced, Your Worship, in the name of Joseph Arthur Markham. He appeared to examine it and he said, "Yes, that is it."

'I said, "When you arrived at Melbourne Airport on the 27th November, 1974, did you present this passport to anyone?"

'He said, "Yes, to the immigration officers."

'I said, "You appreciate that you entered Australia by using a passport which had been obtained by a false representation?"

'He said, "Yes."

'I said, "Did you leave Australia on the following day?"

'He said, "Yes."

'I said, "Did you use this passport then?"

'He said, "Yes."

'I said, "How did you leave Australia?"

'He said, "By B.O.A.C. as I had arrived."

'I said, "Do you have any other passport?"

'He said, "No passport of my own. Mine was left at Miami Beach, U.S.A."

'I said, "Why did you obtain a passport in the name of Markham?"

22

'He said, "It was my wish to establish a new identity and to come to Australia in that name."

'I said, "Why was that?"

'He said, "I was subjected to a great deal of business and political pressure in England and I was also subject to blackmail by certain individuals. I felt I had to escape from them."

'I said, "What do you mean by the term 'blackmail'?"

'He said, "I helped to establish a bank at the invitation of the Bengali community. This was just after Bangladesh had emerged as a country. I had no wish for personal gain but I accepted the position as unpaid chairman to get the bank established. However, before the issue of shares a London newspaper, the *Sunday Times*, published an article which was damaging and that caused the issue of shares to be not as successful as we had hoped. In order to save the institution I had to put all my personal resources into it in the form of shares."

Mr. James: 'As far as your evidence is concerned, Mr. Sullivan, was that "to save the institution" or some other words that you used?'

'In order to save the institution.'

'I beg your pardon. Would you continue please?'

"Subsequently in the last year in England there has been a financial crisis and the smaller banks have collapsed. Our institution was no exception. It did not collapse but certain individuals took advantage of my position in the political world to put me under extreme pressure. I felt it would be much better for my colleagues if I removed myself from the scene so that they would be spared embarrassment."

'I said, "What did you do in that connection?"

'He said, "I went to Miami and staged a disappearance. I went swimming and left my clothes lying around. Then I went off and assumed the identity of Markham and eventually arrived in Australia."

'I said, "Why did you leave Australia on 28th November then?"

'He said, "First I wanted to establish whether I could enter Australia. I left Australia and went to Denmark via Singapore because I wanted to see what the reaction to my disappearance would be like in Europe.''

Jim Patterson then cross-examined Inspector Sullivan and ascertained the crucial facts that 'it is possible in England for any person to obtain a birth certificate for any person' and that, as in Australia, 'you do not require the authority of any other person to obtain that particular birth certificate', and that in the State of Victoria it is not an offence to adopt another name. Mr. Patterson pressed the point.

'The situation is this, is it not: that a person can change his name daily if he so desires?'

Inspector Sullivan replied: 'In this State, yes.'

'And you do not even require a deed poll to actually do this?'

'That's right.'

'And at that time Mr. Stonehouse told you, did he not, that he had adopted a new identity?'

'Yes.'

'Did he discuss this disappearance with you? I think your evidence only confines it to the . . . ?'

'No, he didn't, no.'

'To the fact that he staged the disappearance?'

'No, it wasn't discussed at any length at all.'

'He just said he went swimming and left his clothes on the beach?'

'That's right, yes.'

'Mr. Stonehouse told you, did he not, that he had been subjected to a great deal of political and financial difficulties?'

'Yes, he did.'

'And intimated to you that he believed that his disappearance would assist his colleagues in England?'

'Yes.'

'He told you, did he not, that one of the reasons he believed the bank failed was because of a certain article . . .'

'That's correct.'

'He told you, did he not, that when he established the bank he was going to be the unpaid chairman?'

'That's right.'

'He would not accept any sort of monetary consideration in relation to this matter?'

24

'That's right.'

'And through your general discussions with him, did you gain the impression that he had been approached to form this particular bank mainly because of his high standing with the Bengali people?'

'That's correct.'

At that point the examination went further back in the chronology of the events with the calling of two policemen from the Fraud Squad of the Victoria State police: Sergeants Hugh Morris and John Coffey. They revealed that their enquiries had started on 11th December, 1974 as a result of information from two Melbourne banks, who had noticed a customer operating accounts under different names.

Mr. James guided Morris through his account:

'On the 12th day of December, a Thursday, at quarter past ten in the morning, did you go with Coffey and other police officers to a position outside the Bank of New South Wales at the corner of Marks and Collins Streets, Melbourne?'

'Yes, we did.'

'What took place there, Mr. Morris?'

'We there saw a man . . .'

'The man you saw, is he present?'

'Yes, he is Mr. John Thomson Stonehouse, and he was a man at that time we believed was Joseph Arthur Markham. And we later learnt was also Donald Clive Mildoon. We saw him enter the Bank of New South Wales' premises, shortly later leave the bank, walk down Collins Street and enter the premises of the Bank of New Zealand at 347 Collins Street.'

'Did you maintain your surveillance after he entered the bank?'

'Yes, he was then followed around the city and returned to 500 Flinders Street.'

'On the following day, Friday, 15th December last, did you see Mr. Stonehouse again?'

'Yes.'

'Where was he when you saw him?'

'We saw him in Collins Street and he was entering the premises again of the Bank of New Zealand.'

'Was Mr. Coffey with you on this occasion?'

'Yes.'

'Did you cause to be despatched on Tuesday, 17th, a message to Interpol in London seeking certain information about a person, Markham?'

'Yes, the message was sent to establish the identity of Markham.'

'Was a reply received to that on Saturday, 21st December?'

'Yes.'

'And to your knowledge Mr. Stonehouse was placed under police surveillance on Monday, 23rd, also, is that correct?'

'That is so.'

'On the Christmas Eve, on Tuesday, 24th December last, at about quarter to eleven in the morning, were you with Detective Sergeant Coffey in the vicinity of the St. Kilda railway station?'

'Yes.'

'And did you see Mr. Stonehouse there again?'

'Yes, we saw him enter the St. Kilda railway station and board a train for Melbourne.'

'Did you speak to him on that occasion?'

'Yes.'

'And who spoke, you or Coffey?'

'Mr. Stonehouse was asked to leave the train and stand in the entrance to the station. Coffey identified us to him and he said, Coffey said to him, "Are you Joseph Arthur Markham?" Mr. Stonehouse replied "No".'

Morris revealed that the defendant had a letter in his possession when he was apprehended. The court spent some time in analysing the curious fact that the prosecution had a photostat copy of the letter – which had also been leaked to the press – although their own witness confirmed that the original had been returned immediately to the defendant and never seen again. The mystery of the photostat was explained by Sergeant Coffey and it also threw unusual clarity on the methods of operation of the Victoria police.

Jim Patterson asked: 'As I understand it, Mr. Coffey, what you said was that the original was photostated before Mr. Stonehouse was actually interviewed, was actually arrested on that day; is that the situation?'

26

'That is correct.'

'Well, I take it then that what had occurred was that the mail had been intercepted?'

'That's right.'

'And the mail had been opened?'

'Correct.'

'By yourself?'

'By myself.'

'And what had been returned then into an envelope?'

'Resealed, the same envelope, yes.'

'And had it been done so that there was no trace left of the actual opening?'

'To the best of my ability.'

'And did you go through all the mail which Mr. Stonehouse was receiving at that time, go through the whole lot and photostat it and do all this sort of thing?'

'Well, the whole mail – all that I could intercept, yes.'

'Tell me, is that a normal sort of police procedure, to intercept mail?'

'No.'

'There was some special reason for it in this case, was there?'

'There was, yes.'

'Did you have any authority?'

'I believed I did have, yes.'

'Where from?'

'From my own knowledge of the law.'

'Did you have permission from the Attorney General of the Commonwealth to do this?'

'No.'

'You appreciate, of course, that it is an offence to interfere with mail, do you not?'

'Yes.'

'You say from your own knowledge of the law that you are entitled to do this; could you tell me and perhaps enlighten me where you gained this knowledge from?'

'Yes. I believe from Elias *versus* Passmore. I can't quote the exact reference, but I think you'd know it.'

'To just go along and intercept mail, take it out of a post box?'

'No.'

'Whereabouts did you intercept it?'

'At the Bank of New Zealand.'

'And was it being held at that time?'

'Yes.'

'Was it done with the connivance of the bank officers?'

'I wouldn't say connivance; it was done on my authority to the bank, at my direction to the bank officer to hand the mail to me.'

'Let us get this particular thing straight, because we believe that this is an objection that any citizen can actually take. What was happening was this, was it not, that mail was being sent to the bank?'

'That's correct.'

'The Bank of New Zealand?'

'The Bank of New Zealand.'

'The Bank of New Zealand?'

'Yes.'

'And you have gone down there and spoken to a person down there and told him that you wanted to examine the mail before it was delivered to Mr. Stonehouse?'

'Delivered to Mr. Mildoon.'

'Mr. Mildoon?'

'That's correct.'

'Not Mr. Markham?'

'No, only Mr. Mildoon was receiving mail at the Bank of New Zealand.'

'Did they agree to that?'

'They finally handed the letters over to me, yes.'

'And did you return them?'

'I did.'

'To the person whom you spoke to at the Bank of New Zealand and gave you authority to do this?'

'And gave me the authority to do it.'

'Who you actually saw?'

'Who handed the letter to me.'

'Who handed the letter over to you?'

'Mr. Davenport.'

'Mr. Davenport? And what capacity is he?'

'He is an officer of the Bank of New Zealand.'

'What capacity though; manager, general manager, managing director?'

'I'm not sure of his exact title. He is a witness; I'm not sure of his exact ...'

'And he said that you could do this?'

'I directed him to hand me the letters one at a time; there were four letters altogether.'

'Did you say where you got the authority to direct him?'

'As an officer of police investigating a possible fraud being committed at that particular time.'

'Well, when you say demanded that he do that ...'

'I directed him.'

'You directed him?'

'Yes.'

'And this was on your own authority?'

'That is correct.'

'As a Detective Sergeant of Police?'

'That's correct.'

'No authority from the Attorney General?'

'No.'

'And you say that at that time you believed a fraud had been perpetrated by Mr. Mildoon?'

'Was contemplated or being perpetrated, yes.'

'But this subsequently was found to be untrue, was it not?'

'I am unable to answer that affirmative or negative.'

'When you say you directed him, was any objection taken by the bank official in giving you this mail?'

'Yes, there was.'

'Did he say that he'd have to get authority from higher up, or some such thing as that?'

'Yes. There was another gentleman that I also spoke to, Mr. Banks, and Mr. Manderson was another officer of the bank. Now, what their respective ranks are I am unable to say. I think Mr. Banks may be the senior officer of the bank.'

'And did you subsequently communicate with Scotland Yard and tell them that what was happening in Victoria was that you were interfering with the mail to check up on these sorts of things?'

'Subsequently to what, Mr. Patterson?'

'Subsequently to actually going into the bank, taking these letters out, examining them, examining the letters, photostating them?'

'No. Scotland Yard at that time had no knowledge whatsoever of our movements in Victoria.'

'Subsequently did you send the contents of these letters to Scotland Yard or hand them to Scotland Yard detectives?'

'Yes, I did.'

'Did you tell them how you had obtained them?'

'Yes, I did.'

'Was there any objection raised by Scotland Yard to the manner in which you had obtained this evidence?'

'No.'

'None whatsoever?'

'No.'

'Tell me this: when you go to a bank and you ask to see somebody's account the bank invariably refuses to supply this information, does it not?'

'That is correct, without a warrant.'

'You had no warrant on this occasion?'

'No.'

'Did you seek to obtain a warrant?'

'No, we were unable to. There was no authority to obtain a warrant.'

'Did you seek advice from more senior officers of the police force?'

Witness: 'I can't recall who exactly I spoke to. I think the most senior officer I spoke to was Detective Senior Sergeant Willingham who was then acting officer in charge of the Fraud Squad.'

Mr. Patterson: 'Did he condone what was happening?'

'Yes, he did.'

'Don't you think it would be more prudent for you to obtain advice perhaps from some member of the Legal Department of the police force?'

'No.'

'You were quite prepared to do that?'

'Yes.'

'Do you know from your own knowledge whether it is an offence to interfere with the Queen's mail?'

'Well, from my study of the whole circumstances I do not think I have committed any offence whatsoever.'

'You don't?'

'No.'

'Tell me this; say for instance there had not been any sort of offence committed by Mr. Stonehouse in either the name of Markham or Mildoon. How would you then justify the interfering with the mail?'

'That's completely hypothetical, Mr. Patterson. I don't know. I can't answer that.'

'At the time when you actually interfered with this mail you had no evidence, did you, that there had been any attempted fraud that had been perpetrated in any way?'

'We had a great deal of evidence at that time.'

'What I suggest to you, Mr. Coffey, is this: that all you had was some sort of wild sort of speculation, suspicion?'

'Certainly not wild speculation, no.'

Later, pressing his cross-examination about the legality of intercepting mail, Mr. Patterson said to Sergeant Coffey:

'How could you not obtain a warrant?'

'There was no way I could obtain a warrant in the specific circumstances existing at that time,' was the reply.

Mr. Patterson: 'You had insufficient evidence at that particular time that would prevent you from going before a magistrate or Justice of the Peace and explaining the exact circumstances which existed and allowing a magistrate to use his discretion to issue a warrant?'

'I did not have sufficient information at hand to go before a magistrate with anything.'

Mr. Patterson added: 'Tell me, Mr. Coffey, you appreciate, do you not, that the reason why warrants and search warrants are in vogue in the law is to protect individuals from over-zealous police officers?'

The prosecution counsel, Mr. James, jumped up to protest: 'I object to this. It is a comment, not a question, even if it was asked in an interrogative tone of voice.'

The magistrate said: 'I suppose there is something in that,

Mr. Patterson;' he would not allow the defence counsel to develop the theme, although the subsequent exchanges show he had a good try.

Mr. Patterson: 'It may not go ultimately to Mr. Coffey's credit, sir, though I think it probably would, but it most certainly could have some relevance with the proceedings which may subsequently be taken in England, and particularly because there is a suggestion of a political connotation in this particular case, and in those circumstances, of course, we want to explore the situation as far as that is concerned.'

His Worship: 'Are you suggesting that this was a political move, are you, or inspired by some pressure from somewhere else on a political basis?'

Mr. Patterson: 'Well, at this stage, sir, I can't really say as far as Mr. Coffey's action is concerned, but most certainly all our investigation – or perhaps not so much our investigation but the situation to which we have been subjected, seems to suggest that there is far more in this matter than just an ordinary criminal investigation, and that there is an overtone of political pressures being exerted upon the defendant. Now, this is, of course, what we have to explore.'

His Worship: 'I am inclined to think that you have gone just about as far as you should go in this matter.'

Mr. Patterson: 'I am not suggesting, sir, at any stage that we would be taking any sort of defence – at least at this time – that this is a political manoeuvre as far as the British Government is concerned, and as far as the defendant is concerned, but there is an overtone right the way through this investigation, perhaps not at the time when Mr. Coffey was investigating the letters but subsequently, that political pressures have been brought to bear on certain persons, and this may well have affected their judgment and could have affected the course of conduct which they have taken.'

His Worship: 'I think you have gone as far as you should go on this particular matter.'

Defence counsel went on to argue that as the original of the letter was not available and as the photostat was not confirmed as a true copy of the original, it should not be admissible as evidence. The magistrate surprised everyone when he firmly ruled: 'I propose to reject it. I do not think it should be admitted'.

The defence had won a skirmish in the legal battle; but it was only a Pyrrhic victory for the prosecution had, in effect, secured their own prime objective. The existence of the letter was by now well publicised and, as a result, the inevitable web of innuendo and suspicion was tightening around the defendants. Only later, at subsequent hearings, at other courts, would the defence be able to question the relevance of the letter's contents to the actual charges.

CHAPTER FIVE

The image of the typical British policeman used to be that of a clodhopper who pursued his victim stoically and without much imagination. The image dies hard, for the police still prefer to choose as their weapon the indiscriminate blunderbuss rather than the subtle stiletto.

The technique of police investigation is to seize everything, and to have long interviews with every possible contact, and then to throw every scrap of information – relevant or irrelevant – into the attack, like a fusillade of wasted bullets. The hope is that something will stick on the target. The only information as evidence likely to be rejected by the police are facts that may be favourable to the defence. It is certainly not considered part of the prosecution's public duty to bring all the circumstances of the case to the attention of the court. But it is part of the game to use anything and everything to harm the defendant.

Early in the extradition proceedings in Melbourne, my lawyer had to fight tenaciously to eliminate material which Scotland Yard had, in my view indiscriminately, tendered as evidence.

Of the papers and documents in the 'unit' at Toorak Road, which were seized on the day of my arrest, some were returned after a few days, following a press conference I had called to protest about police high-handedness. If the prosecution had succeeded in denying me bail, I might not have succeeded in getting my material, and my book, *Death of an Idealist* (W. H. Allen, London 1975) might never have been written. As it is, to this day I have never received a receipt for the property taken.

The particular documents to which my lawyer objected were scraps of paper prepared in February, during the Department of Trade Inquiry. The Inspectors had asked that a note be made of a series of cheques – dates and figures –

about which they wanted more information if I could later recall it. Mr. Patterson explained:

'I object to the admission of exhibits "A35" and "A36". The basis of the objection on exhibit "A35", sir, is that this document was prepared not by ourselves but by an officer who is in the Department of Trade Inquiries, and as far as we are concerned, sir, it would have no relevance to this particular case, the case before the court. It cannot be shown that the writing is in the hand of Mr. Stonehouse, and, indeed, if evidence was necessary, we could refer to the Department of Trade Inquiry to show when and where this particular document was actually prepared. Perhaps if I could create some sort of example: if this is evidence against us, the type of thing which could happen would be that the police could in some particular case make a statement or some form of confession, leave it at the person's premises, then subsequently raid the place and then produce it in court and say, "This is what we found," and use it as evidence against him.' He went on: 'It cannot be shown, sir, and it has not been shown, that it was written by Mr. Stonehouse, and if necessary we will call evidence to swear that it was not in his handwriting. At the time when these documents were seized it was brought to the attention of the investigating police that they were seizing documents which were privileged documents so far as the police were concerned, and apparently they totally and completely ignored that allegation and just took the documents without any sort of explanation having been given.' Mr. Patterson added: 'The second exhibit, sir – that is "A36" – to which we are objecting, is a list of cheque numbers which were written out at the dictation of Mr. Sherrard, the Q.C. who was conducting the enquiry. We can show from the transcript where Mr. Sherrard instructed the defendant to write out this list of cheque numbers. This is in the handwriting of the defendant, sir, and if Your Worship cares to see that, we will certainly show it to you. Again, sir, on the same basis we object to the admission of this document. The document would have no relativity to this case.'

Notwithstanding the defence arguments the documents were allowed as evidence.

The prosecution appeared to be on surer ground in detailing the transfers of funds effected by Markham/Mildoon from one bank to another in Australia. It was never suggested that any of the transactions were illegal, but sheer repetition of money movement builds up an impression of criminality. A succession of bank managers and clerks were called as witnesses to this end.

On a cold winter day in mid-June, Chief Superintendent Kenneth Etheridge, who had been in charge of the case in Scotland Yard, was called to give evidence. He was a skilful witness, but there were several key revelations extracted by Jim Patterson's cross-examination. On the first Select Committee's findings that an expulsion should not take place, Etheridge was asked whether there was an outcry in the press about it. He replied revealingly: 'I think most of the national newspapers expressed their disgust, yes'. Later he said that the warrant for the arrest was issued on the same day as the Select Committee reported, but as to coincidence added: 'I know nothing about coincidences.'

Etheridge was reluctant to be drawn into discussing the coincidence that the arrest came a few days after the publication of the first extracts of my book in the *News of the World.* Mr. Patterson was blunt:

'Was anything said to you, or did you receive any information or intimation from any person that the reason why they wanted to arrest Stonehouse and issue a warrant for his arrest was to stop the publication of his book?'

'I have never heard of anything like that, sir.'

Chief Superintendent Etheridge who had already ploughed through mountains of turgid material, was extremely coy about the *News of the World:*

'Would you agree with me that at that time there were certainly articles criticising certain members of the Government appearing in the *News of the World*?'

'I don't recall, I don't read the *News of the World.*'

'Mr. Etheridge, whether you read the *News of the World* or not, you would agree with me that a person in charge of an enquiry of this nature would be aware that a person whom you were investigating was now writing a book and certain excerpts of that book were being published in a Sunday newspaper?'

'No, I don't think I was aware of that.'

'The *News of the World* has got the biggest circulation of any paper in Great Britain, has it not?'

'I don't know, sir.'

'You agree with me that, if it doesn't have the largest circulation of any newspaper in Britain, it would have one of the largest circulations?'

'I don't know.'

'Very well known?'

'Certainly, it is well known.'

'Mr. Etheridge, as a Detective Superintendent are you going to suggest to the court that, having come out to Australia, having been investigating the matter for some considerable time, investigating – if I may say so – a person who is prominent at that time, who had received a tremendous amount of publicity right throughout the press – becoming aware that he was writing certain articles in a newspaper, you would not have made it your business to read them?'

'No, I can tell you this, that I think I may have read one article which was taken by our press cuttings' section – I think that maybe the first article that the *News of the World* printed – but that is all. However, I think that is some time after the event.'

'Newspaper articles were written and published prior to the issue of the warrant, would you deny that?'

'Articles on what?'

'They had appeared in the *News of the World*. The articles to which I am referring written by Mr. Stonehouse?'

'Well, if they were, I have no knowledge of them.'

'Would you agree with me that if you wanted to stop the publication of any newspaper articles – not perhaps you personally – but perhaps if any member of the Government wanted to stop the publication of any newspaper articles, the easiest and most effective way he can do so, is to have the author arrested and make the whole matter *sub judice*?'

'I would submit that that is impossible.'

Jim Patterson pressed the point by referring to another example of attempt at Government censorship:

'Were you aware that there was a politician, now deceased, called Crossman?'

'Yes.'

'He was quite a well-known politician, was he not?'

'I believe he was, yes.'

'Were you aware that around about Christmas or the early part of this year Mr. Crossman's diaries were published in the *Sunday Times*?'

'Yes, I have read some of them.'

'The British Government at that time tried to suppress their publication?'

'I don't know.'

'I could refer you to an article which appeared in this morning's *Age*. This is the *Age*, Melbourne, in which it states that the Government seeks to suppress the Crossman diaries. Have you read that at all?'

'No.'

'I say that in view of the fact that the Government wants to suppress the Crossman diaries that they may have wanted to suppress the Stonehouse publications.'

Mr. James jumped to his feet to object to that question: 'Nowhere has there been demonstrated a desire on the part of the British Government to suppress the Crossman diaries,' he said, apparently blissfully unaware that the Government in London had tried to do just that.

Defence counsel then took up the matter of the release of the Department of Trade Inquiry transcript to the police. Chief Superintendent Etheridge confirmed he had already read it. It was an extraordinary situation, particularly as I had understood that the Queen's Counsel conducting the inquiry, Mr. Michael Sherrard, had given an undertaking that all material would be kept confidential until the persons concerned had been given another opportunity to comment. They had not only not been given any such opportunity, they had not even been advised that the police had been given advance copies. One might almost have thought that the Department of Trade had been acting in liaison with the police.

Although the police had taken steps to examine the transcript of the inquiry, they took no interest in other aspects of the case. Mr. Patterson pressed:

'Were you asked to, or did you consider that you should look into the psychiatric difficulties which may have existed?'

Chief Superintendent Etheridge replied: 'That is a job, surely, for eminent medical people, it is not a policeman's job.'

'I appreciate that and I am not suggesting for one moment that you should do a psychiatric analysis or become a psychiatrist or anything like that, but what I was wondering about is whether you would take these factors into consideration – or whether the Director of Public Prosecutions would want to know anything such as this before they authorised a prosecution?'

'No, I don't think this would in any way weigh in the Director's mind as to whether or not he should prosecute.'

Mr. Patterson then lead the Scotland Yard Chief Superintendent into why he failed to ask me to return to England voluntarily. The answers were very revealing. 'You didn't say, "Unless you return to England we will issue a warrant for your extradition"?'

'No.'

'I can't ask you whether you would consider that a common courtesy, I suppose this is not the way the police force works?'

'Well, if you want me to answer that, sir, only those people – the Queen and those afforded diplomatic immunity – are afforded immunity from proceedings. Perhaps that is a blessing of living in a country such as Great Britain and perhaps Australia, I don't know.'

'What my client puts to me is this, that if you had shown him the common courtesy of telling him that an enquiry was in existence and that you were seeking an extradition, he would have returned to England with you or without you to answer these charges within England, and so eliminated this great deal of trouble to which you and the courts have been put?'

39

'I think, sir, if you were to study Mr. Stonehouse's quotations to the press from January onwards, I don't think there would be any question of him returning with anybody, if those quotations are correctly recorded.'

Mr. Patterson went on:

'There was a tremendous amount of adverse publicity directed against Mr. Stonehouse in England wasn't there?'

'There has been a lot of publicity and some of it has been adverse, yes.'

'There has been a suggestion made to me that some of the publicity which has been directed against Mr. Stonehouse has been created or has been suggested by certain members of the Government. What would you say about that?'

'I can't answer that.'

'You can't answer that?'

'No.'

'There has been one newspaper at least which has been extremely violent against Mr. Stonehouse, has there not?'

'It depends on the definition of "violent", said Chief Superintendent Etheridge. 'which newspaper?' he added.

'Perhaps I could specify it,' said Mr. Patterson. 'The *Daily Mail* has been very anti-Stonehouse, hasn't it?'

The Chief Superintendent said: 'I am not in a position to comment on what the paper's policy is in relation to reporting...'

It seemed to me that, in those replies, Scotland Yard were demonstrating how influenced they had been by what had appeared in the newspapers – however incorrect – for at no time did the police make any independent assessment of the defendant's willingness to return to London, if warned that charges were to be laid. Mr. Patterson then drew out the point that my reluctance to travel to England, when I had been assured no charges were in the offing, was because of my psychiatrist's advice, that such a journey before I had recovered would do damage to my health.

As the defence counsel pressed the Chief Superintendent from London on his own associations with the press, the Australian newsmen in court became more attentive. They knew how police authorities often work closely with the media

40

to get mutual benefit. It now transpired that the man from Scotland Yard had gone specially to the Melbourne Hilton hotel one night to meet Mr. Harry Longmuir, the chief crime reporter of the *Daily Mail*. But it took some getting out as the exchanges show:

'The *Daily Mail* seem to have been able to get a lot of information before any other newspaper, possibly through a gentleman by the name of Longmuir. Do you know him?'

'Yes, I know him very well.'

'He came out to Australia with you?'

'Yes.'

'Did he return to England with you?'

'On which occasion?'

'On that occasion?'

'Yes.'

'Were there any leaks to Mr. Longmuir by yourself or any other member of Scotland Yard?'

'There certainly wasn't any leak to Mr. Longmuir by myself. I can't answer for other members of Scotland Yard or anybody else who may give information to Mr. Longmuir.'

'Do you recall Mr. Longmuir having dinner with Mr. Stonehouse at the Hotel Hilton, Mr. Etheridge? Do you recall that day?'

'Yes, I do.'

'In fact were you waiting in Mr. Longmuir's room for dinner to terminate?'

'No.'

'Would you deny that you waited and you were in Mr. Longmuir's room waiting for the dinner to terminate?'

'I would deny that, yes.'

'Then I should rephrase the question. Would you agree with me that Mr. Longmuir that night discussed with you the contents of the conversation which he had had with Mr. Stonehouse?'

'That is a different matter.'

'Did you discuss it that night?'

'Yes.'

'Early that morning?'

'Yes.'

'Were you waiting in Mr. Longmuir's room at the Hotel Hilton?'

'No.'

'Were you staying at the hotel?'

'No.'

'Where did the conversation take place?'

'I forget the time but I went there for the specific purpose of hearing what he had got to say.'

It was in fact on the day following the secret late-night discussion between the chief crime reporter and the Chief Superintendent that the *Daily Mail* came out with a daring front-page spread: 'Stonehouse blows his top – Short a pusillanimous twit – Mellish a crude bore.'

The dinner Mr. Longmuir was reporting was meant to be a purely private one; the other journalists present – including those from the *Daily Express* – respected the occasion. They knew that I was emerging from a trauma and the first social meeting with pressmen was not to be treated as a press conference. Mr. Longmuir, however, treated the occasion differently. As he had to rely on memory of what was said at the dinner table, there were several inaccuracies. For instance, I had called Bob Mellish, the Government Chief Whip, an uncouth bully, not a crude bore.

Such incidents of *Daily Mail* reporting do not in themselves sound very serious, but taken together with other examples of press reporting which came out in later hearings, they build up a picture that puts a defendant in the worst possible public light, possibly handicapping the position of an accused in the eyes of a jury. The police are entitled to be very careful about the off-the-record information they feed to certain elements of the press, sometimes even *after* an arrest has been made.

CHAPTER SIX

I had agreed with my defence counsel that every effort – short of taking long-winded legal arguments to the High Court of Australia – should be made to throw out the extradition warrant in the Melbourne Magistrates' Court. If we had achieved such a victory my hand would be strengthened and I would return to London, as I had anyway intended, as a free man. If Scotland Yard then chose to arrest me, as I expected they would, the eventual trial would get underway without my suffering the awful stigma of being called a fugitive from justice. The police, and sections of the press, had done their utmost to create that impression in the public mind, and I needed to undo it.

Jim Patterson therefore mounted a powerful case against extradition before the magistrate, whose sole decision it was whether such a recommendation should go to the Australian Attorney General. His attempts to get some dubious evidence ruled as inadmissable did not succeed, but he went on to argue that even if the admissions made by his client about applications for birth certificates were accepted, it would still not be sufficient evidence to say the documents were forgeries. He went on:

'Even if the court concluded from the evidence which is available to the court, that the applications in each case were written by the respondent, there would still not be sufficient evidence to say that the documents were forgeries. A birth certificate, sir, is a public document and, as I understand, can be obtained by any person. The name on the application of the person seeking the birth certificate is totally and completely immaterial and is used only by the office concerned to identify the application. Our submission, sir, even if the respondent signed and tendered the application at the appropriate office, it still would not amount to forgery or the uttering of a forged document. It is not a forgery to put a fictitious name on the application. The situation, sir, is that the person requiring a birth certificate in England pays an appropriate fee and the person with whom he is doing business or conducting this transaction, would believe that they were doing business with the person tendering the application and they cannot in any way say that they were defrauded or deceived, because it is of no consequence to them who the person is who is making the application.'

And later he added:

'With regard to the Extradition Act, sir, the prosecution has to specify that the offence for which they are seeking extradition is an offence which can be committed within the State of Victoria. It is my submission, sir, that the offence of uttering a forged application for a birth certificate is an offence which is not covered by our law.

'In relation to the passport,' Mr. Patterson said, 'it is neither an offence in England, nor in Australia, to have more than one name, more than one surname. A person can use as many names, aliases, or *noms de plume* as he desires without committing any offence whatsoever within Australia and more particularly within the State of Victoria. A person with whom the Passport Office was transacting business was the applicant by whatever name called, or whatever name used, and it is not an offence or forgery to use the name Markham, or any other name in making such an application, or to supply details on the application which are not specifically correct.'

Mr. Patterson went on to analyse the other charges against me and, in doing so, brilliantly anticipated arguments which would be used in later trials. On the charge of obtaining a pecuniary advantage (a bank overdraft for my export company) by 'falsely pretending that his personal guarantee was a guarantee of value,' he pointed out that there was absolutely no evidence before the court to show that my assets were – or were not – sufficient to meet any guarantee I may have signed.

He also made the point that if the virtual sole owner of a company obtains an overdraft for it by giving a personal guarantee, the increase in the value of the monies made available to the company must also increase the worth of its owner. So his personal guarantee must therefore be of value and the charge drops.

On the insurance charges Mr. Patterson said:

'In our submission there is no evidence whatsoever which would allow Your Worship to find a probably presumption of guilt in relation to these charges against the respondent. The information, sir, read, "Dishonestly attempted to obtain by deception, by fabricating evidence from which his death would be presumed and falsely pretending that the death benefit on a life assurance policy was payable by the said insurance." The only evidence which could possibly be concluded is that the respondent intended to fake the death in the depositions of Mr. Charlton. His evidence is confined to say, that Mr. Stonehouse did not keep an appointment with Mr. Charlton who looked into a shed or some form of kiosk and saw some clothing which he believed had been Mr. Stonehouse's. In relation to the evidence which has been produced by the Victorian and the Australian police, the words "faked his death" has never been used. It has never been questioned in relation to this matter, never been questioned in relation to his intentions in this matter and at most there is admission that he wished to stage a disappearance. At no stage did he say that he intended to fake his death, nor has he ever been questioned by any member of the police force in relation to this matter. Any suggestion that he had created a factual circumstance from which his death could be presumed would depend entirely and completely upon the imagination of the person concerned.

'The insurance policies in the main were taken out by Mrs. Stonehouse for her own benefit. Whether a contingent liability would arise, would be dependent upon the evidence of her husband's death and the presumption of evidence, sorry, sir, the presumption of death, would not arise on the simple fact of her husband's disappearance.

'Death, sir, or presumption of death, does not arise, could not possibly arise until seven years after the person has last been seen.'

Mr. Patterson pressed home the point and the five insurance charges were beginning to look extremely thin; later, however,

45

an extraordinary aspect of the case became clear. Doubtful the charges might be but this only seemed to increase the tenacity with which the prosecution pursued them.

When he came to the charges that I had stolen cheques from my own company, Export Promotion and Consultancy Services Limited (EPACS), Mr. Patterson was absolutely firm. He said that: 'The prosecution have failed to produce evidence from any person who can say that they spoke for and on behalf of the complainant company or the alleged complainant company, and who can say that the respondent did not have permission to take this money, and he did not have a claim of right to this money, and that the money was not used in the interests of the company. Mr. Hayes, sir, who is a solicitor, and Mr. McGrath, a chartered accountant, who are co-directors of EPACS do not say the respondent did not have permission to take or use this money.'

He went on:

'It is also admitted in evidence that the defendant has had a loan account with the company since its inception, that he used the loan account during the period of time when he was in control of the company and that the loan account was in debit and in credit during that period of time. It is significant, sir, that Mr. Hayes and Mr. McGrath placed the company into liquidation and yet we don't have any evidence from the liquidator to say that his enquiries show that the respondent did not have permission to take the money referred to and indeed, sir, the liquidator has debited such money to the respondent's loan account with the company. As I intimated, sir, there is no evidence whatsoever that the money was not used in the best interests of the company. Furthermore, the overdraft of the company was guaranteed by the respondent and it has not been shown that the overdraft of the company account cannot be met by the respondent.'

Mr. Patterson added:

'Mr. Stonehouse had total and complete control of the company, was construed to be the actual owner of the company, and could use his own discretion in the business activities of the company.'

It was then the turn of Mr. George Hampel, the counsel

for Sheila Buckley to address the court. The charges against her were conspiracy on the drawing of cheques from EPACS, as she had signed them as the authorised signatory. Mr. Hampel made a powerful case against Mrs. Buckley's extradition. He wound up his argument with an important general point:

'Your Worship, if every secretary or clerk or person in an office who signed cheques were to be committed for trial if it were found that the cheques were illegally dealt with subsequently, there would be a great many people in gaol or awaiting trial at any rate, merely because of that supposition, and it just can't be done unless there is strong evidence to support it.'

It remained to be seen if the magistrate would uphold the defence.

CHAPTER SEVEN

It was now the turn of Mr. James to address the magistrate on behalf of the prosecution. It was by now 19th June and, since my arrest, the Crown had spent three months working on the case for extradition. This time-scale of events – the long-drawn-out delays – is an aspect of criminal proceedings most galling to defendants. No expense, as well as no time, is spared by the authorities in pursuing their attempts to win; no thread of argument, no shred of seemingly insignificant evidence is wasted. The normal rules of cost-effectiveness which guide other sectors of society are totally ignored by the prosecuting bodies. Because they sanctify their activities as 'upholding the law', they consider themselves in no way bound by the need for economy.

Chief Superintendent Etheridge, who had been put in charge of the case at an early stage, flew to Australia no less than three times. With another senior officer he spent over three months in and around Melbourne, when all the initial Scotland Yard enquiries could surely have been dealt with by the Australian police.

When it came to the actual proceedings, Mr. James was given a 'reading brief' for several weeks before the case opened, so that he could be fully primed. The prosecution were determined to leave nothing to chance, and were certainly not reluctant to incur heavy legal fees. So when Mr. James rose to speak he had the full resources of the Crown and months of work behind him. His *tour de force* was disappointing; on sheer merit of performance the defence barristers, who had been working with totally inadequate resources, deserved to win, but in truth we all knew that the odds were stacked against us from the start. However badly Mr. James might do, the chances of the extradition request failing were remote; very rarely, if at all, in Australian history had a request from the United Kingdom been rejected, and it was unlikely that a magistrate would want to make legal history with me.

Early in his statement Mr. James reiterated the strongest card in the prosecution's case at that stage: the fact that under extradition law the case does not have to be proved, as all that is necessary is that evidence is produced which shows there is a case to answer and that a trial would be justified. On the birth certificate applications he put it that:

'In making those applications with those documents in relation to deceased persons and causing the Registrar to issue a false document in relation to a person not legally entitled to it, that he was intending to defraud in the sense of causing the Registrar to act contrary to his duty'.

Mr. James went on:

'I can only put to Your Worship that what is said about a man being entitled to use a name other than this own is not to the point. We are not here discussing a person who, for some reason or other, wants to book into a hotel and calls himself Robinson because he doesn't want to meet an unwelcome relative or for some other reason of privacy.

'It was said that forgery at Common Law no longer has any significance and I sought to say to Your Worship what I wanted to about that and it was asserted that even if there was evidence that he read the document, that is Mr. Stonehouse, it was not sufficient they were forgeries and Mr. Etheridge sought to dissuade Your Worship that the birth certificate was obtained by right by any person so far as these matters are concerned. It is put that what is established here is in fact the foundations of a plan, the culmination of which was to be the disappearance of Mr. Stonehouse from the face of the earth in November and his re-emergence, from what he said to Mr. Sullivan, in whichever of the new identities suited best the circumstances.'

He returned to re-emphasise this line of action in relation to the charge of providing a personal guarantee for a bank overdraft:

'I ask you to turn to the totality of the evidence where it is said that the acquisition of the overdraft increases and later on the negotiation of the cheques, the subject of the other group of charges, was the means by which Mr. Stonehouse could provide himself with funds to prosecute the plan

49

that he conceived of, effecting his disappearance and emerging with a new identity, with evidence of that new identity by way of passport and able to leave behind not only political and business pressures, but financial liabilities and obligations that he had incurred in England.'

On the actual disappearance Mr. James took issue with Mr. Patterson:

'My learned friend sought to make somewhat light of it in saying that the witness Charlton had seen clothing that he had inferred was Mr. Stonehouse's and sought to indicate that that part of the matter had not been terribly well proven. I would ask Your Worship to pay regard to the account given by Charlton. You will recall that it was he who said that he has known Mr. Stonehouse since 1967 and has known him in business since 1961. This was no mere acquaintance and when you look at the account he gives, it is open to me and open to you to find that it is a reasonable inference open to any jury that Mr. Charlton was a singularly apt choice as a man to report the disappearance once the disappearance was effected. . . .

'When my learned friend was, with respect, discussing it and speaking of this gentleman seeing a few clothes that he inferred were Stonehouse's, the impression was calculated to be given that he told a tale which hardly hung together and didn't prove very much, whereas I ask you to look at the whole account that he gave.

'Where the point is reached where the appointment to have a drink at 7 p.m. was not kept, he said, "After about half an hour I left the bar, thinking Stonehouse had either overslept or taken rather longer about his shopping than expected. I was by no means alarmed – possibly a little annoyed. Having telephoned his room, I received no reply. I wandered about the hotel grounds," and so on. You will recall the detailed way in which he describes his movements, the presence of the woman attending in the early morning, the way in which the clothing had been placed there by Mr. Stonehouse then and it was in the same position when he, Charlton, saw it later that evening.

'You will recall his account of opening Stonehouse's

50

attaché case and listing the contents and so on, and that account is not to be dismissed as saying that a witness saw some clothes that he inferred were Stonehouse's. It was a detailed and, on its face, convincing account of what took place and the evidence that followed was that Mr. Stonehouse was by the early part of December of last year, that is to say, approximately three weeks after the events described by Mr. Charlton, in a bank in this city, depositing the sum of $22,000 in large denomination issue notes and that is what I meant when I say the totality of the evidence here has to be looked at.

'It is possible to dissect probably interminably every syllable uttered by every witness but when the evidence is fitted together, it is impossible, in my respectful submission, to argue in respect of Mr. Stonehouse that there can be no consideration by a jury of the matter so produced; where what is demonstrated is that in July of last year, he took steps which point unerringly to his equipment of himself with passports in names other than his own, where he arranges with Mr. Charlton to accompany him on a trip which was, in our submission, to result in his apparent disappearance, where as I say even a matter of weeks after that, it is clear he has communicated with Mrs. Buckley and with no one else or anyone else that will admit to being communicated by, where three weeks after these events at Miami he is in Melbourne seeking to deposit $22,000 in high denomination notes. Now so far as the matter of the cheques is concerned, the Crown says that on the whole of the evidence these cheques were almost solely the means by which Stonehouse provided himself with funds to prosecute the plan for a new life under a new identity.'

Dealing with the insurance charges Mr. James said:

'It was put by my learned friend yesterday that the only evidence from which a faked death could be inferred is that of the witness Charlton, and that evidence only shows a failure to keep an appointment with Charlton and discovery of clothes in the shed. Then Mr. Patterson went on to point out that as far as such a death was concerned, that any claim upon any insurer would meet with the difficulty of the presumption of death, the probable lapse of seven years, and he referred to difficulties of the law in Florida and the obtaining of probate. What is put in relation to these matters is this: the evidence amply establishes Mr. Stonehouse's active part in the securing of those policies of insurance. Where the rest of the evidence establishes, as it does in my respectful submission, a plan to disappear and re-emerge in this country, a plan which is evidenced by the conversations with Mr. Jones of the Bank of New South Wales, to the effect that Mr. Markham was making plans to emigrate to Australia long before the urge to swim at Miami overtook him. . . .'

On the question of the company, Export Promotion and Consultancy Services, he said:

'When it was incorporated it became a separate legal person, Your Worship, and if the fact were that every single penny of its capital was contributed by Mr. Stonehouse himself, that person would remain legally separate and apart.'

On the overdraft facilities he said:

'When it is said that the evidence does not establish an incapacity on Mr. Stonehouse's part to furnish the required guarantees out of his own assets, that has to be read in context with the fact that what is to be looked at is his illegal or deceitful intent at the time. If the effects remain the same, Your Worship, if a millionaire deceives a person into lending him threepence or a pauper achieves the reverse, if at the time Mr. Stonehouse was penniless or fabulously wealthy is not really to the point. The point is that the evidence establishes that within a comparatively short time after seeking those additional facilities and increased amounts available to the company, Mr. Stonehouse was to put himself in a position where his assets would not be his to dispose of and his personal guarantee would have died with him, so far as the facts appear to have demonstrated.

'There is ample evidence from the bank concerned that had they known of the true circumstances those facilities would not have been granted. When that is the case, it is proper to argue that they have thereby been induced to offer that increased credit, when it is clear with full and fore-knowledge, as it turns out, of what the situation was to be, they would not have so acted.

'When those increased facilities were sought, it was a matter of comparatively short time to elapse before, as I say, if things went as it is suggested they were planned, Mr. Stonehouse would not be able to be called upon for his personal guarantee when he would have lost control of the disposition of his assets and would not be in a position to assert that he was alive.'

Mr. James summed up the essence of the prosecution case against me by saying:

'In the Crown's contention, the events start in July with the efforts to obtain birth certificates and later passports and are carried on through September and October where Mr. Stonehouse as Markham disclosed to the Bank of New South Wales, what his true plan was to be; that is, that he was intending to go to Australia, and that is why you have to look at the significance of the trip to Miami in a somewhat less simplistic light than that urged yesterday by my learned friend Mr. Patterson. That is why that event achieves complete significance, because understanding of that is the only way to see the plan that had been put into operation at least as early as July. Its middle stages are evidenced by the actions of Mr. Stonehouse in making these arrangements with the Bank of New South Wales in London, and explain so much of his intention as to say that he intended by some means and at some time to live in Australia.

'By that time he had the means to live as whoever he chose out of Markham and Mildoon. By that time, in the Crown's case, he had either achieved, or was about to seek, increased overdraft facilities and it is said that the cheques, subject of the five charges, were negotiated to provide him with the necessary funds to finance that immigration to Australia that he had confessed to the Bank of New South Wales in London.'

When the court resumed ten days later to hear the Magistrate announce his decision to recommend extradition, Mr. Patterson called psychiatrist Dr. Gerard Gibney. It was another of his brilliant moves in establishing evidence which would be eminently valuable in later hearings. He was demonstrating his concern for the final outcome and not merely the tactical encounter.

'What degrees do you hold?' he asked.

'I have a Bachelor of Medicine and Bachelor of Surgery from the University of Melbourne, and a post-graduate Diploma in Psychological Medicine from the University of Melbourne.'

'Are you a practising psychiatrist?'

'I am.'

'You practise at 428 St. Kilda Road, Melbourne?'

'Yes.'

'Mr. John Stonehouse has been a patient of yours for some considerable time?'

'He has.'

'When did you first examine Mr. Stonehouse?'

'On the first of January of this year.'

'Was it shortly after his release, as far as you understand, from the detention centre?'

'I understand so.'

'Did you come down especially to interview and to examine Mr. Stonehouse, notwithstanding it was a holiday?'

'I did.'

'Was it a fairly long and detailed interview you had with him?'

'It was a long interview, yes.'

'Was it actually spread over two interviews?'

'Yes.'

'Of some five hours duration?'

'That's so.'

'What was your diagnosis, as far as Mr. Stonehouse was concerned?'

'I thought that at the time I saw him he was suffering from a depressive illness of quite significant severity. I felt this illness had been a response to a number of stresses that he had been subject to for a period of more than a year before I had seen him, and I was quite concerned about his emotional condition at the time I saw him early in January.'

54

'When you were discussing the case with Mr. Stonehouse, did you go into his earliest life and what may have caused these depressions?'

'I took a complete history of his early life and cited the significant features in his development.'

'Would it be true to say that Mr. Stonehouse would be what would probably be classified as an idealistic sort of person?'

'His history certainly indicated that he had been an idealist and a person who had associated himself with a number of campaigns and movements of considerable humanitarian value through his life, yes.'

'Would some of these humanitarian movements with which he became involved, would they cause some degree of unpopularity with certain sections of the community?'

'They had, yes.'

'Notwithstanding this fact, did he indicate that he still carried on his functions, his humanitarian functions?'

'He persisted with them very often to his own detriment socially, politically and financially, yes, I think so.'

'Had he devoted a great deal of his time, his earlier life, to under-privileged people in some of the under-privileged countries?'

'Yes.'

'Under-developed countries?'

'He had.'

'Subsequent to that, did he become a Member of Parliament?'

'He did.'

'And was a Member of the Labour Party, was he not, in England?'

'Yes.'

'Again, did he become associated with certain aspects of under-privileged people and humanitarian problems?'

'While he was a Member of Parliament he did become associated with such movements in Africa, and he became involved in Co-operative movements in England as well.'

'Subsequent to that, was he associated with the difficulties which arose in Bangladesh?'

'Yes, it was in 1971 that he developed his interest in the

55

welfare of the people of Bangladesh. He became deeply involved in bringing relief to the starving people of Bangladesh. He visited refugee camps and began to organise relief projects. He appears to have spearheaded a campaign to have Bangladesh recognised by the British Government. As a result of these activities, Mr. Stonehouse was lionised by the people of Bangladesh. There were at that time 83,000 Bengali nationals in England, and a group of these people approached him to set up a banking organisation to cater for their needs. Mr. Stonehouse agreed to do so, and he now considers that this decision marks the beginning of a dramatic turn in his political and financial affairs.'

'Did he discuss with you difficulties which were created in the formation of the bank and difficulties which he was subjected to by business and political pressures?'

'He did, yes.'

'Did he indicate to you that there was a general disillusionment of the situation which existed, not only in his own life but in political life and business life in England at that time?'

'I think this sense of disillusionment was beginning to evolve at that stage, and certainly he was becoming disillusioned about the outcome of a number of his activities throughout his life and the result of them, and the attitudes of people towards him after he had devoted a good deal of energy and activity on their behalf, and I think it was about this stage that emotional difficulties began to appear in his life.'

'Could I put it this way, Doctor: did he more or less indicate to you that he had started out with Utopian ideals to build up and to assist under-privileged people in Africa and in India, and these sort of countries, and that what he had seen was not the realisation of his ideals but the taking over by vested interests and factions in these countries?'

'Yes, I think he was disillusioned because idealism seemed to have been replaced with corruption in a number of countries that he had helped. People who had been very grateful to him originally became critical, and in general this sense of disillusionment had a considerable impact on him emotionally.'

'Did he more or less indicate to you that in some cases he

was disgusted with what had occurred in some of these African States?'

'He was.'

'And that all his work, particularly his earlier life had seemed to have gone to nothing in relation to these people?'

'He felt that a good deal of his efforts on behalf of these people had been wasted or corrupted in some way.'

'Did he also indicate to you that at this time he was being subjected to a great deal of business and financial pressures in relation to the bank?'

'Yes, he gave me details of those pressures.'

'Did he indicate to you – whether this is right or wrong – that it was a certain article which appeared in a newspaper which created these difficulties?'

'Yes, he felt that that article had been a very significant factor in the creation of a lot of financial difficulties that he had experienced.'

'And there was a Department of Trade Inquiry, was there not, for some time by a member of Scotland Yard in relation to the bank?'

'There was quite a prolonged inquiry, and I think this caused him a great deal of worry and added to the emotional distress that he was experiencing.'

'It appears from the evidence that at this time Mr. Stonehouse adopted another personality – let us call it the Markham personality?'

'He told me that he decided to do this around the middle of 1974, yes.'

'Perhaps, Doctor, you could describe it to the court: why would a person who has one personality wish to develop a second personality?'

'I think that Mr. Stonehouse was quite significantly depressed at this time, in the first half and towards the middle of 1974. I think he was conscious to a realisation that he was just unable to cope with the emotional and practical pressures under which he was living. I think it was difficult for a man with his personality to make a public admission that he may have made mistakes or errors of judgment in certain areas, and for those reasons he evolved the idea of escaping from the whole thing, and the mechanism which he used was to adopt this new personality.'

'And this would be some form of an escape, would it not, some form of relief?'

'Yes, it was a relief from the emotional pressure and the practical difficulties that he was experiencing at the time.'

'If a person is subjected to a great deal of psychological pressure and business pressures and worries like this, and if they become too great for him, do people occasionally try to escape in this manner?'

'I think people use a number of escape mechanisms to handle severe depression. The commonest one, I suppose, is suicide. A very common reaction to depression is one of withdrawal in which a person will stop seeing friends, stop functioning from the point of view of their occupation, withdraw from a family and close themselves in a shell. I think that very often in middle-aged men this sort of mechanism which Mr. Stonehouse evolved is used, but it is part of the general withdrawal from depression, an effort to hide away from your own feelings, almost.'

'You mentioned the word "suicide", Doctor, is it quite commonplace that a person subjected to these pressures would go through the physical act of terminating their own life?'

'It is one of the common outcomes of a depressive reaction, yes.'

'And in Mr. Stonehouse's case, was it more a depressive destroying of a figure which he had created, a public figure he had created?'

'After speaking to him, I almost regarded his actions as a suicide equivalent. He did look at the possibility of suicide, but for a number of reasons decided against it, and I believe that this action he took was in a way a self-destructive thing and a suicide equivalent.'

'Doctor, dealing with the individual, perhaps, and the personality which is projected as a public image, do you see a conflict between John Stonehouse as an individual and the projection of his image as a politician and a Privy Councillor?'

'Yes. My impression of him, especially the history I obtained of his early life, indicated that he had always been a person suffering from some degree of insecurity, that he had had feelings of anxiety and perhaps depression through his life. As opposed to this, as a political leader and as a very successful public figure, he had to, if you like, wear a mask of calmness and great confidence in public. Very often, when you get this sort of combination, you will get a build-up of depression and of anxiety, until these disorders reach quite dangerous levels within a person, but very frequently in depressed people, and I think particularly with successful men and business executives and public figures, very very few people, even their most intimate acquaintances, can be unaware of the level of depression from which they are suffering until something fairly dramatic happens to bring it to everybody's notice.'

'Would the adoption of a new personality by an individual or a person who has been subject to those pressures, like Mr. Stonehouse, offer some psychological relief?'

'Yes. He told me when he was adopting this new personality, he had a great feeling of relief. He said, "It was a tremendous relief to me." There was an immediate reduction of tension. He relished the experience of going into a restaurant or a hotel, not as a public figure, but as a private citizen with this new name, and he did find some good deal of emotional benefit from this sort of behaviour, I think.'

'Well, doctor, you know that Mr. Stonehouse came to Australia and for a time, the allegation is, he lived under the name of Markham and under the name of Mildoon?'

'Yes.'

'Subsequently he was detected and was arrested in December. You saw him one week later. How would you describe his condition when you actually saw him on 1st of January?'

'When I saw him in January he was still significantly depressed, but I gathered from the evidence that he gave me and from the evidence of his wife, whom I also interviewed, that his depression then was probably not as severe as it had been during the last half of 1974. I felt that after coming to Australia there was certainly a part of him that hoped for detection. I think this was largely because of the feelings he had towards his wife and towards his children, and he told me that when he was detected, he experienced something like relief to know that the whole experience was coming to an end.'

'As I understand it, doctor, perhaps I can say from my own personal experience – if there is no objection from my learned friend, Mr. James – the situation was this, was it not: in reality he endeavoured to destroy a personality, which we will call the Stonehouse personality; is that so?'

'Yes.'

'And that notwithstanding this fact, he still had a great deal of affection and ties with the Stonehouse personality?'

'Yes. I think it is absolutely understandable that a person cannot drop all of their old life, all of their family connections, all of their beliefs and ideals without a good deal of ambivalence of liking and disliking what is going on, and very often feelings of regret at having made the move, I think.'

'Even though you more or less extinguished one personality, would that prior personality still draw on your new personality, trying to pull you back into the old personality?'

'I do not want to make too much of this. He was the same person; he was operating in a different environment; he was living a different sort of life, but he retained the same personal characteristics, the same strengths and weaknesses that he had before.'

'Subsequent to 1st of January, you saw Mr. Stonehouse during January? You had further discussions with him?'

'I saw him a number of times through January. I saw him quite regularly after that date. By the middle of January I was quite concerned about his condition. I then thought there was an increasing risk of suicide and I arranged for his admission to Trentford Private Hospital at Caulfield for several days because of my concern about his condition.'

'At that time was Mr. Stonehouse being subjected to a fair amount of press publicity?'

'I understand so, yes.'

'And was a fair amount of pressure being brought on him from the British Government to resign his seat in the House of Commons?'

'I think this was at a stage when there was pressure for him to resign, yes.'

'And his future at that time was most uncertain, was it not?'

'Yes.'

'Did you believe that if he had resigned his seat at that time, that suicide was a big possibility?'

'I think a combination of factors were influencing him – certainly, the decision as to whether or not he would resign his seat was one that held a great deal of emotional content for him, and it was one of the factors that made me concerned about the possibility of suicide.'

'And for this reason and other reasons due to his depression, was he admitted to hospital some time?'

'He was, yes.'

'Well, since that time has there been any improvement in his condition?'

'Yes. I felt that even while he was in hospital there was evidence that he was re-integrating. He seemed to get the emotional defence mechanisms, which had stood him in good stead in the past, working properly again. He began to read and to function and to take an active interest in what was happening to him, and increasingly he wanted to play an active part in what was going to happen to him. Before this, the process of withdrawal and just wanting to opt out of the whole situation was predominant, but, I think, in the latter half of January, he drew himself together and began to function at the sort of level at which he is capable.'

'As a public figure, I take it he would be able to pull himself together to show a face?'

'This is something of necessity he has become a past master at. He can project calmness and confidence when these qualities aren't necessarily present under the surface.'

'He would have a veneer on the outside but underneath there might be a turmoil?'

'That is right.'

'What do you consider the situation is now as far as the respondent in these proceedings, Mr. Stonehouse, spending some time in gaol awaiting extradition?'

'It has been proven that he is an emotionally vulnerable person and as his treating doctor, I think it would be to the detriment of his emotional health to be in gaol at the present.'

'There would not be any risk of suicide if he was there?'

'I don't regard him as being an active suicide risk at present.'

'I think that early in the piece you stated in one of your reports that it would do irreparable damage to him if he returned to England, perhaps at that stage?'

'I am not sure if I used that phrase. I thought that in January a return to England would have caused him a great deal of distress, and in all probability would have led to a worsening of his depression and a feeling of great despair.'

'Has he now got more or less the control of a person who could build himself up to some great eminence now, seeing the whole of his life falling around him?'

'I think that is precisely what is happening.'

'And in the intervening time since January to now, the end of June, has he more or less built himself up to the situation where he can more or less face the experience of returning to England and the resultant publicity it would create?'

'I think he can cope with that quite competently now; in fact he tells me that he wants to return to England. He feels capable of stating his case and he feels it is very important to himself as a man to do this.'

'What effect would a period of time now – a period of time in gaol – have on his personality at the present time?'

'Mr. Stonehouse is a proud person. He is a person who has enjoyed considerable eminence. I think it is just a matter of commonsense that a period of being in gaol would be a distressing experience for him. He is subject to feelings of depression and I feel that being in gaol would put him at risk for a recurrence of significant depression.'

'And most certainly, as far as his psychiatric health and mental health are concerned, it would be far better if he remained out of gaol until he was actually extradited?'

'It would. I wouldn't want him there as his doctor, no.'

'The only times that Mr. Stonehouse made utterances in relation to England were to the effect that he never wanted to return to England?'

'Yes.'

'Would this be somewhat of a love hate relationship as far as

62

he was concerned, that he considered that he had been totally and completely rejected by England at that time, say January?'

'He was in a state of great disillusionment then and his reaction was a very emotional one. I think in his more recent calmer emotional condition, he has re-thought the situation and come to different conclusions about it.'

'And has he expressed the opinion that he now believes that what he should do is go back to England and to face the whole consequences and the whole situation as it now stands?'

'He has come to that conclusion and he has come to that point as a man in control of himself and in control of his feelings.'

'He considers, does he not, that his duty still lies with the House of Commons?'

'I think he is aware of his responsibilities there.'

'And recently there was an attempt by Mr. Stonehouse to return to the House of Commons?'

'I understand so.'

'Do you believe that he believes quite honestly and sincerely that what he should do is return to the House of Commons and to make the speeches which he desires?'

'I believe so.'

'And when he attempted to go back to England, that this was what he intended and fully wanted to do?'

'I think he wants to return to England for that reason, yes.'

Mr. James then asked two questions which, to some extent, acknowledge that the prosecution recognised the value of expert psychiatric opinion:

'So far as the matter that you were asked about Mr. Stonehouse's confinement in prison, I gather from what you said you no longer consider there is any significant risk of him attempting to destroy himself, is that right?'

'Not in his present emotional state, no.'

'So that it would be in your professional opinion not dangerous to his life to commit him to prison?'

'I don't think it would be dangerous to his life, but I would like to point out that depression is a most distressing illness.'

At the end of these exchanges the magistrate decided to

exercise his discretion and commit me to the Detention Centre rather than prison for the fifteen days' mandatory period. Under the law – even if the defendants volunteer to leave immediately – they must be locked up while the case is considered by the Attorney General. It is a curious provision which allows of no exceptions. As I preferred to spend the fortnight with my new-found friends in the cell at Pentridge Prison, I refused the invitation to return to the cold, inhospitable Maribyrnong centre, the scene of my incarceration over the previous Christmas.

Sheila Buckley was sent to the Fairlea Womens Prison. It seemed particularly unfair to me that she should suffer the hardship and indignity of imprisonment when the evidence against her was, so I thought, tissue-paper thin, and as she was, anyway, on the point of flying to London at about the time she was arrested. If the law is an ass, the extradition law which specifies a minimum of a fortnight's imprisonment is an obstinate jackass. None of the experts – however they tried – could devise a way for Mrs. Buckley to have bail and stay out of prison. It made me wonder whether we are not all prisoners of the bureaucratic systems we have devised.

CHAPTER EIGHT

Two women police officers were flown out to Australia for a week just to accompany Mrs. Buckley on the flight back. We had no less than four police escorts on the journey to London by British Airways' jumbo jet. On arrival at Heathrow airport, all the passengers left by the front exit except the two 'prisoners', who were made to walk down specially arranged steps onto a tarmac where over a hundred pressmen and television crews were gathered behind neatly arranged barriers.

The plane had been delayed and it was already Friday evening. We were rushed to Bow Street for a hearing before the magistrate and both defendants, in their innocence, thought bail would be granted that night. It was too late for a hearing, however, and we both had to spend the night in the filthy police cells facing the Royal Opera House at Covent Garden.

On the following morning the prosecution raised no objection to bail for Mrs. Buckley, but I was horrified to realise that the Director of Public Prosecutions was opposing bail in my case. The two Australian counsel, Jim Patterson and George Hampel, who had both flown to London at their own expense to assist us prepare the defence, were shocked. They were surprised that English courts should be asked to deny bail when the Australian courts had consistently granted it.

The main court at Bow Street was absolutely packed with pressmen and public who had waited several hours through the crop of petty crimes and prostitutes' and drunks' cases, which are the normal agenda for a Saturday. The place is so intimate that the reporters sit immediately behind the dock and could – and at later hearings sometimes did – pass notes to the defendants. Only the magistrate sits in isolation. It is not a splendid isolation, for he looks like and acts as a very mundane person. But his word rules and there is precious little opportunity of questioning his decisions – as I was to discover during the following seven long weeks.

Anthony Whitfield, a large florid man, acted for the Director of Public Prosecutions, and George Hampel, the barrister from Melbourne who had been quickly admitted to the English Bar, represented me. Mr. Whitfield said:

'It is not in the public interest that he should be granted bail with all the attendant risks that he could abscond a second time and thereby compel a repetition of the protracted and very expensive extradition process.'

Mr. Whitfield made no reference to my earlier offer to return to London voluntarily, nor did he make clear that there were no criminal charges at the time of my disappearance, and that charges were not laid until four months later. He did however describe the applications for birth certificates and a passport in the name of a dead man, the opening of a bank account in Melbourne and the reappearance on Christmas Eve. As, by then, all these details had appeared in the newspapers several times, they did not surprise the court, nor did the fact that 'shortly before his arrest he had approached the Swedish Prime Minister for a Swedish passport.' That particular application had received world-wide publicity as my personal letter to Olaf Palme had been read by a Swedish journalist even before the Prime Minister saw it, under the strange Swedish system of 'open' government. The letter had also figured in the House of Commons Select Committee report.

Mr. Whitfield went on: 'He had also made overtures to Mauritius and there is evidence that he had at least been sniffing at Bangladesh as a haven.' He claimed it would be easy for me to obtain a passport at any branch passport office in a false name or a visitor's passport at any employment exchange. 'Amid the teeming millions of the small island it would be easy for him to disappear.' He claimed that my conduct had consistently shown my intention not to appear and that in Australia I had said it would be impossible for me to obtain justice in Britain.

As for my right to appear in the House of Commons and make a statement, Mr. Whitfield quoted from a former Clerk to the Commons who had given three previous instances in which MPs in custody had applied to attend. They were a Mr. McHugh, gaoled for three months in 1902, Horatio Bottomley in 1922 and Captain Ramsey, who was detained under a wartime regulation as a Nazi sympathiser.

Mr. Hampel very soberly explained the case for bail. His client had 'consistently, openly and honestly made every effort to get back to Britain to face the House and the charges,' and he said that as a man of 'ability, ingenuity and intelligence,' I could have skipped bail in Australia without much trouble. He argued that an MP's position provided a very important and special reason why bail should be granted, and to refuse it would effectively prevent me from putting my case to the House of Commons.

At the point the Magistrate, Mr. Evelyn Russell, interrupted: 'Do you say he is entitled to special consideration above that of a normal citizen because he is an MP?' Mr. Hampel replied not and Mr. Russell added: 'I certainly hope not. I misunderstood you. He is in the same position as an ordinary member of the public.' This comment from the bench revealed the extremely difficult position I was in: the court felt it had to lean over backwards not to show any special consideration, although my position as a public figure had ensured that I had received incredibly damaging press publicity which an 'ordinary' person would never have suffered.

Mr. Russell refused the application for bail, saying: 'You might not surrender and secondly, the serious nature and the number of charges and the large amount of money said to be involved.' In reporting the decision the newspapers of course gave the details for the umpteenth time: '21 charges alleging fraud, forgery, theft and conspiracy involving a total of £172,000.'

To the uninitiated the charges seemed awesome and daunting but those who had analysed them were less impressed. My Australian lawyers, now assisted by Michael O'Dell, a solicitor newly in separate practice and on his first big criminal case, decided to appeal urgently to a judge in chambers. They thought that a judge, looking at the case dispassionately behind closed doors, might see things differently from a busy magistrate in open court. They were to be cruelly disappointed.

Mr. Justice Kerr, who was the judge available on the following Monday, normally disposes of bail appeals in a few minutes and may have been somewhat alarmed when Mr. Hampel addressed him for fifty minutes. Although he was surprised that the insurance charges had been laid, since no claims had been made, he still rejected the application.

Although the courts and judges were against me, a certain amount of public sympathy was beginning to make itself felt. A Mr. Colin Lord Amery hit the headlines by offering £250,000 as surety for bail, and dozens of other people from all over Britain wrote to me in Brixton gaol to offer their support. My cell there, incidentally, had been prepared for my single occupation before the court appearance.

Newspapers reported that I had gone on a hunger strike, which was incorrect, but – acting on these reports – the prison staff were preparing to move me to the hospital and I wrote to the Governor to explain my position. It was a sign of the slight shift in media attitudes to me that my letter, which was smuggled out, was printed by the press. It read:

'Dear Sir – I would like to make it clear that I have no quarrel with the prison authorities: in fact your officers have treated me with courtesy and consideration. As far as I can see the food is excellent and make no protest about the food.

'My accommodation is quite satisfactory and I am content with it.

'According to a report in the *News of the World* and other newspapers, I requested to be transferred to the hospital on my arrival here. This report is not correct. I made no such request whatsoever. I have been advised that it is now reported that I will nevertheless be transferred to the hospital. I would object most strongly to this as I am perfectly fit.

'My objections relate solely to the conduct of the British Government in not making it possible for me to make a statement in the House of Commons. I should make it clear that such a statement would not be on my own case. My own case will be conducted in the courts of law. The statement will consist solely of such facts of which the House is not yet aware.

'The denial of bail was on the instruction of counsel acting for the Director of Public Prosecutions. Those instructions came from the Attorney General and it was therefore a political act designed to frustrate any bail appeal.

'Conversely, if the Attorney General had given instructions that bail was not to be opposed, bail would presumably have been granted.

'Since my arrest on 21st March I have consistently been granted bail by the Australian courts: It would be extraordinary of the English courts to grant me less. The opposition to bail in England is clearly politically inspired. Yours faithfully, John Stonehouse.'

The next try for bail came on the following Monday – 28th July – my fiftieth birthday. I decided to conduct the application myself, and this time the Bow Street Court was presided over by the same man who months before had issued the warrants for my arrest which had formed the basis for the extradition proceedings. It did not seem particularly auspicious to appear before him but I did my best.

The bail application saga went on for another six weeks including appeals by Mr. O'Dell, Geoffrey Robertson, who had been appointed as my barrister for the case, John Mortimer, the Queen's Counsel and playwright, and myself. Each time we tried to raise new points: O'Dell on the problems of consultation and preparing a defence in Brixton; Robertson on the fact that Poulson, Bloom and Savundra had all been granted bail and that, 'He has no money, no passport and a face that has launched a thousand Fleet Street headlines.' Indeed, he added, 'The press would probably follow him 24 hours a day.' All these appeals were to no avail.

Not until well into August, and after the House of Commons had risen for the summer recess, did the magistrate, without any forewarning and without any application being made, suddenly grant the bail which had been consistently refused for weeks. His decision was welcome if illogical.

I was learning that the courts of England work in curious ways: it is difficult for any layman defendant to reason the hows and the whys of the mysterious ways of the legal system. But, at least, I was free for the first time in over two months.

CHAPTER NINE

We now had to wait for the next stage in the trial drama, the committal proceedings which are usually held in a magistrate's court. These can either be under Section One of the Justices Act, which means no evidence is called and the business is fairly formal, or under Section Two, which involves calling prosecution witnesses for cross-examination by the defence. After consulting my lawyers, I had decided to opt for the second alternative as this would provide an opportunity, perhaps, for some of the charges to be thrown out and, as reporting restrictions had been lifted, would enable a lot of poisonous accusations to be fully ventilated. It would help to clear the air long before the main trial before a jury at the Old Bailey.

It is usual for the barristers on both sides of a case to consult about suitable dates for a hearing. This is a matter of convenience more than anything else; professional men have a lot of commitments and when they can oblige one another they invariably do so. But in my case there was no consultation. At one of the routine appearances at Bow Street, we were suddenly presented with a date for the committal hearing. It was 13th October – the date Parliament was due to resume after the summer recess and the first day that I could make my long awaited statement to my Parliamentary colleagues. It was either just a coincidence or a contrived date to prevent me going to the House.

My suspicions that it was the latter were increased when the DPP counsel, after having the coincidence pointed out to him, consulted his superiors about changing the date and came back adamantly saying 'no change'. The Attorney General, I suspected, had been asked and had refused to budge.

In the court itself, Geoffrey Robertson suggested 3rd November, but to no avail. 13th October was fixed.

Some weeks before, while I was in Brixton Prison, my solicitor had submitted the usual forms requesting legal aid, and as I was without available funds, apart from my Parliamentary salary, the application was granted. When the news came out a few MPs protested and there was some confused comment at the Liberal Party Assembly then taking place.

The problem of legal aid was also to plague me as soon as I arrived at the new Horseferry Road Courts for the committal proceedings. Before they could commence, two new charges were laid against me, claiming I had made false statements about my means. It was even more of a shock to my solicitor than to me, for he had reason to know that all my available assets, whatever they were, had been seized by creditors. I felt that the new charges had been brought more as part of a technique of intimidation rather than as serious in themselves.

On the opening day, as at most subsequent hearings, the Horseferry Road Court was packed with journalists. The press gallery, however, was hidden high under the ceiling as the architect had apparently believed that reporters should be read but not seen. In the well of the court we could occasionally hear them exchanging comments as they strained to follow the proceedings far below.

The public queued up for seats in a tiny box at the back, but it was quite inadequate and only the regulars who came early could be sure of a place. Among them was a young Ugandan law student who was born about the time I was working in his country for the Co-operative movement. He gave me much encouragement by reminding me that my efforts for Africa had not been completely forgotten or wholly obscured by the trial.

His dark handsome presence helped me to keep my sense of balance during the unsettling early stages of the committal. The prosecution's technique of making a wholesale condemnation of the defendant in a long speech setting out the 'facts' as they interpreted them, is naturally designed to establish a momentum in favour of the Crown from the very start. Listening to the catalogue of the cunning and calculated crimes for which I was supposed to be responsible, I could easily have begun to doubt myself. But the black man stood out as a reminder of the part of my life which the prosecution chose completely to ignore.

David Tudor-Price, the counsel for the prosecution, allowed

no respite in his attack on me, developing his theme from the closely typed speech which, I noticed, had been circulated in advance to the other members of the DPP team.

'Stonehouse,' he said, 'had become acutely aware of debts incurred by him and his companies and he planned to leave them behind in an elaborate scheme to fabricate evidence of his death and to take Mrs. Buckley with him to his new country where he would have a new identity.' Substantial sums, he went on, had been provided in false names overseas in Switzerland and Australia, at the expense of creditors.

'In the course of implementing this plan he committed many criminal offences of which the charges before the court were representative.' Tudor-Price put them into four groups, firstly: uttering forged documents to obtain birth certificates and passports in a false name; secondly: theft with Mrs. Buckley; thirdly: running up large debts on credit cards with no intention to pay, and fourthly: taking out five large life-insurance policies when 'it was Stonehouse's intention to disappear and considerable money would have been paid if he had not been discovered.'

As I sat in the dock, listening to this attack, I could easily have become dispirited by its carefully spun web of innuendo. However, I made a conscious effort to remember that the final trial – before a jury – is what really counts: the preliminary skirmishes, either in Melbourne or Horseferry Road, are no more than the manoeuvrings of junior officers, deploying the arguments on the field in preparation for the coming decisive battle which only the generals can direct. Already I could see openings in the armour Tudor-Price had brought forward but it was too soon for the defence to attempt to exploit them. Our turn would come.

There was, however, one small tactical advantage Geoffrey Robertson secured for me. The earlier denial of bail had prevented me going to the House of Commons to make a personal statement, and Bow Street Magistrates had for weeks given short shrift to the arguments that recognition should be given to my Parliamentary responsibilities. With the help of the Commons Library, I had unearthed the 1967 report of a Select Committee which had recommended that 'the courts, whether civil or criminal, should give appropriate weight, when exercising their discretion over such matters as the fixing of dates and the granting or refusal of bail, to the importance of the Parliamentary function of a Member who may be involved.' Armed with this document Geoffrey requested the adjournment of the court at the appropriate times so I could attend the House and make my statement. Mr. Kenneth Harington, who treated me much more sympathetically than the Bow Street Magistrates, readily agreed and promptly adjourned the court for the rest of the afternoon.

I was thus enabled to walk into the Commons Chamber – the first time for eleven months – and to hear a Labour MP, Max Madden, urging that I should not be allowed to make a personal statement. Although my situation was far from easy, his attack seemed curiously out of date, like a hustings speech repeated long after the General Election is over. In truth, the political campaign against me was gradually crumbling: the Speaker, Selwyn Lloyd, saw me that afternoon and promised that I could make a statement if he first agreed its terms. Step by precarious step, I was climbing back into the Parliamentary process if not yet into Parliamentary respectability.

It took three days of negotiation with the Speaker, through the Learned Clerks at the Table, to get the text of my statement approved; it was also agreed that it should be made on the following Monday, immediately after question time.

On that day I took a seat on the Tory benches, both to demonstrate my independence from the Labour Members who had demonstrated such hostility towards me, and also to return to the place where I had actually sat for most of my years as a back-bencher. By a strange quirk the man who happened to be sitting next to me, Peter Tapsell, had been my Conservative opponent at the Wednesbury bye-election when I was first elected nearly nineteen years before. At that time neither of us had anticipated we would someday be next together in such circumstances.

The House was very crowded considering it was a Monday and there was only a one-line whip. The Prime Minister had just made a statement about the setting up of a Royal Commission on the National Health Service and then promptly left the

Chamber. Only one other Member, a Labour man from Liverpool, left as I was called and his reasons might have been wholly unconnected. What was clear was that the mass walkout threatened in the media had not materialised.

I had an attentive House and they heard me, as is customary for a personal statement, without interruption. Mr. Speaker, however, intervened four times when he suspected I had departed from the text he held in his hand.

I started with an explanation:

'I think I should first explain that the fact that I am speaking from the benches of the Opposition side of the House has no party political significance whatsoever, I am standing here because this is the place that I occupied for most of my time in the House in the last nearly nineteen years, and indeed it was from this bench that I made a personal statement when I returned from Rhodesia some sixteen years ago on 13th March, 1959.'

Mr. Speaker stood up in his place and I sat down:

'Order.' he said. 'The rules are very, very strict. The Rt. Hon. Gentleman must say only what has been passed by me.'

I went on:

'I simply wanted to say that as there were some inquiries as to why I was at this bench, in particular from some hon. Members who were already sitting here, I felt that I should explain why I chose to speak from this side of the House.

'I am grateful to you, Mr. Speaker, for your agreement to my request to make a statement. It is not easy for me; nor is it easy for the House. The events surrounding my disappearance last November, and since, have created tremendous press publicity, and everyone's consideration of my experience has been coloured and influenced by that media treatment. There have been incredible allegations made against me . . .'

Mr. Speaker again was on his feet:

'Order. The Rt. Hon. Gentleman must be very careful. He is not now reading from the text which has been agreed with me.'

I said: 'I have made a few textual changes.'

Mr. Speaker: 'Let there be no misunderstanding about this. The Rt Hon. Member is entitled to say only what I have passed.'

74

To be on the safe side I returned to the exact text:

'In particular – you will see this in the text, Mr. Speaker – I deny the allegation that I was an agent for the CIA. I deny the allegations that I was a spy for the Czechs. I can only regret that the original stories were printed. The purpose of this statement is to explain, as best I can within the traditions of the House, why I was absent from the House for such a lengthy period.

'The explanation for the extraordinary and bizarre conduct in the second half of last year is found in the progressions towards the complete mental breakdown which I suffered. This breakdown was analysed by an eminent psychiatrist in Australia and was described by him as psychiatric suicide. It took the form of the repudiation of the life of Stonehouse because that life had become absolutely intolerable to him. A new parallel personality took over – separate and apart from the original man, who was resented and despised by the parallel personality for the ugly humbug and sham of the recent years of his public life. The parallel personality was uncluttered by the awesome tensions and stresses suffered by the original man, and he felt, as an ordinary person, a tremendous relief in not carrying the load of anguish which had burdened the public figure.

'The collapse and destruction of the original man came about because his idealism in his political life had been utterly frustrated and finally destroyed by the pattern of events, beyond his control, which had finally overwhelmed him. Those events which caused the death of an idealist are too complex to describe in detail here, but in the interests of clarity as well as brevity I refer to them as follows:

'Uganda was a country in which I worked for two years in the development of the Co-operative movement. I was active also in developing political progress and became, for instance, a character witness for one of the accused in the Jomo Kenyatta Mau Mau trial in Kenya.

'Later, as a back-bench Member of Parliament, I campaigned vigorously for African independence and became vice-chairman of the Movement for Colonial Freedom. Much of my back-bench activities at that time – conducted, incidentally, from this bench – were concerned with advancing this cause. I believed in it sincerely and passionately. But those ideals were shattered in the late 1960s and the 1970s as Uganda and some other countries I had helped towards independence moved from democracy to military dictatorship and despair.

'The Co-operative movement in Britain had been a great ideal for me from an early age. Co-operation was almost a religion for me. It was not only a way to run a business; it was a way of life from which selfishness, greed and exploitation were completely excluded. I became a director and later president of the London Co-operative Society, the largest retail Co-operative society in the world, in active pursuit of those ideals. I did not do it for money. The honorarium was £20 per year.'

But the Speaker did not want any domestic political controversy. 'Order,' he said. 'The Rt. Hon. Gentleman must say only what I have passed.'

I quickly abandoned any hope of adding points of substance, however vital to my narrative, and went on:

'That time was a most traumatic one for me and wounded my soul deeply. It had become cruelly clear that my Co-operative ideals were too ambitious, for, in truth, they could not be achieved, given human motivations. I felt as though my religion had been exposed as a pagan rite.

'Bangladesh is a country which I helped to create, and, with my Hon. Friend the Member for Mitcham and Morden (Mr. Douglas-Mann), I was one of the first in the House to take up the cause of self-determination for East Pakistan following the terrible events of the military crack-down in March 1971, when ten million people had to flee for their lives to the safety of India. I became deeply involved as a result of first-hand experience in Bengal during the struggle for freedom. I sponsored several early-day motions concerned with Bangladesh, including one which attracted over 100 signatories, calling for the recognition of an independent and sovereign Bangladesh. That motion, in July 1971, was most significant in the progression of events towards the independence which finally came in December of that year.

'Bangladesh made me a citizen in recognition of my identification with the cause. I was enthused at that time with hope, but the hopes turned to tears as the conditions in that country deteriorated. Another of my ideals had collapsed.

'After the Labour defeat of 1970, I became active in export businesses, a field in which I had been successful as a Minister and one in which I felt I could make a contribution in assisting British exports. I had hoped to establish personal financial security after a few years and then return to full-time political activity. My enterprises were successful.

'However, early in 1972, I was approached by Bengalis residing in this country who wanted me to assist the establishment of a bank to cement relationships between Britain and Bangladesh. This involved me in very great problems, which could have ruined my career and public standing, and I was left a broken man as a result of the nervous tension I suffered throughout that period. That experience contributed heavily to my breakdown.

'In 1974, with the collapse of many secondary banks and the problems of the British economy, the strains became even worse. There seemed no escape from the awesome pressures which were squeezing the will to live from the original man. Everything he had lived for and worked for seemed to be damned.

'In this House itself, I felt a big weight bearing down on me. It was physically painful for me to be in the Chamber because it was such a reminder of my lost ideals. I was suffocated with the anguish of it all. The original man had become a burden to himself, to his family and to his friends. He could no longer take the strain and had to go. Hence, the emergence of the parallel personality, the disappearance and the long absence during the period of recovery.

'That recovery took time, and in the early stages the psychiatrist in Australia advised that I should not return to England until I had recovered, as a premature return would inevitably do further harm to my health. At the time of the disappearance, no criminal charges were laid or anticipated; they did not come till four months later.

'In view of the facts I hope that the House will agree that the Rt. Hon. Member for Walsall North had no intention of

77

removing himself from the processes of justice as established by Parliament.

'I am not allowed by your ruling Mr. Speaker, to refer to what you consider to be controversial subjects, and of course I accept your judgment; but I remind you, Mr. Speaker, that one man's meat . . .'

Mr. Speaker would not allow me to add, 'is another man's poison'. 'Order,' he said. 'The Rt. Hon. Gentleman is again departing from the text.'

But I was on the last words:

'Yes, Mr. Speaker. I am simply explaining that I accept your judgment entirely, but a personal statement is a personal statement, and I must advise the House that half of my original statement was deleted by you. However, I fully appreciate your position, and I am deeply indebted to you for your sympathy, understanding and forbearance in the difficult circumstances which I have involuntarily created for you and the House during these past eleven months. I am very grateful to those Hon. Members who have extended understanding in my turmoil – especially to my Hon. Friends the Members for Mitcham and Morden (Mr. Douglas-Mann) and for East Kilbride (Dr. Maurice Miller), the Rt. Hon. Member for Down, South (Mr. Enoch Powell), and the Hon. Members for Chippenham (Mr. Dan Awdry) and for Horncastle (Mr. Peter Tapsell). I express thanks also to the Rt. Hon. Member for Worcester (Mr. Peter Walker) and the then Foreign Secretary, who both helped me through a terrible crisis in 1973. I thank the Clerks at the Table and their assistants, who have been exceptionally helpful in recent months.'

I sat down glad that at any rate I had been able to pay a small tribute to the few MPs who had tried to help me in one small way or another.

The crowded House rapidly dispersed as Barbara Castle stood up to start a debate on one-parent families.

The *Evening Standard* headlined its report in the last editions: 'Jekyll and Hyde', and the *Daily Telegraph* took up the phrase: 'Death of an Idealist'. The forum of the nation had heard from the only 'runaway MP' who had ever returned to its midst: through Parliament I had reached my fellow citizens outside. The committal trial might be proceeding in a small crowded courtroom in Horseferry Road, but the ultimate jury in the judgment of my actions would be not there – nor even merely in the Old Bailey – but in those teeming millions in the country at large.

CHAPTER TEN

Procedure in a committal trial allows the defence counsel to cross-examine all prosecution witnesses, and of this we took full advantage. Every morning I set my alarm to awake at five or six, and for two or three hours wrote out questions which Geoffrey Robertson was to ask later that day. The system worked well and many of its victims were, in reality, converted to being more useful to us than to our opponents.

We even had an unexpected bonus during Crown counsel's own cross-examination of one of his key witnesses. Mr. Alfred Gundry, the bank manager from Lloyds Bank in St. James's, had been called to confirm that he took a personal guarantee from me for an overdraft granted to EPACS. Tudor-Price asked: 'If you had known he was planning to disappear, would you have authorised the overdraft?' Gundry was precise in his reply: 'If it was the fact that he was planning to disappear and I had known of the fact, then of course I would not have authorised the overdraft.'

The clerk sitting below the magistrate was meanwhile reading the witnesses replies as a statement on to a tape-machine. It was a tedious process but had the advantage of allowing both counsel and witness to reflect, momentarily, on the next exchange. Tudor-Price continued, trying to establish a vital point: 'Did you believe his personal guarantee to be a guarantee of value?' Gundry said: 'I believed his personal guarantee to be a guarantee of value,' and to Tudor-Price's surprise went on: 'I still believe it to be of value.' Prosecution counsel, realising he was on to dangerous ground, tried to move to another subject, but the magistrate intervened: 'What did you say, Mr. Gundry, you still think it of value?'

'Yes,' said the impressive bank manager, 'I still believe it to be of value.'

'Why?' said the magistrate.

Gundry: 'That is because I think Mr. Stonehouse has a good life ahead of him, he has a potential force for good,' and making his point emphatically clear, he added: 'If in the event I have to rely on the personal guarantee, I do not consider it necessarily to be bad in the long term.' Tudor-Price sat down, abandoning further questions. Seldom in a court of law can a prosecution witness have so neatly turned the tables on the prosecution.

Under Geoffrey's steady cross-examination, other witnesses such as Jim Charlton, my bland erstwhile co-director, and Alan Le Fort, the diminutive accountant, had to admit that almost all the business in the companies had been obtained by me. They also demonstrated that I had made every possible effort to assist the bank to survive, during a period of unprecedented difficulty for secondary banks. It was valuable material to get on record.

Geoffrey's examination of Inspector David Townley was also brilliant. He concentrated on the Inspector's visits to the Dover Street offices. 'I cannot recall the dates,' Townley said, 'I did not make notes every time I went there. I did not make notes subsequently. I am required to write up my activities in my diary but not a notebook ... I visited the premises of EPACS before the date of the interview between Mr. Stonehouse and the Board of Trade Inspectors ...

'I cannot be specific without my diary, I do not recall the first occasion I went to the premises ... It was an occasion after it had become known that Mr. Stonehouse was alive and well in Australia ... I am not certain whether I took possession of any documents on that occasion ... The first occasion was purely an exploratory talk and discussion ... There came a time when I did take possession of documents from the EPACS office ... They were not taken from a safe at 26 Dover Street.'

It seemed to me that Townley was not helping the prosecution case, and then he admitted; 'I don't know which is Mr. Stonehouse's desk.' On the crucial point about documents he said: 'I at no stage went to the premises and made a top-to-bottom search of every document on the premises. I had no need to. There were certainly documents on the premises that I did not see.' He went further: 'I certainly did not specifically go and look in Mr.

81

Stonehouse's desk,' he said, and 'I cannot say whether the papers said to have been in Mr. Stonehouse's desk existed or not.'

Townley admitted that he had read the transcript of the Department of Trade Inquiry in which I had told the Inspectors that receipts were kept in my desk, and then said, surprisingly:

'I have made no further enquiries since reading the transcript.'

The cross-examination was adjourned so he could get his diary. When he returned, he was made to read out the dates on which he had visited the Dover Street offices in 1975. It was a startling revelation: January 3rd, 6th, 7th, 10th, 15th, 17th, 24th, 28th and 29th and in February, on 3rd, 4th, 6th, 7th and 19th – no less than fourteen times, and yet he said he had never identified my desk nor checked all my papers.

Evidence was read out from Ian Ward, the *Daily Telegraph* reporter, who claimed he had seen Sheila Buckley's clothing in a trunk sent out to Melbourne by Joseph Markham, my parallel personality. It was the most titillating item for the press, who were informed by the prosecution as to when it would be reached. Nevertheless, many of them missed the full lurid details and one of the DPP lawyers held an impromptu press conference, after the court adjourned, to read the Ward statement out at dictation speed.

After our protests at this extraordinary exercise in public relations, using court documents, the magistrate censured those in the DPP who were responsible. But the reporters already had their titbits and next day the headlines read in the *Mirror*: 'The Night Stonehouse Danced with Sheila's Undies', and the *Mail*: 'Tango with a Black Slip', and the *Express*: 'Runaway MP's Petticoat Polka'. It was a perfect example of journalistic embellishments on another journalist's imagination or of the media feeding on the media in an orgy of Fleet Street cannibalism.

The press also had a heyday describing the contents of letters sent by Sheila Buckley to Donald Clive Mildoon during the period I was living under that name in Australia. Clive was, in fact, the third parallel personality that I had adopted.

Sergeant John Coffey of the Victoria State police confirmed to the court that he had collected the letters from the Melbourne branch of the Bank of New Zealand, had opened them, photocopied the contents and returned them to the bank. The first letter was collected, he said, on 19th December and was postmarked 'Chippenham, Wiltshire, December 13th, 1974'. It said, in part:

'The rags are hounding. I have come away for everybody's sake. This is all because of my friend's death, which seems incredible. I have the most terrible problem. I don't have a friend in the world except you. My boyfriend is away at the moment and I have heard the most dreadful things about him from his former wife.'

At a later point the letter said:

'At the moment she is being questioned on our self-service project. He lied about the insurances to me. They suspect her of murder because of insurance. S. has had to promise to retrieve if she is accused.

'Industry is in 27 going through the whole project. JCM probably arranged that. Don't know quite what will happen. All I know is that I don't know about my boyfriend. Sorry to burden you. I know you must be going through it but you are my only friend. Shall write with an address. Don't worry about not writing.'

The second letter said, in part:

'I completely forgot to tell you of the end of the book I was to tell you about. The mystery was never solved and the verdict was never reached, so it was all rather unsatisfactory.

'The dilemma with my man still exists. He has not yet returned although he will do in due course, although I hope not. The thing that confused me mainly was the double life, so completely unnatural and so hurtful.

'My biggest problem apart from industry – like flies – is insurance. Mr. Fuzz wants to see me but I am not agreeing since I am not well enough. Mr. Michael agrees this is best but soon Mr. Fuzz will demand since Mrs. Boots is also front rag.

'Next morning: Mr. Michael has just called. Mr. Fuzz insists on seeing me on instructions of Mrs. Miampol. I am a link so must be OK with concrete thing.

'May well be J and Miss S is therefore territorized by Royal, etc. contract. Will never forgive that one for it automatically costs existence on junior contract.'

The prosecuting counsel explained that a policy with the Royal was the last of a series of policies taken out on my life.

A third letter said in part:

'I am in Brighton staying with uncle, the heart one. Mr. Rag is after me like crazy still. Mr. Fuzz wants to see me. I have no option to agree. George insists on stealing the scene on that other thing, front page in the local circular, every dayline head. I am so lonely, I shall wait for you for ever now.'

The fourth letter, which had a Christmas card tucked inside it, said, in part:

'I am only sorry I haven't better news about my friend. Ports project is still OK but frankly I can't see why, although it is only Mr. Rags who is blowing things up king-size. I believe my friend is still kicking somewhere and this is terribly disturbing.

'MGH rang me just before I went out and said Mr. Fuzz wants to see me definitely before Christmas. Just can't avoid his advances any longer. Will have to give up in London on Monday.'

It was becoming obvious that the prosecution were relying heavily on the letters to lend support to the allegations of conspiracy. Neither my counsel nor Sheila's – Mr. Jeffrey Gordon – were prepared to reveal the defence to this allegation. That would be reserved for the jury at the Old Bailey.

Some evidence from the prosecution witnesses was very useful to me. Inspector John Sullivan of the Australian Commonwealth police, for instance, reported that on Christmas Eve 1974, I had sent a cable to the Prime Minister, Harold Wilson, saying: 'I have had a breakdown. Apologies to all concerned for trouble caused. Thanks for your statement denying allegations of Czech spying which denial is correct.'

The Australian Inspector also told the Horseferry Road Court that on that fateful day, I had told him that I had been suffering from political and business pressures and was being blackmailed by certain individuals. Both statements were of enormous significance to the defence but, as on so many points, we could not use them until the Old Bailey many months ahead.

The committal trial lasted over six weeks and ended on a heartwarming note. My counsel, Geoffrey Robertson, had spent many hours arguing on legal grounds against the conspiracy and insurance charges. It was an impressive performance but, frankly, we had not expected him to win. As the defence cannot afford to reveal its plan of campaign for the final trial, its attack on the prosecution's case at committal is hardly full-blooded. When Kenneth Harington, the magistrate, announced that he was throwing out the five insurance charges, we could not believe our ears. All the other charges stood but to have a quarter of the famous twenty-one charges removed – especially as they involved seven-tenths of the monetary figure bandied about on my case – was a signal victory.

However, our delight was shortlived. Within weeks the *Daily Telegraph* reporter assigned to the case rang me to say he had heard a rumour that the five charges rejected by the magistrate were being put back in the indictment. The story was checked by Michael O'Dell, my solicitor, and the DPP was made to admit that it was his department's intention to pursue the insurance cases at the Old Bailey. It is extraordinary that this procedure is allowed and, even more, that the defendant concerned is almost the last one to be informed.

Despite the long committal trial, and all the arguments deployed by counsel, we were back just where we had started, simply because of the whim of the DPP. Again I was learning – in the hardest possible way – that the legal process is an esoteric mystery which can only be fathomed by that special breed of men who have eaten the requisite number of dinners at the Inner Temple or Lincoln's Inn.

PART TWO

The Trial

CHAPTER ELEVEN

During the seven weeks before the Old Bailey trial I consulted a Queen's Counsel, Richard Du Cann, whom it was intended should represent me, along with Geoffrey Robertson as the junior counsel. Such consultations on a complex case are essential if the advocate is to understand the points to make; certainly they cannot be obtained merely from a brief prepared by the solicitor. But the defendant immediately comes up against immense problems of timing. If his chosen counsel is successful, and therefore is in demand – and, according to Mr. Du Cann, they all have to be on a sort of taxi-cab rank waiting to be hired – he is almost certainly bound to be committed to other courts in the period up to the hearing of the case.

In the event I was only able to see Mr. Du Cann on eight occasions of about two hours each. It was hardly sufficient time for me in which to tackle the myriad of points which might be raised in a marathon trial taking, perhaps, three months – twelve weeks – sixty days or a total of three hundred hours. The idea of defending myself, and thus removing the barrier between myself and the jury, had appealed to me from the early days. What finally decided me on that course was seeing the transcript of the first long interview I had with Victoria State policemen on Christmas Eve, 1974. It came into my hands – after repeated requests over the previous seven months had been rebuffed – only five days before the trial was due to open.

In my view the transcript contained political dynamite: confirmation from Scotland Yard to the Australians that they had no other charges to prefer against me other than a false passport offence. In the letter I wrote to Mr. Du Cann, which was released to the press, I expressed my appreciation for his efforts. I said:

'As my trial opens next Tuesday, the time has come for me to make a decision as to who to appoint for the defence. I have not, as you know, made any announcement of an appointment. As the charges were originally brought against me for political reasons and now the prosecution have shown by the depositions they have brought forward that they want this to be a political trial, I have decided to defend myself.

'It is the best way, in my view, to bring out all the facts for the benefit of the jury. It is very important that they should appreciate the full circumstances surrounding this case rather than being asked to judge the defendant on a narrow legal intepretation and argument which may confuse them and distract them from their wider duty. Besides being jurymen, they are representative citizens of the nation as a whole.'

So when, on the morning of Tuesday, 27th April, just after ten, I walked into court Number One at the Old Bailey, I knew, without any shadow of doubt, that the key to my future was held only by myself. It was both a sobering and an exhilarating thought.

It took some time for the hearing to get under way as the judge – a slightly built man of fifty-eight – had first to hear some applications for bail. Sheila Buckley and I were allowed to sit at the rear of the court to hear them. For an hour or so we were in the audience looking on the dock, where we ourselves would soon be the object of all attention. It was thus possible for us to assess Mr. Justice Eveleigh; and what we saw did not dismay us. Two bail applicants were allowed against police objections, which showed a likeable independence of mind.

When it came to our turns, bail was granted willingly and furthermore – to our surprise – we were allowed freedom of movement during lunch breaks provided we remained with our respective solicitors.

I had agreed that Du Cann could make one last application before withdrawing; he was allowed to do so as *amicus curiae*, which can be freely translated as 'friend of the court'. His was a motion to quash the reinstatement of the five insurance charges which the Stipendiary magistrate had thrown out. He said the fact, even if accepted, amounted to no more than a preparation and could not constitute an attempt to defraud as no application or claim had been made by my wife to any of the companies.

Michael Corkery QC, the senior Treasury counsel appearing for the prosecution, argued that in taking two steps – in arranging life cover and staging my death – I had done all I could do towards defrauding the companies. The legal argument, with the ritualistic quoting of precedent cases from the well-worn law books of the Old Bailey Library, went on for nearly four hours with the judge, who had intervened several times to clarify points, eventually ruling in favour of the Crown.

When my two barristers had left I asked the judge to consider a short adjournment so I could master the defence that I had just inherited. I explained that the transcript of 24th December had only recently come into my possession and touched on the political nature of the case which this attempt to suppress information seemed to indicate. The word 'political' seemed a red rag to a bull for Mr. Justice Eveleigh and his friendly manner suddenly became most stern. I attempted to amplify my request but he said, 'You will sit down or be taken down and there you will stay until you decide to obey the directions of this court. If I am wrong, there is another court which will put me right.'

I tried to explain that I had been advised to apply for the adjournment precisely at this stage but he said firmly, 'You will sit down or be taken down. You must make up your mind. You are not going to delay these proceedings. Any point you may wish to make may be made after arraignment.'

The judge had exerted his authority and demonstrated who was in charge. After all he could not appear to be less severe than the Deputy Speaker of the House of Commons who had recently had me banished from the precincts under the little used Standing Order number 23.

On the next day I apologised for my misunderstanding of the procedure, and the judge said very kindly, 'Think nothing of it, Mr. Stonehouse.' I hoped I had established a tenuous rapport with the judge, which is no bad thing in a criminal trial – he is, after all, only human although wearing a red cloak and a wig.

The first day ended with the reading out of each charge and the pleas, all Not Guilty. My counsel had advised me to plead Guilty at least on the birth certificate and passport offences which I had already virtually admitted in statements to the Australian police and in my book *Death of an Idealist*. But I considered there would be no real advantage. I certainly did not want some squalid deal with the prosecution – that would have been right up their street – and the medical evidence, particularly Dr. Gibney's from Australia, could only be introduced on a Not Guilty plea.

Then there was a scurry at the rear of the court. The prospective jury had entered – all fifty of them. I looked round from my seat in the front of the huge dock, standing like a raised stage in the centre of the court and providing a good vantage view. In my hand was the list of those summoned for jury service which my solicitor had obtained for me the day before. Although it showed only full names and addresses and no occupation I had discerned, from checking the addresses in an A–Z book that Tooting, Hackney, Charlton and Barking were most likely to produce working-class people. Women predominated on the list by two to one and their first names – Edith, Amelia, Ella and the like – indicated the older age group.

These were the sort of people we wanted least as they would be most likely to be prejudiced at the outset.

Lord Wigoder, QC, for Mrs. Buckley, had the same idea and objected to five women, including, I was sad to see, a black lady. I challenged four women, and the Crown surprisingly, one. Others, and also a man, were allowed to excuse themselves on grounds of taking care of sick relations or holidays arranged early in July. One self-employed consultant was excused because long jury service would harm her work. The list started with precious few professional people or anyone with experience of business and I despaired that we would get anyone who could appreciate the strains of running even a small company. A jury, I was learning, is a gamble – as with other aspects of life – except that it is most unlikely to be a fair cross section of the community.

In the end we secured, thankfully, a majority of men by seven to five, including three in their twenties, and all were from working-class addresses except for one lady from Blackheath. Of the rest no less than six were from Barking and two from Hackney and Stoke Newington, two from Wandsworth and Tooting and one from Willesden. The 'professional' belt of Dulwich, Canonbury, Hampstead, Fulham, Chelsea, Kensington, Twickenham, Kingston and Richmond were not represented; some of those are catchment areas for other Crown Courts.

As we left the court one bewigged wag was heard to remark cynically, 'we do have some experts on Company Law on the jury,' but, frankly, I was much heartened as the members of jury gave me a strong first impression of being genuine. One would not hope for more than that, for with a fair jury I had a good chance to get my defence across.

CHAPTER TWELVE

The trial, now over the preliminaries, began to get into its stride on the second day. The twelve jurymen (or should it be jurypeople?) were in their seats looking smarter and more alert than on the day before. So all the elements were present: judge, jury, counsel (I counted seven barristers of whom five were retained by the Director of Public Prosecutors) the press and the public and the two defendants.

Each daily session is preceded by a few formalities. The entrance of the judge, whose sword or mace of authority is already fixed in position on the wall behind his seat, is followed by a court usher's voice intoning the morning greeting in archaic phrases.

The defendants actually never hear the greeting, as part of the ritual demands that they only enter the court when in session from the direction of the cells below. It meant depositing my case and papers on the table, which had been kindly provided for·my use in the dock, and descending the steps to meet Sheila on a bench below. It was a welcome chance to have quiet words with her and as the days went by I changed my original resentment to the procedure. We had agreed we would not speak to one another in the court itself as the press – or indeed the jury – might misinterpret. The brief conversations we had each time the court resumed were therefore very useful and sometimes we had a laugh about the improbability of the situation – sitting under a signature, indelible but probably false on the wall above, of Crippen, the notorious murderer, who had heard the death sentence in the same dock we were about to enter.

The judge delivered a homily to the jury. 'Cast out of your minds anything you may have heard or read. Do not talk to anyone about the trial. You must not do it. You must not talk to anyone else until it is over.' And Michael Corkery opened for the prosecution with the well-worn phrases: 'The judge rules on the law and the jury must listen to the arguments and apply commonsense. Only consider evidence you hear from witnesses, cast out of your minds any matters you may hear about outside this court.' He went on with references he considered more specific for this case. 'Ignore comments in the press, in magazines, on TV; ignore reported interviews with family and friends. Cast out of your minds any prejudice and do not be influenced by political beliefs. This is a crucial trial involving grave dishonesty: politics do not come into it whatsoever.'

Leaning over the immense pile of files and papers on the desk in front of him and speaking slowly and deliberately so the jury would follow each and every syllable, the Crown counsel developed his theme with simple analogies. 'I want to give the story in outline,' he said. 'It is like a jigsaw puzzle with the true story on the outside of the box. Sometimes bits of evidence are missing but the story is one of overwhelming dishonesty.' The jury looked towards me at this point, sensing the dramatic confrontation between the Queen's Counsel and a Privy Councillor, but I did not sense hostility in their eyes.

Mr. Corkery left no stone unturned in the search for adjectives to build the image of the criminal in the dock but fell back time and time again on the words fraud, deceit and dishonesty. After describing the defendant's 'distinguished career' as a Minister and MP, he said, 'He faced bankruptcy, disgrace and ruin and decided that his only course was to flee to Australia and start a new life with Mrs. Sheila Buckley, his secretary. He arranged a new identity and set about plundering funds of companies, of which he was a director, at the expense of creditors. He insisted in arranging insurance policies which would bring in £125,000 for his wife in the event of his being presumed dead.'

Mr. Corkery then gave an analysis of the setting up of my companies in 1970 and the British Bangladesh Trust in 1972. As he spoke, I rapidly wrote a longhand record of his remarks, pausing every now and then to make a marginal note of points I would subseqently want to make in amplification or reputation. I had said it was a political trial; in fact my political training would help me to reply to this sustained attack from the Crown counsel. As Mr. Corkery spoke, my spirits rose. On almost every page of his speech I detected what I believed to be inaccuracies. I know that most people would be distraught if they had to bear the torrent of abuse still coming from his lips in a never-ending flow – the phrases came around again as on a roundabout and punctuated his narrative: 'very clever, very ambitious, very elaborate and utterly dishonest' – but I had schooled myself to take a professional stance towards this attack. The House of Commons had been a good training-ground for nineteen years; one needs a thick skin to survive there for so long.

In any case, I reflected, in one sense, the experience of the trial had to be welcomed as an opportunity to let it all come out and be exposed. Like bursting an ugly boil. I was able to listen calmly as Mr. Corkery spoke about the ingenuity of preparing Company minutes, showing people present when they never were and, he went on, 'Like so many documents in this case they are bogus, false, spurious, dishonest.' That word again. I thought wryly that Mr. Corkery should look up Roget's *Thesaurus* but probably he already had, for his vocabulary of terms in the the field of fraud seemed to be remarkably complete.

Mr. Corkery outlined the alleged crimes: stealing cheques from EPACS – 'Some of them signed by Mrs. Buckley who was not signing blindly or because she was a stooge. The prosecution case is that she knew perfectly well that what she was doing was to help Stonehouse to remove those funds to hide them away until it was convenient to meet her in Australia.' He spoke of a cheque for $12.500 from a Los Angeles corporation, Garrett, which had wanted to use me as a consultant, how the cheque had been paid into my own bank account and how I had been questioned by the Department of Trade Inspectors on the matter in Australia. I was delighted to hear this reference as, under legal procedure, once the prosecution have referred to a document it becomes relevant in full, and later I wanted to refer to the inquiry.

Then he described count five – obtaining pecuniary advantage by deception – the personal guarantee for an overdraft to EPACS – and solemnly read from the banker's standard form of guarantee: 'the amount will be payable on demand', and as he did so the absurdity of it struck me. I noted on the margin, 'What is the point of overdraft facilities if the guarantor has the liquid resources available on demand? Confirms the old adage: Banks only want to lend to people who do not need to borrow.'

'Notice his signature on the guarantee form,' said Corkery. 'Perhaps the jury might like to ring it. That signature on a document is utterly worthless. It was part of a plan to steal from EPACS and put money safely away.' It was coming up to four o'clock and adjournment time, and Corkery concluded with a flourish: 'This is not a political crime; it is a criminal trial.'

The whole court stood up with the judge standing in his place facing the assembled participants of the drama which was to be played out below him for several succeeding weeks. The usher intoned the traditional closing remarks, entreating all those present to return next day, and then the judge walked out, the jury and public gallery dispersed, the press and the TV commentators left to meet their deadlines and the barristers sorted out their papers. The two defendants waited ten minutes, as instructed by the judge – so they would not bump into jury members on the stairs – and also left to prepare for more verbal onslaughts which would certainly follow on the next day.

In fact the attack was just as severe as on day one. For five hours with only one short morning intermission and an hour for lunch, Corkery pressed home his case. 'The various birds came home to roost after his disappearance. The overdrafts for his various companies were just under £200,000; the schedule of personal debts showed £375,000 and his contingent liability in personal guarantees was £729,000.' The sums quoted sounded vast to jury members whose annual budgets would all be in single thousand figures.

He went on, referring to the British Bangladesh Trust shares deposited at the banks for security, 'I am not going into details but the BBT shares are of very limited value.' As he continued, I made a red underlining of his phrase 'not going into details' to remind me to do so at the appropriate time.

Corkery then spent time describing the activities of Mr. Markham – booking into the Astoria hotel, St. George's Drive, London for one night a week, opening of bank accounts at the Post Office Giro, Midland Bank and the Bank of New South Wales and establishing a business address in Regent Street. 'This is all good, clever stuff or perhaps I should say bad clever stuff,' he added with a grimace.

Corkery went through various credit card transactions – amply demonstrating that in this computerised and over-documented age *American Express*, *Diners' Club* and *Barclay Card* are the sleuth's best friends. 'These credit cards in his hands,' he said, 'were nothing more than the instruments of fraud.'

Corkery spent the third day of his introductory speech analysing the various applications for insurance policies, pointing out that two different doctors' names were given on different applications, but failing surprisingly to point out that all the forms except one were completed by the applicant, Mrs. Barbara Stonehouse, and not by the defendant.

Then moving on to four 'coded' letters written by Sheila Buckley to Donald Clive Mildoon at the Bank of New Zealand in Melbourne, counsel's voice picked up, for he knew that, whatever else, the jury from now on would give him close attention. He was right. They sat intrigued and entranced as he read them through, sometimes pausing to omit passages which he said would be embarrassing to the defendant, but which I felt would be favourable to Mrs. Buckley in revealing the full context of her situation at the time of writing.

Most of the letters had been released at the committal proceedings. The *Daily Mail* and the *Daily Mirror* had both received the full texts months before the committal. The *Mail* had quoted from them at length in July 1975.

The newest twist to the prosecutor's case was their interpretation of the £125,000 life insurances and of the words 'to retrieve' in one of Sheila's letters. Next day the *Daily Express* gave the story the main position on the front page under the heading: 'Stonehouse jury told of confession fear if wife Barbara was accused of killing' and a banner 'MURDER, LOVE AND SHEILA'. 'To retrieve?' asked Corkery. 'Did that mean that Mrs. Buckley promised to tell the truth about the disappearance if Mrs. Stonehouse faced charges?'

The use of the evidence of the trunk from *Daily Telegraph* correspondent Ian Ward, was also not neglected with Corkery, almost apologetically, adding the words: 'He picked up a black slip and did a little jig,' himself seeming to jig a little with his arms as he said it. He then quoted from my denial written in Sydney just after the original story had appeared in the *Daily Telegraph*, when I had said that the clothes belonged to my wife who had returned to London with only hand luggage. Corkery went on, 'Mr. Ward will tell that he saw the clothing before Mrs. Stonehouse had even arrived in Australia, so this passage could hardly be true.'

Sitting in the big dock, I retained my composure outwardly but inwardly I was elated: Corkery had now made what I believed to be a glaring mistake and this on top of his analysis of Sheila Buckley's current bank account at about the time of my disappearance, presumably designed to show how impecunious she was, but failing to bring into evidence her deposit and Building Society accounts.

After an hour and a half of legal arguments on admissibility, which I had opened by quoting, in my best Queen's Counsel style, from the Old Bailey law books, the court adjourned for the weekend. Strange to relate, I was happy. The prosecution had done their best to damn me in a fifteen hour speech, and I was happy. It was unbelievable but true. That evening, I fried myself a supper of sausages and tomatoes and hummed the melodies from Eugene Onegin. I was happy.

Corkery had ended his marathon address with the words. 'Members of the jury, in this case there is no sudden breakdown. This is a story of crime where a very able and talented man over a period of at least four months covers up his disappearance and spins a web of deception in which almost every single strand is fashioned with ingenuity and great ability. Obviously when caught on Christmas Eve there was a great deal of sorrow and torment. You will decide the case on the evidence you will hear. Apply your commonsense to the evidence and if you do your honest best no one can complain.'

I was happy because on that basis, and with a fair jury, I

felt I would be acquitted. The prosecution in fifteen hours had done their worst. In due course we would see whether the edifice they had erected would stand up to examination. I found I was positively looking forward to the next stage of the drama in court Number One.

CHAPTER THIRTEEN

The second week at the Old Bailey opened with legal arguments on admissibility. Armed with *Cross on Evidence* and another lawyer's book with a name like a TV Western series, *Hogan and Smith*, I posed the question whether material on the activities of the British Bangladesh Trust and the London Capital Group was relevant. I know there are general rules about what can be brought into a case – obviously there has to be a limit otherwise complicated charges, particularly fraud, could go on for ages – but in the last analysis it is for the judge to decide.

One firm rule, however, is that the material sought to be presented by the prosecutor must not be prejudical to the defendant in another connection. For instance, if a man is charged with burglary, evidence which suggests he committed a murder can not be introduced unless he is also being charged with that crime. This legal point was to be of profound significance.

I was in a split mind about my application to stop the Crown drawing in all the details of the audit of the bank and I said so in my remarks confirming that I wanted the totality of the issue to be revealed and nothing hidden. In my mind was the realisation that the court could better understand the causes of my breakdown if the hoary and harrowing facts came out. But lawyers had told me that the admissibility point should be canvassed as it might become an issue for Appeal Courts at a later date.

My speech – largely consisting of quotations from past cases – was therefore somewhat perfunctory but had the effect of creating an exchange between judge and Crown counsel which somewhat put the latter in his place and it was a pity the jury had to be absent for this stage. The judge ruled, somewhat obliquely, that some of the material could come in but the Crown should proceed with caution; thus I got the best of both worlds.

In the process of this argument both judge and Crown counsel had to confirm that there was no suggestion of illegality in any of the bank's transactions or activities which were about to be revealed. It was more than a good beginning as far as I was concerned; it was the most secure base on which to build my defence and I was able to take full advantage of it.

The first prosecution witness was a man called Albert Stokes, a Fellow of the Institute of Chartered Accountants, who had conducted the last stages of the audit of LCG in the second half of 1974. Corkery guided him through documents with the intention of demonstrating that there had been a deliberate attempt by the defendants to delay the audit completion so – as he had put it earlier – they could steal more money. A great deal of emphasis was put on the fact that a Miss Sheila Black had operated an account for the purchase of Stock Exchange shares and the auditors had never known, until they asked the question, that she was Mrs. Sheila Buckley acting as a nominee. All this was unravelled as though it was extremely sinister evidence of conspiracy. A telephone call by Stokes to the EPACS number in which he asked for Miss Black and Mrs. Buckley answered to say there was no one working there of that name was described. For it was the most powerful, if not only, point in the whole bank material which they alleged supported the conspiracy theory.

As Corkery skilfully held the hand (or rather the tongue) of his witness through his evidence my confidence grew by the minute. If this was, in fact the worst they could do with their first key witness, on whom they were trying to build the edifice of their case, then my task would be easier than I thought. Furthermore Stokes looked nervous and when it came to my turn for cross examination it began to look as if he were the defendant in the dock.

At the beginning I persuaded him to concede that attitudes to an audit are altered by changes in accountancy practice and also by changes in the general economic environment. I opened up the second point by going through the saga of the collapse of secondary banks. The names of the companies which had gone under in the debacle of the last two years came pouring out in my questions: London and County, which had started the trend, and Jessel, Triumph, Burston, Keyser Ullman, First National Finance Corporation and nearly a dozen others. Had not these banks received support from the Bank of England and the big clearing banks? 'Yes,' said Stokes, remembering a figure of £1,200 million. Did LCG need or receive any of this support. 'No,' said Stokes. And it survives today? 'Yes,' said Stokes, admitting more specifically later that his intensive investigation on audit matters was brought about because he was surprised the bank had no great problems although others had been undermined through the catastrophic fall in the value of property on which much of their advances were made. It seemed odd that a client company should be penalised because it floated without support when all around were sinking.

For hour after hour, I took Stokes through the file of exhibits on the fateful audit in 1974 revealing how the auditors, Dixon Wilson, had raised one series of quotations, receiving the directors' replies invariably by return of post, only to ask another set of questions. The exchanges showed how some auditors work – nitpicking their way through a maze of transactions towards a final confrontation. Early in my questions, I called the process a 'cat and mouse game' but later the pain was so apparent I amended the description to Chinese torture.

Stokes was in the box for ten hours over three days and for about eight and a half hours under my cross examination. At the end I went through the charges against me broadly by categories. 'Do you know anything about these alleged offences?' 'No,' he answered, 'Not at all.' 'Why are you here then?' 'The prosecution asked me to come' was the final, curiously revealing reply.

The second witness, Leslie Powter, a manager with Dixon Wilson, the auditors, went through the same hoops. I was not nearly so severe on him as his role had been more of a functionary. After pointing out that the judge had confirmed that no illegality was alleged in relation to bank matters I asked Powter did he know anything about the actual charges. 'No,' he answered to each category, 'No, not at all.' 'Why are you here, then?' 'The prosecution asked me to come,' he replied.

I also had a bonus in the exchanges with the auditors. Time and time again they revealed that their memories could not cope with detailed quotations without recourse to documents or diaries. The fact that the defendant had been denied access to his files would later emerge as a vital item.

The judge made few interruptions to my line of quotations and almost all of those were helpful in gaining clarification. I upset him only once when analysing what Powter remembered about a particular conversation by emphasising how much depended on his recollection: 'A conspiracy charge carries a maximum penalty of life imprisonment,' I blurted out. 'Now, Mr. Stonehouse,' said the judge, shifting his place slightly in his seat, 'you can't say that.' It was only a gentle admonition and, anyway, I had made my point for the jury to hear.

Gerald Hastings, who had been with me thirty years before in the Royal Air Force and had subsequently contacted me when I was Postmaster General, next appeared hot-foot from Brussels. His evidence was on the acquisition of LCG shares for which he had been granted an overdraft by the bank. The prosecution wanted to demonstrate malpractice in the handling of documents and the unauthorised transfer of the proceeds from the sale of the shares to my own company, EPACS.

Hastings, admitting he was impulsive, conceded that when he had signed the loan agreement, I had given him the opportunity to take documents away to study them first. He also acknowledged that although subsequently he had thought the signature on the debit slip was probably a forgery he now knows it was his, although he could not recall the amount of £5,180 being on the slip at the time.

Crown counsel played up Hastings' dismay that he might have lost a profit of over £5,180 and sought to confirm that he had been only a personal friend of the defendant and in no way a business agent. Both flanks looked decidedly shaky after my cross-examination. Hastings fell into great confusion when he said he had understood he was a nominee because he had not yet paid up the full value of the shares and therefore would not expect the profit. The judge displaying a great interest at this stage took over the questioning to the defendant's great advantage. 'How did you interpret your position as a nominee, Mr. Hastings?' he asked and the witness virtually admitted he had no rights in the transaction.

It came out loud and clear that he was delighted when he heard it was cancelled at a meeting with Mr. Stonehouse in Brussels in September 1974. He had even broken a bottle of champagne to celebrate. And he had incurred no loss except that after Mr. Stonehouse's 'breakdown and disappearance' the bank had sent him a demand for £17,000 and then frozen the £600 he had left in his current account.

I then turned to two devastating pieces of information. Firstly, Hastings sheepishly confirmed he had introduced me to a business lawyer, Oswald Bühler, in Liechenstein, to set up an agency called VICTA and confirmed 'there is nothing exceptional in a multi-national business concern using such agents in international trading.' Secondly, he was handed his own handwritten letter showing his own detailed investigations into arms supplies for Bangladesh, way back in 1971. 'I only did it for a friend,' he remonstrated. 'Well, I would have expected commission if the deal had gone through,' he conceded. Would you like to amend your statement to Scotland Yard to the effect, 'It is totally false to say that I could be described as his business agent in Brussels or anywhere else for that matter.' He would not and, in some confusion, added from the box, 'I did not expect these matters to come up.'

There was laughter in court when he acknowledged that the letter was signed '1066'. There was also a hearty laugh after Hastings had said that personal tax in Belgium is 20% and the judge, smiling, said, 'May I congratulate you on living in such a splendid part of the world.'

The press, thank goodness, had largely turned to other subjects as the case got into its long stride but the *Mail* and the *Sun* ran reports likening me to Perry Mason, the American TV lawyer of yesteryear and the *Express* used a headline 'Stonehouse, QC'. It was certainly better than 'Runaway MP' which had been the staple diet for newspaper headlines during the year before.

CHAPTER FOURTEEN

In the third week the trial is getting into its stride; everyone is settling down. We all know we are going to be together for a long time and whatever the idiosyncracies of the other participants in the drama we must make allowances in the interests of a smooth passage towards the final destination. It is rather like the atmosphere in a cruise liner on a long voyage with passengers, who had previously no particular knowledge of each other, thrown together for hours on end, day after day. After the first awkward days they learn to respect and even like fellow travellers, although normally they would have no time for them, because they know that such commitments will be no permanent strain on emotions for the time will inevitably come for the final 'goodbyes' and everyone will scurry back to the havens of their own lives.

Under the eyes of the captain, attempting to keep everyone to the rules of his ship steaming over the oceans of paper, the deadly contest continued as the witnesses, called like pilots at each port of call, guided the newcomers over the shores of new evidence. For myself, I felt more and more at home as the days went by. The awe inspiring atmosphere becomes mundane after the passage of time and one also begins to appreciate the intensity and rich humour of the human relationships thrown up by the unique atmosphere in court Number One at the Old Bailey.

The friendly City of London policemen on the door, like the stewards on the cruise liner, had seen it all before. 'We take an interest in the game,' one said, 'and it is a game,' he emphasised. 'But we can't afford to get emotionally involved on one side or the other – that would be too wearing. We like to see who's winning.'

'How am I doing?' I asked incautiously.

'Very well on the first few witnesses, you were scoring good points, but . . .' he hesitated.

'Go on, tell me,' I said.

'Well, not so well in the last two days,' he added frankly. He was referring to my encounter with my nephew Michael Hayes who had appeared a somewhat hostile witness. The prosecution had highlighted the points considered to have adverse reflections on me: minutes of meetings where directors were not physically present, transfer of Bank shares and the ignorance of the directors of EPACS of a Stonehouse loan account. It was part of the general campaign of innuendo and as the nephew did not appear to want to defend the uncle it became, to that extent, more effective than with earlier prosecution witnesses.

In my cross-examination I brought out the exceptionally valuable point that no sensible contact had been allowed between the defendant and the witness, so as to enable any explanations to be given on the penalty of prison for the defendant for the bail offence of 'interfering with witnesses.' I hoped the jury, at least, would ask the question: 'How could the nephew possibly understand the uncle unless they were allowed to talk?' The operation of the 'course of justice' cuts across families with impunity and it became obvious that as far as Michael Hayes was concerned the breach was deep.

However, he did confirm to the court that all the consultancy business in EPACS – the contracts with Dowty, ICL, Britten Norman and the rest – were obtained by me without any help and serviced by me. 'Was EPACS then just an extension of Mr. Stonehouse?' I asked. 'Oh yes, it was wholly his company, he did with it what he wished,' he answered, helpfully. But on the voluntary liquidation of EPACS decided upon during December 1974 and confirmed at the meeting of two Directors – John McGrath and Michael Hayes – on 2nd January 1975, he was less than helpful. 'It came about because you took out money and left the company insolvent,' he emphasised.

'But were you certain it was insolvent?' I pressed, drawing into evidence the report produced by Philip Gay, the Secretary of the company in October 1974 which had shown the value of the leases owned by EPACS at £128,000, on certain 'conservative' assumptions. He floundered a bit on that as well as on my questions about which creditors were pressing for repayment and why the banks did not allow time for the company to sort things out.

'And why didn't you seek explanations from Mr. Stonehouse the owner of the company, before pressing ahead with liquidation?' I asked.

I then sought to bring into evidence the newspaper reports which appeared during the period of my disappearance as confirmation of the vicious atmosphere created around my name at that time and inevitably influencing the nephew against his uncle. He confirmed he had read the reports about a million pounds alleged to be missing from the Bangladesh Fund, that he had read the denial put out by the former President of Bangladesh, Abu Sayeed Choudhury and that he had seen the *Daily Mirror* reports on allegations that I was a Czech spy. But when I came to a report about the sale of a house near Salisbury the judge intervened: 'Now, Mr. Stonehouse, you must try me no further. This is not evidence for this witness.'

Mr. Justice Eveleigh, assuming firm command of his ship, sent out the jury and the witness, to give me another little lecture. 'There are ways of doing it, you see, but not this way. I see the point you are making, and I think you have made it.'

The jury filtered back and the witness returned. My point that the two directors had taken their fateful decision to liquidate in the context of a great deal of confusing and damaging publicity, had I thought, got across. There was no point in pursuing it. But the text of a minute passed by the directors on the fateful day of 2nd January and which had only come my way through an extract from the Department of Trade Inquiry, was still to be brought out. It called for an explanation from Mr. Stonehouse for his borrowings from the company.

'Do you know how this request was conveyed?' I asked.

'No, I presume the Secretary did it.'

'Do you know the reply?'

It was clear that he never checked any reply.

'So you just passed the buck to the firm Cork, Gully, renowned as company undertakers, without bothering any more?'

'I had a lot of other things to do,' he answered.

'Exactly,' I said.

Michael Hayes, as solicitor to my wife Barbara, was invaluable as a witness on the insurance matters. It was significant that the prosecution had asked him no questions on this score although they had previously made great play with the importance of a letter written by Stewart Green also on December 12th, 1974 to the six insurance companies. It had been according to Corkery, the inevitable first step towards a claim under the policies. But under my cross-examination the solicitor, rather than the nephew, confirmed that no claim was in mind and that the letters were written only after press publicity and to divert any inquiries from Mrs. Stonehouse, who was most harassed, to himself. His evidence also confirmed that most applications were almost wholly written out by Mrs. Stonehouse who was also the proposer in every case and paying the premiums from her own resources. All were valuable defence points which prosecuting counsel had deliberately failed to notice.

My final quotation to the nephew was a daring one in view of his apparent hostility. 'Did you complain to the police about the EPACS cheques?'

'No,' he said.

'It was merely a civil matter then?' I pressed.

'I prefer not to answer that question,' he replied, probably feeling that he had done enough to help me. It had been a thoroughly disagreeable encounter for both uncle and nephew and we were both heartily glad it was over.

One witness who turned out to be an unexpected bonus to the defence was the inoffensive and neutral Mrs. Ash of the Registry at Somerset House. She had originally merely produced a formal written deposition on birth certificate applications. Before the trial my defence counsel Richard Du Cann decided it would be pointless to call her as an oral witness but when I took over I changed that decision. It turned out to be a good move. Firstly, she acknowledged that if she saw a sick person on the pavement on her way to work she would give help even if it meant being late for work. 'You would not regard this as a deflection from your public duty?' I asked pointedly.

'No,' she answered, perplexed and still innocent of my purpose. 'There are others in the office to do my job if I'm late.'

She also agreed, surprisingly, that it could be possible for an application form for a birth certificate to go through without a signature of an applicant on it. I handed her a birth certificate for Michael Patrick Hayes O'Dell which my solicitor had obtained in his own name through an unsigned application and the receipt so she would come back with that particular form. The prosecution looked as worried as cruise tourists who had suddenly lost a point in a bridge tournament and even more so when I handed over another receipt for a certificate obtained with an application form without signature or applicant's address. It began to look as if the alleged forgery on an application was as irrelevant as the allegation to deflect a public servant from her duty.

It was interesting that the newspapers failed to report any of the evidence about the irrelevance of signatures on official application forms. It made me curious: perhaps a 'D' notice had been put on the information to prevent it reaching the eyes of the public.

Ronnie Harker, who had been an executive with Rolls-Royce, was called by the prosecution to give evidence on a proposed nominee holding. What he had to say was apparently totally unconnected with the charges but the Crown had done me a favour as he became my own character witness. After he had talked about my work for British aircraft exports I asked, "Did you regard Mr. Stonehouse as a man of integrity?' 'Yes,' he replied. 'Do you still regard him as a man of integrity?' 'Yes, indeed,' he added.

With such witnesses for the Crown I wondered whether I needed to call any one for the defence. As the case seemed to be coming within my control I could, in a sense, 'relax and enjoy it.' 'Enjoy' is hardly the appropriate word and 'endure' might convey a more accurate meaning. But there are moments of amusement for me: Seeing the warder sitting behind me in the dock reading a paperback hidden in the drawer of his little table and the young DPP barrister sneaking a look at *Private Eye* in the middle of a bundle of depositions. I had an invitation from the proprietor of the New Court Restaurant, facing the Old Bailey, to have lunch there. He had the name of Alibi (actually spelt Allibhai) and I found this very amusing, but on reflection perhaps it is not all that funny. Maybe to be subject to a long session at the courts heightens the sensations and makes one a little intoxicated. If so it is something I must learn to control as I 'relax and endure' the long and intricate voyage through the labyrinthine ways of my recent experiences.

CHAPTER FIFTEEN

Week ending Friday, May 21

The processes of law are supposed to operate like pieces of machinery which are well-oiled and maintained in perfect running order by the barristers and judges who are the mechanics to the industry. Although the professionals strive to keep it mechanical, they do not always succeed because the fodder is not some inanimate material which can be moulded or analysed according to definite rules of science. The throughput of the court's sausage-machine is the testimony of witnesses and the evidence they bring forward is never, and could never be, pure unadultered fact. The truth is elusive, as it can only be conveyed by human beings who are bundles of emotions and not just flesh and blood automatons.

In some trials the near-truth may be easier to come by than in others; in conspiracy and fraud cases it is certainly obscured by the mists of motivation which are most difficult to clear even with the strongest lights of understanding. And everyone suffers from quirks of memory and feelings of disgust or respect for the accused which inevitably colour what they say.

As the prosecution witnesses were brought forward one after the other, I became fascinated by this aspect of the proceedings. Each person in the witness box became a reflection of the same series of events which had taken place two to three years before, but no two mirrors showed the same image. The passage of time – and more significantly the particular vantage point of the individual concerned – had distorted the actual truth in an intriguing way. As the story unfolded I also became painfully aware that my immediate associates in the Dover Street enterprises had all been operating in compartments in which they were largely insulated from the tensions and pressures which had grievously affected me.

In their single-minded and resolute quest for a conviction the Crown counsel always seek to elicit from their chosen witnesses only those points which serve their sole purpose. If the information the witness has might be favourable to the defendant, it is only a clumsy or incompetent prosecutor who will allow it come out. The way Corkery and his junior, Tudor-Price, guided the string of company employees who were brought to the box confirmed their skills as prosecutors. Alan Le Fort was asked to confirm his role as accountant always acting under instructions from Mr. Stonehouse; the loan account and the inter-company transfers were the creations and instruments of Mr. Stonehouse and Mr. Le Fort became 'very concerned about the insolvency of the companies and the extent of Mr. Stonehouse's personal guarantees'. He had resigned because of his concern and although he had told Mr. Stonehouse he might join his father's practice he was surprised that a statement had been circulated among staff mentioning that as a fact. His evidence did not amount to a great deal but from the Crown's point of view aimed to show the defendant's Svengali-like direction of the staff towards, they implied, a devious purpose.

My cross-examination of Le Fort, which took two and a half days, turned him into a most effective witness for the defence. It was fortunate that, having resigned before my disappearance, he did not suffer the resentments of the other staff members and could speak more objectively. Firstly, I got him to confirm that minutes for small companies are usually regarded as a mere formality and in the case of EPACS Annual General Meetings were produced by the auditors as routine without regard to the physical presence of directors. It was beginning to make a nonsense of Corkery's opening on the 'spurious, bogus minutes'.

When I turned to the consultancies EPACS had with various companies the answers became even more useful. The consultancies were all obtained by Mr. Stonehouse, said the accountant, and Mr. Stonehouse could have taken the money himself or put it into any other company he chose: EPACS was a mere convenience, it emerged. And as Le Fort took the ledger which he had handled so many thousands of times in the years before, he rattled off amounts received from the clients: ICL £13,000, Westland Aircraft £11,000, Mullard £4,500, Leyden £5,500, Shorts £14,000 and many others. And who had worked very hard on the consultancies? 'Mr. Stonehouse.' Gone abroad for them' 'Yes.' The *Daily Mail* in its report added up the totals, which I could have taken personally, to £69,000: it was ironic, at last, to be having such help from the paper which had been, at one time, my most vicious attacker.

As to the notorious loan account it became clear that it worked both ways: for long periods Mr. Stonehouse was owed large sums by the company. At other times, in the years 1971, 1972 and 1973 there were amounts advanced to Mr. Stonehouse which were larger in total than the balance alleged to be outstanding on November 20th, 1974. At the end of each financial year the account was always regularised: clearly it was an accountancy device for advancing and transferring monies for the company's purposes rather than representing 'loans' to Mr. Stonehouse for his purely personal requirements.

Le Fort also confirmed that I stimulated business for Global Imex, the trading company, and that much of the commission carried could have come to me personally. The de la Rue printing of banknotes for Bangladesh, he acknowledged, resulted in over £30,000 being paid in cheques to me personally which I had endorsed over to the company. It was the same sort of story with regard to commission on Fokker aircraft.

On current business prospects the accountant confirmed he would not know of the entrepreneurial efforts being made for electronic sales in the Yemen, fertiliser plants or railways in the Sudan, sales of Rumanian cement or work anywhere else. He would only know of these enterprises when they resulted in successful contracts producing income for the companies and he appreciated that expenses would be incurred in advance.

On credit cards he confirmed that *Diners Club*, *Barclaycard* and *American Express* would invariably be paid monthly from EPACS as the expenses were incurred for the companies, and for personal use of the cards I would provide my own cheque.

The prosecution had made great play with an investment in Stock Exchange shares through a British Bangladesh Trust subsidiary called Finsec Securities apparently to imply malpractice in that Miss Sheila Black had become the nominee for the holding. But Le Fort remembered that the project had been approved as an investment for the benefit of BBT at a meeting of bank officials just after Christmas 1973. What was even more valuable was that he remembered the memorandum which had given rise to the scheme and this enabled it to go in as an exhibit. When I came to my questions about Sheila's involvement, Le Fort honestly remembered that she had taken over the portfolio merely in an attempt to assist the bank by hiding from the auditors a heavy loss which had by April 1974 been incurred, following the collapse of share prices. He confirmed that up to October 1974, £40,000 had been paid in on Mr. Stonehouse's instructions from EPACS and associated companies to make up the loss on the shares.

The prosecution's allegation that I was stealing money from the companies was beginning to look decidedly thin. It seemed even more pathetic when Le Fort, who had also been accountant to the bank, confirmed that when depositors came to withdraw sums which were simply not in the tills due to liquidity problems, Mr. Stonehouse actually paid in cheques on his personal accounts to help the bank over the crisis.

When Philip Bingham, the Cambridge graduate who became my P.A. appeared, I thought I was in for a difficult session. The prosecution had clearly spent a lot of effort in getting his evidence as useful as possible for their purposes. In fact there was little really adverse he could say although he did show his hostility. When my turn came, I opened by demonstrating that there had been no communication between us since my re-appearance and therefore no opportunity for me to explain my bizarre conduct in November and December 1974. I then quoted from various newspaper reports of the period – the Czech spy story and the account of the alleged one million pounds missing from the Bangladesh Fund as a means of demonstrating that Philip Bingham had been adversely influenced by the prevailing campaign of hate at the time.

The judge, as ever vigilant to keep within the rules intervened and took over the questioning, 'Let me put it like this,' he said, 'were you deflected from doing your duty by what you read in the newspapers?' 'No,' was the predictable reply but later Bingham acknowledged that he had lost 'respect' for me and it was difficult for anyone not to see that the press must have played some part in his change of heart.

From my position in the dock, I passed a series of papers via the court usher to Bingham standing twenty feet away in the witness box. First a blotting pad. 'When did you last see that?' 'In my office, it has my signature on it.' 'And these photographs?' 'Yes, they are like the ones in Stonehouse's desk.' 'And this sign?' I handed over an old EPACS sign. 'In Number 6, Dover Street, probably in January 1975.' 'And this letter?' I handed over a letter from the solicitors to the company Aeromaritime, of which I was chairman, dated 24th December, 1974 – the day I was reported discovered in Australia.

'I saw that in the offices.'

'Why was it not sent on to Mr. Stonehouse?'

'It was not my responsibility to do so.'

As I passed over more envelopes – some still unopened and postmarked February and March 1975, months after my re-appearance in Australia the judge said kindly, 'What is it you are getting at, Mr. Stonehouse? Members of the jury and I are mystified. You have been following the same line for fifteen minutes and we don't see where it's going.'

'This is the reason,' I said, becoming more emotional than I wished to be. 'This is the reason,' putting a big plastic bag of rubbish on the dock ledge, and then a cardbox of documents, then another. 'These are the reasons. I found this rubbish just a fortnight before this case started in Your Lordship's Court and it contained my private papers and letters addressed to me which had not even been opened. Thrown out any old how onto the pavements of Dover Street because those people, – I pointed to Bingham – 'had no concern for my interests.' I sat down. 'Sorry to be overcome,' I said to the judge, who had so kindly allowed my outburst without interruption. He defused the electric atmosphere by turning to Bingham, 'Have you seen this rubbish before?' 'No,' he said.

The judge turned to me with his now customary steely smile. 'There you are, you see. There is a way for you to bring this in; at the appropriate time you can either make a statement from that dock or take the oath in the witness box but we can't deal with it now.' He adjourned the proceedings – it had already reached 4.15 pm – and after we had all stood to see out the judge, with his little hat and white gloves clasped in his hand, I stowed the rubbish away under my table in the dock to await another day.

For the next two days I cross-examined Bingham in detail and secured many valuable points. He acknowledged that the bank had been formed to assist Bangladesh and the Bengali community and that I was idealistically involved in the cause of Bangladesh when it gained its independence.

He confirmed that the information handbill in the Bengali language was not a prospectus and that no money had ever been collected on it. Only Barclays Bank (London and International), the receiving bankers, had actually handled applications, and the forms in that connection had always been distributed with the official prospectus.

All this was valuable material to get on the record in view of the need to bring in the effect of the devastating article in the *Sunday Times*. Bingham, who by this time had shown himself to be the most pressy and pedantic witness, did admit that the attack in the week before the applications opened did have the effect of discouraging many potential shareholders and created the shortfall on the minimum requirement of £500,000. He then ever so reluctantly agreed that nominee holdings were arranged to make up the balance but his manner made the fact as elusive as a slippery eel.

I went on to get on the record the Department of Trade investigation which had 'sent shivers down the spines' of BBT officials but that there was relief when the allegations were not substantiated. Then, he confirmed the arrival on the scene of Detective Inspector Grant and I asked was he aware of the harassment, tension and persecution I had suffered from Scotland Yard over the allegations. The investigation, which he thought lasted two months, was merely concerning the Bengali translation in the handbill. He also agreed that I had produced a long memorandum for the Director of Public Prosecutions detailing BBT transactions; and that later the matter was dropped, but only after prospective customers had been frightened off because of approaches by the Fraud Squad.

As we went through the ludicrous and thoroughly unjust episodes which had caused me so much anguish at the time, I could feel the tension building up within me. I had to fight them back so as to maintain the illusory appearance of control in the conduct of the cross-examination. I had already allowed emotion to take over during the demonstration of the rubbish and I could not afford too many such outbursts.

I next took Bingham through the list of consultancies and export prospects being pursued in 1974 simply to demonstrate to the jury that he knew precious little about how the business was obtained. When I asked whether he knew Hafeez, the undercover agent in Bangladesh, and anything about inducements to get contract he answered, 'I do not know that. I have read in the newspapers that it is a common practice in some countries.' It was the best I could hope for from an obviously unco-operative witness, but it was useful. So was his answer to the direct – and daring – question, 'Did you at any time after 20th November go to the police and complain that you thought a criminal act had been committed in relation to the loan account or anything else?' 'No, sir,' he said and I breathed a quiet sigh of relief to myself. Eleven prosecution witnesses so far and not a single complainant.

The week's performance closed with Philip Gay the ex-major who had joined me a month after leaving Army service in Belfast. His military voice boomed so much in the amplification system (installed only in the witness box) that the judge complained of the oppressive noise and had it toned down.

Corkery took Gay through his evidence on the appointment by the Garrett Corporation of America as though he were revealing some terrible frauds. 'Yes,' the fee was shown on the appointment letter as $25,000; 'No,' that amount was not shown as being paid into EPACS bank account. At this point Corkery seemed oblivious of the fact that according to the evidence already before the court that only the first $12,500 had been paid over by Garrett anyway. Obviously the learned counsel for the Crown was getting lost in the bogs of business which were foreign country to him. Gay soon put the matter into perspective by confirming that Garrett only wanted me as consultant and that I would have chosen to take the fee myself or pay it to any company I chose.

Gay was also useful to me in cross-examination as I used him to open up the huge range of business opportunities being followed up in 1974. It sounded like an extract from a Chamber of Exporters Report: Racal Electronics, value £4 and commission of £400,000, to the Yemen; Rumanian cement, profit potential £500,000, to Iran or Nigeria; Marconi Transmitters to Bangladesh; Cyprus cement to Libya; hotel complex on the Gulf; General Dynamics buoys for the Bay of Bengal; fertiliser plant, value ten million pounds, for the Sudan; British Rail railway equipment for the Sudan; bailey bridging for Mauritius; whisky for the Yemen; textile mill for Tanzania and so on. The court was boggling, the potential business ran to millions.

Gay also confirmed the list of EPACS creditors made out by him on 9th December, 1974, showing the credit card accounts of *American Express*, *Diners Club* and *Barclaycard* payable by the company as normal practice. As I was charged with defrauding these companies, this was a vital piece of evidence. But as I looked down the list I noticed another item which had previously escaped my attention, 'Inland revenue £333.10' which was in respect of my past salary of £1,050. 'Wow,' I thought that was one of the cheques deducted from the loan account and the entry showed the officials as believing at the time it was past salary and Gay duly confirmed it was. I was chalking up little victories along the way and to cap it all, Gay also averred that he did not, at any time, complain to the police, despite his obvious hostility. 'I did not pass on Mr. Stonehouse's mail after his re-appearance because it was immaterial to me,' he had replied to the question about the non-delivered mail. 'I did not seek any explanation from Mr. Stonehouse, I felt he had walked out on us,' he added. It was a telling phrase which exactly demonstrated my situation: condemned by my own once loyal staff without the opportunity of communication.

If my own associates would so condemn me for my bizarre behaviour about which they had read in the papers with a particular slant, who could blame others for doing likewise.

The case was beginning to plumb the depths of human sensitivities – or should it be 'insensitivities'.

In the lofty corridors I met Chief Superintendent Kenneth Etheridge, the Scotland Yard Fraud Squad chief in charge of my case, who sits in the well of the court all day every day. On the air journey from Australia he was my escort and I had carefully refrained from uttering a word to him so he could not do a 'verbal' on me. Now we talk and he is most affable. He asks me for a copy of *Prohibited Immigrant*, the book I wrote in 1959 on my experiences in Uganda and Rhodesia, and also for a signed copy of *Death of an Idealist*. I oblige with an inscription 'To Kenneth Etheridge with personal regards and regrets that we did not meet earlier (say in January 1975 or even Chapter 11).' I am of course referring to the first trip he made to Melbourne after my re-appearance and when he failed to interview me; the chapter reference was to the Fraud Squad investigation into the Bengali handbill.

When I saw the superintendent again he said, wreathed in smiles, 'You've given me the first valuable contribution to the Etheridge archives.' I said, 'You must wait around for the next book, you might find yourself in it.' I wondered later, 'Are superintendents usually so friendly with defendants in court Number One at the Old Bailey?' and come to think of it, 'are defendants usually so pally in return?' It is a strange trial; soon I will have the superintendent in the witness box and my questions must in no way be tempered by the corridor conversations. There is too much at stake for that.

CHAPTER SIXTEEN

As the judge had announced that his court would be adjourned for three extra days during Whitsun, I decided to try to use part of the time to finish consultations on the 'Policy on the Irish Problem' which the English National Party was preparing. The need to find solutions to a running sore that had lost fourteen hundred lives in terrorist attacks in eight years, and which cost the English tax payer six hundred million pounds a year in subsidies, was uppermost in my mind. Already in the House of Commons I had put questions on the redrawing of the boundaries in Northern Ireland and in the Army debate had argued for European troops to replace British soldiers on law and order patrols. Any realistic policy, I thought, should involve the European community as both Northern and Southern Ireland were members of the EEC and, perhaps, could edge towards an understanding of the historic dilemmas under that umbrella.

But to pursue these ideas I had to talk to politicians in Dublin. Accordingly I politely enquired of Mr. Justice Eveleigh whether my bail conditions could be amended over Whitsun to enable me to go to Ireland. The prosecution did not actively object but limited themselves to saying it posed 'great difficulties', but the judge rejected the application without more ado, emphasising, in a gesture towards the press boxes, that his ruling was not exceptional and would apply in every case: 'The defendant cannot go outside jurisdiction.'

I was not surprised by his decision but I had thought it was worth a try; later in the week I was to bitterly regret that I had raised the issue. The week, in any event, was an exhausting one. I was spending nearly five hours a day on my feet in the dock using cross-examination to dig out the essential facts for my defence and then going on to the House of Commons for a further five hours of hectic politics. On Monday evening I arrived just in time to sit in front of Enoch Powell as he spoke on immigration with all his customary flair for dramatic revelation. On Tuesday I spoke on the Whitsun adjournment debate – but only for seven minutes not wishing to repeat the ridiculous episode at Easter when the Deputy Speaker had excluded me from the House because, he claimed, I had spoken too long and repetitiously. In fact I had been stopped as soon as I referred to the association between the Prime Minister and Sir Julian Hodge, the banker of South Wales. Enoch had put the record straight by putting down a motion, mildly condemning the ruling, and insisting it be debated which, it was generally agreed, resulted in my being vindicated. This time he sat behind me and tapped me on the shoulder to say with a smile, 'Now, don't let me down this time.' My speech on the pyramid selling scandal, which had badly affected a constituent who had lobbied me that evening, passed off without incident.

On the following day the Government's business on the Aircraft and Shipbuilding Industries Bill collapsed due to a procedure wrangle and the Bail Bill was suddenly put in its place, For the second day running I found myself seeking to 'catch the Speaker's eye'. And the Speaker himself, ever courteous, sent me notes, signed 'Geo', to say when he would call me. When I spoke to him in the Chair later to thank him, he was extremely friendly about the case saying, 'I do hope you are acquitted; there has been so much prejudice against you.' His words were acutely apposite, as the cross-examination was currently demonstrating.

Mr. Fuller, the manager of the Midland Bank in Victoria Street, had revealed that his bank's confidential notes on clients had recorded the word 'prejudiced' in relation to me because of the adverse effect of newpaper articles at the time of the launching of the British Bangladesh Trust. And he went on to admit that the formal demand made on me to honour the personal guarantee in relation to the EPACS overdraft was without the usual preliminary negotiations because of the atmosphere generated in January 1975 by both the press reports and the police inquiries. It was again confirmation as to how prejudice had worked against me.

But the bonanza of the week was not on the point of prejudice but on the value of the leases at 26 and 27 Dover Street.

Philip Gay, who had become Secretary of EPACS, had written a report in October 1974, estimating the value at £128,000, assuming the landlords did not obtain permission to re-develop. In January 1975, a firm of valuers put in a report to the liquidator saying the landlords were not now intending to redevelop, showing the rents received for 27 Dover Street at £26,000 per annum, with two vacant floors, and putting a typically cautious estimate of the least value at £11,000. As the profit rental per year was in the region of £20,000 this seemed to be an under-estimate.

When the liquidator revealed, under my cross-examination, that the lease had been sold for only £5,000, I was astounded. For several dramatic seconds I was quite lost for words. The 'pest' became ever more curious when it transpired that the lease had not been offered around nor advertised, and the Midland Bank had willingly accepted £5,000 because their own rights under the mortgage they held had been undermined by their own negligence in failing to register their interests with the landlord four years before. It was a tangled story but one totally relevant to my situation for I was charged with obtaining a pecuniary advantage by deception in giving a personal guarantee to Midland Bank for the EPACS overdraft. If the facility had been paid off by the sale of the lease for £17,000 or more, then no charge could have been laid. Or, better still, if EPACS had been kept going then it would have met its liabilities from rental income.

The succession of witnesses from insurance companies helped to demonstrate one essential fact: all the policies on my life were taken out by my wife with the premiums paid by her and the benefits payable directly to her. They also confirmed that no claim was ever made. In his long opening speech Corkery had made great play with a letter written on 12th December, 1974 from Stewart Green and Co of Winchester by Michael Hayes, acting as solicitor to my wife. He called it the 'inevitable first step towards the submission of a claim'. When a Mr. Pextow the actuary for the Yorkshire Insurance Company, was in the witness box he confirmed that the letter was in fact written as a result of publicity in the *Guardian* newspaper about insurances and was not a claim. Very daringly

I chanced my arm with the question, 'Did you regard this letter of 12th December as the inevitable first step towards the submission of a claim?' For a long time he hesitated and I feared the worst. Michael O'Dell looked up at me from the table in the well of the court with apprehension all over his face. It was a tense moment – so much depended on his interpretation of my question. But the answer eventually came back exactly as I had hoped: a simple and gloriously definite, 'No.'

Other evidence that no claim was contemplated was given in the letter written by my wife Barbara to the Canada Life representative after he had written expressing condolences. She replied that the news had been a 'nightmare' and 'depressing and nervewracking' and the press had been 'unbelievable' but more 'searches were continuing'. The same representative also threw light on the original reasons for insurance which he gave as the fact that the existing insurances were all pledged to the various businesses and that my car had been blown up at Heathrow.

In any case involving fraud allegations, it is, I suppose, inevitable that every witness does his best to protect his own position. From a succession of participants in the drama of the British Bangladesh Trust came the impression that their roles had always been perfectly pure. Against this evidence which was, after all, from *prosecution* witnesses it seemed to me vindictive and discriminatory to attack me for my conduct of the bank's affairs. Everyone acknowledged that I was, after all, only an unpaid non-executive chairman.

On the Thursday evening, just before the Whitsun Parliamentary recess, the House of Commons was the scene of unprecedented uproar. I found the opposition parties in voting against a Government device to circumvent Parliamentary rules on the hybridity of the Aircraft and Shipbuilding Industries Bill. On the first vote there was a dead heat of 303 votes against and the Speaker gave his casting vote with the Government. It only won the immediately following division by allowing a whip to vote, although the Conservative whip claimed he was paired. The ensuing bedlam, with Labour members singing the Red Flag in the Chamber, a Tory front bencher seizing the mace and members exchanging a few blows, was incredible.

As I left the crowded chamber a Tory member turned to me and said, 'I hope you conduct yourself better at the Old Bailey than this.'

On the following day I had a severe test of self-restraint. Just two days after I had spoken for half an hour in Parliament on the iniquities of the bail system, my own bail was called into question. The judge cleared the court to ask me searching questions about Ireland and a proposed writ to Walsall. 'I require you to report twice a day and to remain throughout the Whitsun within the Metropolitan Police District.' Furthermore, he added, residing at my home address meant sleeping there. As I had never had to report more frequently than once a day, and after comittal only once a week, the judge's conditions were unecessarily restrictive. I quietly pointed out my long-standing constituency engagement that very evening, and the judge's questions about that were equally searching. Only when he was told that my solicitor was proposing to drive me to Walsall and to return the same evening did he relent to allow me out of the Metropolitan area just for that visit – but the reporting conditions were not altered.

It would be interesting to know the reasons for the judge's actions but it is unlikely that I will ever be told. Curiously enough I find the imposition of reporting restrictions has depressed and debilitated me more than the trial itself, although a successful political meeting in Walsall has provided some balance to improve my morale. It certainly would not have seemed possible a few months ago that I would have a meeting in my constituency without a demonstration or at least hostile questions. To have had neither does demonstrate the healing process of time and there is a heartening lesson in that for anyone on a long trial.

CHAPTER SEVENTEEN

Whitsun was not much of a respite, even though there was an extra two days of 'freedom' before the court resumed. Reporting twice daily to the police was a tedious chore and the inability to leave the Metropolitan Police Area seemed so oppressive as almost to be an imprisonment. Walking in Kew Gardens one sunny afternoon, skirting the groups of foreign tourists, was the happiest time. Suddenly, for an hour or so, the Number One Court at the Old Bailey seemed a million miles away and totally irrelevant to the real world of laughter, expensive soft ice-cream, glorious rhododendron bushes and Tridents booming overhead on their way to London airport.

I was almost relieved to get back to the hearing, anxious to speed up the grotesque charade so it could be concluded before all the summer had ebbed away. And still the prosecution had not completed their string of witnesses. More bank officials to hear, reciting the details of accounts I had held and facilities I had been granted. Corkery asking the same question, 'Would you, if you had known Mr. Stonehouse had the other liabilities shown in the schedule and was planning his disappearance, would you have granted him this overdraft?' 'Most unlikely,' was the inevitable reply; its value to the Crown limited by its repetition a dozen times. I tried to put the unfairness of the question into perspective by asking, 'If you had known Mr. Stonehouse was going to have a breakdown what would you have done?' The question – designed, of course, for the jury – usually caught the witness unaware and he would mumble: 'Ask to see him,' which suited my purpose admirably.

Then a witness from a firm of stockbrokers gave details of share transactions and 60 per cent advances from banks for investment purposes. Gradually the eyes of the jury were being opened to the intrigues of the world of high finance: it was important for them to realise that whatever share manoeuverings I might have engaged in, they were not exceptional. It was my responsibility to set out the arguments against allowing the material in as evidence, as the prosecution had already won on the issue in the Magistrates' Court and thought they could rest on their laurels. After explaining that I did not want to suppress any evidence but was concerned about the 'route' by which it was presented – and the precedents that would be established if it were allowed – I set out the points. Principally they concerned the rules against hearsay – that is a witness quoting what he has been told at second-hand. Normally this is only allowed if the person being quoted has since died. There was also the question of the admissability of a photograph of a document which was not actually a contemporaneous record of a transaction – a computer read-out, I submitted, was specially obtained and had not been produced in the ordinary course of business.

My trump cards were to quote the Criminal Evidence Act of 1965 and to say that if Parliament had actually intended copies of documents to be admissible then it would have been specifically stated and the fact that the 'evidence' was based on a triple hearsay. The last point concerned the visit by a Detective Inspector Lewis to Zurich where he had seen a Dr. Klingenberg, the bank's lawyer, and obtained from him the photograph of the read-out and other material. The 'evidence', I said, was therefore hearsay upon hearsay upon hearsay, as Inspector Lewis was reporting what someone had told him and in turn Dr. Kingenberg had reported to Lewis what someone had given to him. It was too remote, I submitted, to come within the rules of evidence.

In my preamble to this argument I had pointed out to the judge that the prosecution had relied heavily on inference arising out of innuendo. Seeking to submit 'evidence' obtained in Switzerland was another example, particularly as it was aimed at inferring that cash drawn out in London had been transferred to Zurich, which was untrue. There were no charges relative to the Swiss bank account or to transactions abroad, and the fundamental question must be asked – is it relevant to the actual charges or is it being introduced merely to produce another innuendo? I pointed out that the circumstances were unique and that the judge's ruling, if he allowed the evidence, would break new ground in admissability. I emphasised that the prosecution were bringing in circumstantial evidence to support an inference upon an innuendo and that the defence were constantly at a disadvantage through the Crown digging up isolated transactions of companies not named in the indictment. A lot of time had been wasted, I said, in trying to put those transactions into context. After quoting several cases, for good measure, I concluded, 'I am not a lawyer but I suggest it would be entirely wrong for a fundamental point of law to be decided on the basis put forward by the prosecution. It would be a very dangerous precedent.'

After several searching questions about the actual photographs of Swiss Banking Corporation documents, the judge reserved his judgement. I felt annoyed that he had not ruled immediately; and I had just cause. It was over a week before he gave a preliminary ruling and that showed that I had won the main burden of the argument. The photos of the computer read-out and paying-in forms would not be admissable. Michael O'Dell was pleased. We had won our first major point; it was the watershed of the case and from now on, we told ourselves, we would be coasting downhill.

But there still remained more prosecution witnesses and one, in particular, who was very disagreeable. Ian Ward, a correspondent for the *Daily Telegraph*, had become my friend at a critical time when I was at my lowest ebb in January 1975. He had helped me write an article on the constitutional implications of the setting up of a Select Committee of the House of Commons to discuss my expulsion. He had started producing a book of my experiences mainly by recordings on tape.

When Sheila Buckley was under siege from the press in a Cornish farmhouse, Ward suggested the name of a friend who could help her leave England and the service of his Chinese girlfriend in Singapore who would provide accommodation. He was, at the time, a friend indeed.

The prosecution set great score on his evidence that he saw a trunk being unpacked in my 'unit' in the Toorak Road, Melbourne, that it had just come from the Customs' shed and that I said that the woman's clothing belonged to Sheila Buckley. The inference was, of course, that the clothing had been packed and despatched in the trunk from London before my disappearance and this was a vital point for the prosecution to try to stick to show a basis of conspiracy. In his opening Corkery had said Mr. Stonehouse will claim that it was Mrs. Stonehouse's clothing but that would be impossible as it was 'before Mrs. Stonehouse ever arrived in Australia'.

By this time evidence had been given – by Michael Hayes amongst others – that Barbara had already been in Melbourne. Ward, under my cross-examination, agreed. He also confirmed the close association that existed between us although he said he was only doing his job as a journalist.

My initial examination included the reading of extracts from Ward's articles in the *Daily Telegraph* in 1972 on Vietnam in which he has spoken of the strength of the Thien regime. After some moments on this the judge intervened to ask, in his by now characteristic way, 'Now, Mr. Stonehouse, what is the relevance of this?' 'Your Lordship I am seeking to show that Mr. Ward wrote articles with the best intentions, but which were subsequently shown to be untrue. It is important for the defence to establish that.'

'Well,' said the judge in one of his quick replies, 'Two American Presidents were also wrong about Vietnam.' 'Exactly,' I murmured, hoping the jury had grasped the point, despite the raucous callow laughter in the gallery.

Ward went on to give me surprisingly good material. He had with him a copy of his letter to Jim Patterson volunteering to collaborate on a book. He confirmed the press harassment in Melbourne, saying he wanted no part of it, and accepted that I had had to move addresses frequently to avoid the attentions of reporters.

He would not accept that the events in the 'unit' which earlier he described as 'dancing a jig with a black slip' arose because I had said what a joke it would be if the press thought the clothes belonged to Mrs. Buckley. But he acknowledged that he obtained no further information about the trunk and did not even attempt to question me about it. As he had criticised one of his own colleagues, Kenneth Clarke, for printing a story about £350,000 being transferred from Global Imex to a Swiss bank account without first checking it, the point was a useful one to establish. Especially because on the day Sheila Buckley arrived in Australia he made the same error in telephoning the trunk story through to Fleet Street without any attempt to cross check. Furthermore my cross-examination revealed the priceless information that the story had been phoned from a public phone on the concourse of Perth airport at five in the morning by a reporter who was tired and who had lost a night's sleep. That, it transpired, was the circumstance for an incredibly damning story – possibly leading to a conspiracy charge – and written without any corroboration.

Ward confirmed that there were no other reporters or photographers – apart from his own contact – at Perth airport and that he had thus secured an exclusive story on Sheila Buckley's arrival in Australia and, significantly, that he had obtained the details of her travel arrangements to Perth from his Chinese girl friend in Singapore.

The Ward evidence and my examination of him spread over a three day marathon and it was not without incident. One occurred only ten minutes after I had resumed my questioning on the second day. I was asking Ward questions about an article he had written in January 1975 about Barbara staying with me at the Barletts' home in Yellingbo when the judge intervened: 'Members of the jury, that is not proof that they did.' I went on to ask about another snippet in the article and the judge snapped fiercely at me, 'One reason I don't crack down is that it takes longer, therefore I allow you your head. But if you think you're scoring over the court I shall remind the jury what I said.'

I said I wanted all the information to come out and the judge said, 'Yes, it must be by admissible evidence. You want everything to come out because if we accede to your request we shall be here until Christmas.' At this point I felt compelled to comment emphatically, 'I don't want to be here until Christmas. I didn't ask this witness to come all the way from Singapore – the Crown did.'

'Take him downstairs,' the judge said angrily. 'We shall adjourn for half an hour.'

During the twenty minutes or so in which I sat downstairs in the corridor leading to the cells (it was never the case that I was taken to the cells themselves), I was able to collect my thoughts for the next line of questioning. The break was certainly no particular handicap for me.

On return to the dock the judge put on his stern head-masterly style. But now less ill-tempered, he said, 'When I give a ruling and then say you are to proceed, you do not indulge in gratuitous comment to the effect that you did not want a prosecution witness to be called. That is disrespectful and don't let it happen again.' I replied that I intended no dis-respect to the court, and apologised. The judge – in the absence of the jury – then asked me to give an explanation for my line of questioning. I pointed out that Ward had not told the police in his statement that Mrs. Stonehouse had already been in Australia, although he clearly knew so; that Mr. Corkery had made great play in his opening statement that the clothes could not have been Mrs. Stonehouse's as she had not yet arrived. The facts were, I explained, that Mrs. Stone-house had stayed with me and had left all her clothes with her husband. The judge turned to Corkery. 'Are you denying Mrs. Stonehouse had been there?' He replied, slightly con-fused, 'It may depend on hearsay, but is not denied that Mrs. Stonehouse was there two times.'

Lord Wigoder, who had remained silent through most of the seven weeks proceedings, intervened to say that Michael Hayes had given evidence that he was Mrs. Stonehouse's solicitor and that she had left England for Australia for the first time at the end of December. The judge interrupted saying, 'It doesn't prove she went.' Wigoder pressed home the vital point, 'I clearly understood Mr. Corkery to have said that the clothing could not have been Mrs. Stonehouse's as she had not arrived.'

The jury returned and I continued questions to Ward for most of the day without serious interruptions from the judge. At the opening of the session on the following morning Corkery spent a long time taking Ward through two of his articles in detail, seeking to establish where the information had come from. It was a lame attempt to undo the damage I had done to his witness; it was also more time-consuming than my questioning. After he had finished I asked to raise a matter in the absence of the jury to which the judge agreed. I explained that I wanted him to be under no misapprehension that I wanted to prolong the case in any way. 'It is a living nightmare for me.' Ward, I went on, is a vital witness for the prosecution and despite all the resources of the DPP they failed to bring all the facts about Ward before the court. They had also failed to refer to the article of 12th February (in which Ward had reported on Sheila Buckley's arrival in Perth and the trunk); the defence had raised it and it had turned out to be vital. I added that I was on a conspiracy charge which could carry a sentence of life imprisonment so as to emphasise why I took the defence of Ward's allegations so seriously.

The judge then read a little lecture in the course of which he included this observation, 'Let me make it clear I have not indicated nor formed the view that you are delaying the proceedings. I had in fact made a note to say to the jury at the end that I had not meant to say and nor was there any evidence that you were attempting to delay the proceedings. Your examination of some of the insurance witnesses showed that.'

The earlier encounter with the judge had been disagreeable but in the end I had won something from it. The press, which for weeks had printed the judge's observations implying that I was wasting time, failed however, to publish his statement.

CHAPTER EIGHTEEN

Mr. Edward Cox of the Business Management Services in Regent Street turned out to be a lovely witness. The prosecution had built up the one or two telephone calls to bank managers in which a female voice had said, 'Mr. Markham's secretary,' and the five or six girls at the bureau had been lined up to deny they ever used the expression 'so and so's secretary'. All the ground work collapsed when the manager himself said, in answer to the judge who asked searching questions during Corkery's re-examination, that his girls could say they would put a caller through to the secretary of the person asked for.

Cox also confirmed that Mr. Markham never wore disguises, had the same appearance as the man in the dock and came to the bureau – completely alone – on every other day between the beginning of September to the end of October 1974.

Later we heard that the prosecution were not calling the girls employed by the bureau: it seemed again that the prosecution's witness had been turned to the advantage of the defence. The Crown next sought to play tapes from the Department of Trade Inquiry when the Inspectors interviewed me in Melbourne in February, 1975, and the judge looked decidedly dismayed at the idea. 'Do you realise what you might be letting us in for?' he said in a tired voice. The prospect of sitting through a whole six day playing of the tapes loomed large in his mind. The crown persisted in the request and I took the opportunity of indicating that the defence had argued at the committal proceedings in the Magistrates' Court for the whole of the transcripts to be inadmissible. It was one way to get credit with a judge who had his eye on the clock.

After some legal argument and negotiation, it was ruled that other bits of the tape, which I had requested should be heard, should also be played. The court – with an interval of a few days – thus had two long interludes from the hearing of line witnesses with the booming of the voices from February 1975. For me it was an eerie experience especially as the tape often included the voice of Jim Patterson, my dear Australian lawyer who since died. I could not fathom why the prosecution were so keen on playing back my words from sixteen months before, particularly as they included so many clear denials of criminality. For instance on the sixth day of the interviews I said:

MR. STONEHOUSE: 'I would like to deal with that immediately because one of the reasons why I have been so anxious to co-operate with your inquiry is because I am so bitterly resentful that there has been any suggestion, and that suggestions have appeared in the press, that sums of money are missing from EPACS. This appeared in the liquidation proceedings of the company, a liquidation which I think was unnecessary in view of the assets of that particular concern, in particular the leases on 26 and 27 Dover Street, which were not apparently accounted for, and the enforced liquidation of that company at a time when I was clearly not in a position, in view of my breakdown, to deal with the matter, is something which I find intolerable. And then . . .'

MR. SHERRARD: 'Yes, could we just . . .'

MR. STONEHOUSE: 'Can I complete what I am saying, Mr. Sherrard?'

MR. SHERRARD: 'I am sorry, I thought you had finished that part of it.'

MR. STONEHOUSE: 'What I find is also unacceptable is that certain information has leaked to the press about sums of money that were supposed to be missing, in order, of course, that the issue, as usual, is ganged up against me. And therefore I have some pre-warning of some of the things that you might be saying to me. And one of the reasons why I have been co-operating with you is because I want to deal with this particular matter because I find that any suggestion of criminal charges against me or any accusation of criminal activity is so ludicrous and so against either Stonehouse's or Markham's character that I completely and utterly refute it. And I want you to understand that your inquiry is necessarily, because of the restrictions that you are under and because of the background from which you approach it, is a very restrictive enquiry, not as restrictive as some, and I think the best thing I can do to illustrate the point is to draw a diagram to show you exactly what I mean and what I am trying to say to you, because it is I think relevant to the point that I am trying to make. If we assume that that is the totality of human experience . . .'

MR. SHERRARD: 'You have drawn a large circle on a piece of paper?'

(I had gone on to explain a philosophical point)

MR. STONEHOUSE: 'Yes. We have here a legalistic rectangle, which is the area in which you have necessarily to operate this inquiry, according to legal rules and judging the whole matter against Acts of Parliament which lay down the Criminal Law, you are judging it in that particular rectangle. And you . . .'

MR. SHERRARD: 'We are not simply concerned with Criminal law.'

MR. STONEHOUSE: 'But this is the way the inquiry is being conducted. You have to operate within a procedure, and you have to operate within certain Acts, and you are obviously concerned, as you keep referring to the Acts, quoting sections of them, you are obviously concerned with the law.'

'Now, there is a bigger circle, which is a sort of moralistic area which is given an opportunity of wider consideration.

MR. SHERRARD: 'It is round the inner rectangle, but within the later circle?'

MR. STONEHOUSE: 'That's right.'

MR. SHERRARD: 'And we are saying this so that the transcript makes sense. I can see what you are drawing, the tape machine cannot.'

MR. STONEHOUSE: 'Right, fine. Unusually for an inquiry on this matter you occasionally come out of this legalistic area and you invade the moralistic area, and I say this in fairness to you, you are trying to see it from a wider point of view on occasions, I grant you that, you are coming out.'

MR. SHERRARD: 'Yes, indeed, it is sometimes necessary.'

MR. STONEHOUSE: 'Yes, exactly, you are unusually coming out, but you are coming back again into that legalistic area because this is your training, your background, and you are necessarily, because this is a discipline that you are under, acting almost completely within that particular rectangle.

'The other problem, of course, and this is what you have referred to yourself, certain events that you are dealing with have to be dealt with according to actions at a particular time rather than as part of a flowing story, although you are trying to take into account the time factor, but when it comes to a legalistic interpretation you have to consider that particular moment when a thing occurred, you cannot avoid it.'

MR. SHERRARD: 'It is one of the factors.'

MR. STONEHOUSE: 'Yes, quite. Now the individuals that are concerned with this, the actors on the stage, are all over the place. Right. All over the place, some of them inside the moralistic circle and some of them outside. But, because of the discipline of this inquiry, and of course the other disciplines that are being applied to this business by Scotland Yard and the Fraud Squad who have been very active on this, the attention of these individuals is not related to the total picture. Their attention is directed directly to that inner rectangle, whereas, of course, in normal circumstances, they would either view it within that circle or from outside, viewing the whole totality of the story.

'Now unfortunately, when these individuals have that rectangle uppermost in their minds, the discipline of the Criminal Law, the pressures of your inquiry, the pressures of Scotland Yard and all the other things, this warps their judgment, because they cannot see the story as a whole, they don't want to see the story as a whole, they are being dragged into that area, which is very restrictive. And I have found that you have been doing the same thing with me, you have been dragging me back to an old personality that I left, dragging me back, and I feel the pain and anguish of it, because you are forcing me back to a narrow area, and I am trying to get you to understand, because I want you, because you have been good enough to say your goodwill is present in this whole business, I want you to look at it in more general terms and to understand the total picture rather than judging it merely from that rectangle.'

And then Mr. Sherrard had said, 'Mr. Stonehouse, that was helpful, I understand exactly what you mean.' As I heard his voice booming back from over the traumatic months I wondered, 'Did he really mean that?'

On the tape my voice went on:

MR. STONEHOUSE: 'I have not concluded yet, I am coming on to the particular questions that you asked. The idea that I would frankly steal any money from anybody is ridiculous. The money that I took out and put into the resources of my new personality, Markham, was money that I was fully entitled to from a legal and from a moral point of view, together. And the suggestion that people have implied, and has appeared in the press, that I should have taken money out illegally, some sort of fraud, is utterly wrong and something that is totally against my whole life, and that is why I find it so anathema. And you have been kind enough to bring out the allegations pretty clearly and you have given me cheque details, and I want you to know, although I haven't got the documentation, that every single one of these transactions were legitimate.'

MR. SHERRARD: 'I understand.'

MR. STONEHOUSE: 'The Export Promotion & Consultancy Services was, of course, the pump premier for the activities of Global Imex, and originally the business that Global Imex did was totally based on what EPACS did, the commissions that it earned came from business that Export Promotion had generated. Export Promotion was responsible for maintaining contacts with agents and representatives who obtained the business that both companies enjoyed in various parts of the world, and this had to be paid for, and the moneys that were withdrawn over that period went in expenses and payments to such people, some related to past activities, some related to future opportunities that we were pursuing at that time, all perfectly legitimate. Documentation about this was certainly available.

'We were, and I was, attempting, although I was moving over to the Markham personality, I've already told you that it was my anxiety to get the bank re-organised in a way that it would survive and prosper. As far as Export Promotion and Global Imex were concerned, we had suffered because of some share dealings that went wrong, and we had suffered because some of the deals that we had been involved in hadn't gone as well as we had expected. And I think I have already told you that by having Markham as a parallel personality a new lease of life was available to Stonehouse to press on with all these activities. From about June onwards my wife remarked that things seemed to be very much better, and if you talk to my colleagues they will tell you that things seemed to be very good. I think you've already said that, they were apparently going well because I was putting so much energy – there was a change in the mid-year – putting so much energy behind these things. I was very anxious that the various things that we were pursuing in the exporting field could be successful so that my departure would be smoother and the problems that were left behind for my former colleagues would be that much less. I have already told you I wanted to be the lightning conductor to take away their problems, I didn't want them to have to suffer the sort of tensions that I had suffered. It was apparent to me that they didn't, they came in in the morning, very happy, whistling, cheerful, everything was fine. We discussed problems, but they didn't feel them as I felt them. Do you understand what I mean, Mr. Sherrard?'

MR. SHERRARD: 'Yes, I understand exactly what you are saying.'

MR. STONEHOUSE: 'The pressure was on me totally and absolutely, and I felt that they didn't feel the same. Well, obviously they were not so much emotionally involved as I was.'

MR. SHERRARD: 'And men in positions of effective power and men at the top of the pyramid are usually the men who experience the pressures and have the anxieties, and the tea boy who whistles, wishing he were the boss, probably does not have any idea what he is letting himself in for.'

MR. STONEHOUSE: 'It isn't a question of tea boys.'

MR. SHERRARD: 'No, but you know what I mean.'

MR. STONEHOUSE: 'It's a question of my immediate colleagues. And I wanted, I didn't want them to have to suffer as a result of anything that had gone on before.'

MR. SHERRARD: 'I quite see that.'

MR. STONEHOUSE: 'And clearly, I wanted these businesses to

be successful, so there was a feverish round of activity, to try to get deals, and you would have seen some of these referred to in the press, erroneously, I may say, but certainly there were a lot of negotiations going on, we stimulated activity in all sorts of directions.'

MR. SHERRARD: 'Do not worry too much about the effect of the reports in the press.'

MR. STONEHOUSE: 'No, no, no, I am saying that there were deals being arranged.'

MR. SHERRARD: 'No, I told you we put it out of our minds for this purpose.'

MR. STONEHOUSE: 'Well, the fact is that there were deals, and we can put it on the record, there were deals involving cement from Rumania . . .'

MR. SHERRARD: 'You do not want us to go into that at this stage, we are not equipped to do so.'

MR. STONEHOUSE: 'Pardon?'

MR. SHERRARD: 'We are not equipped to do so.'

MR. STONEHOUSE: 'Well, it's relevant to what you are asking me about these particular transactions.'

MR. SHERRARD: 'Yes, I understand, I follow.'

MR. STONEHOUSE: 'There were cement deals which were involving millions of dollars. There were communications equipment deals in the Middle East which would have involved millions of pounds and commissions to us of tens of thousands, and any one of these deals, if successful, would have given a flush of money to these companies and would have assisted all, including the bank, over a very difficult period. It was very important that every effort be made to get these deals off the ground. After all, we had the base, we had the companies, we had the contacts, we had already achieved a good deal, and more activity for making more use of the contacts that we had could produce the right result. So there was a feverish activity. But for anyone to suggest, as apparently they suggested when EPACS was unnecessarily liquidated, that this money had gone missing, is really ludicrous, it just shows that these individuals, rather than seeing the total story, have now become disoriented and are looking into the centre there, like Mr. Hastings, who has become a little disoriented.'

MR. SHERRARD: 'We understand what you are conveying to us.'

In answer to Mr. Sherrard's questions about rewards of transactions I said:

'What I am saying is that I kept a record and it is either on the counterfoil of the cheque or in other documents in my desk or in the safe at 26 Dover Street. I am not saying that they were written into the books because the accountant, Le Fort, left some weeks before and I am not sure that these accounts were written up in the way they normally would be.'

MR. SHERRARD: 'But what instructions did you leave – what written instructions did you leave to explain the entries that should be made to anyone who would have to fulfil the function?'

MR. STONEHOUSE: 'The documents were all left relating to these particular transactions. And, of course, some of it was related to Global Imex's potential business, where EPACS would make a recovery, either in sharing commission or in actually drawing expenses from the associate company.

MR. SHERRARD: 'Yes. But if the advances were required to pay the expenses of the business, why were not the cheques used, as one would normally expect them to be used, to pay the persons to whom money was due and drawn in their favour?'

MR. STONEHOUSE: 'Because overseas, agents and representatives normally demand to be paid in cash.'

MR. SHERRARD: 'But then are you telling us that these sums of money that were drawn in cash were in each case drawn in order to be converted into currency suitable to be received abroad?'

MR. STONEHOUSE: 'No, no. I'm saying that the cash was paid to individuals in England who insisted on being paid in cash for various reasons.'

In the earlier extracts from the tape which I requested should be played, I described the reasons for the adoption of the parallel personality of Markham. I had said:

'I obtained the passport and I felt this gave me great relief, because I had a document which identified me as another person, who was quite an ordinary person, and in establishing that person, in obtaining an accommodation address and other such normal simple activities, it was just remarkable, it was just such a contrast to everything else that I was doing. To be working in a normal area, without the stresses that I had in my other personality, was a saving thing to me, it really was.'

MR. SHERRARD: 'But how did it change your face, by which you would be recognised?'

MR. STONEHOUSE: 'No, I wasn't. That is the point. That is entirely the point. I wasn't, I was able to go to an address in Victoria, to an address in Regent Street, to a bank even in Threadneedle Street, as Joseph Arthur Markham, and not be recognised. I was being treated as Mr. Markham, as an ordinary fellow.'

MR. SHERRARD: 'What had encumbered you? What you have been describing hitherto is not so much your face as your name.'

MR. STONEHOUSE: 'The name and all the problems which went with it, because as soon as you announced who you were, you had people reacting, not to you as a person, but to you as a public image, which they thought they knew about, and they didn't really. I think every person in public life has this problem, and they learn to live with it, they have their private life and their public life, and the two personalities are separate.'

MR. SHERRARD: 'Mr. Stonehouse, why a passport? You see, there are ways . . .'

MR. STONEHOUSE: 'So I could escape from England.'

MR. SHERRARD: 'Yes, I follow.'

MR. STONEHOUSE: 'I felt England had become oppressive.'

MR. SHERRARD: 'Yes, but you did not need a passport if you wished to lose yourself or create a new personality within the United Kingdom.'

MR. STONEHOUSE: 'No, but within the United Kingdom it was likely that I would be recognised eventually by someone, and then it would all be brought rushing back on me. I wanted to get away absolutely, completely and utterly from the personality that had become intolerable to me as a simple human being. I think we all are simple human beings basically and we develop cloaks as we go along, we put on clothes, we put on new personalities, we develop attributes as a result of jobs that we do, and any one of us who looks back over twenty years may have a shock to think that that was the chap that started off down this road and he is unrecognisable now because he has done all the things that he has done and he has developed all these eccentricities and he is not the same chap as he was before; but basically, stripped of all those cloaks, either of humbug or deceit or ability or whatever, we all put them whatever jobs we do, particularly professional men, if you strip them all off there is a basic human being there somewhere, and I was trying to find him.'

Mr. Sherrard asked:

'Yes, but had it occurred to you that one of the advantages of being Mr. Markham was that if the blow should fall and you found yourself in difficulty, you could disappear completely, avoid bankruptcy, avoid proceedings, avoid disgrace, and yet live on as Markham? Did you ever think along those lines?'

MR. STONEHOUSE: 'Not coherently, but subconsciously it might have been there. But one never actually sat down and worked all these out. All one was doing was creating something that provided relief. It was an irrational, not a rational calculated move. It provided relief, and no doubt the factors you describe were part of it.'

I spoke then of the situation concerning the bank:

'I was very anxious that the bank should survive the crises and it couldn't survive with the old personalities involved in it, apart from John McGrath who had not been in any way effective, through no fault of his own. I mean he just wasn't effective, he was just a name, and he could well go on, if his health improved he may have been able to make a contribution. But all the old ones, including myself, had been an embarrassment, and we were all going.'

MR. SHERRARD: 'Now just tell us how in due course you thought that you ought to resolve the position. Ahmed has gone, Forte is in, Charlton is in.'

MR. STONEHOUSE: 'Well, the death of Stonehouse provides the cathartic experience which pulls the whole thing together.'

MR. SHERRARD: 'Would you care to tell us about it?'

MR. STONEHOUSE: 'He goes, he disappears, he's dead, every-

142

body knows he's dead, so that they have just then to attend to the position as it exists without him there, and he is a lightning conductor.'

MR. SHERRARD: 'But what of the mechanics of this, when do you think about it and how do you go about it?'

MR. STONEHOUSE: 'I just say that I felt that he would be a lightning conductor in disappearing – dying like that, he would take away so many of the problems that existed because he had been present.'

MR. SHERRARD: 'Yes, but this is a fundamental change in your approach to the new personality now. Originally the notion was to enable you to obtain some permanent relief, some anonymity if you like . . .'

MR. STONEHOUSE: 'Temporary relief, because at that time, it was never a coherent plan that Stonehouse would die, there was always a possibility that Stonehouse would survive, and the extraordinary thing was that having a parallel personality helped Stonehouse to go on.'

MR. SHERRARD: 'Yes.'

MR. STONEHOUSE: 'In fact my wife has said to me since that she felt things were improving, because in the summer and early autumn I was getting much stronger and dealing with things far more effectively. That was her impression. She thought everything was really improving and that I was lively and dealing with it. Well, what in fact had happened was because I had Markham there I was much more effective as Stonehouse, I was playing that part very much more effectively.'

MR. SHERRARD: 'You were able to rest, in a way?'

MR. STONEHOUSE: 'Yes, exactly.'

MR. SHERRARD: 'Switch off the one and switch on the other?'

MR. STONEHOUSE: 'That's right, but the other one became more, I suppose, of an actor than he normally was. Most people in public life are seven/tenths actors.'

MR. SHERRARD: 'Which other one?'

MR. STONEHOUSE: 'Stonehouse became more of an actor, he was playing the part, doing the job which was expected of him.'

MR. SHERRARD: 'Are you really saying that the real person

143

was becoming Markham, the shadow was becoming Stonehouse?'

MR. STONEHOUSE: 'Well, if you put it like that, it could have been that, yes, it could well have been that.'

MR. SHERRARD: 'The role you were creating, the role you were playing, was becoming the reality, and the actor – the physical actor, John Stonehouse, was being submerged in it. This is the impression you are giving me by what you are now saying.'

MR. STONEHOUSE: 'Yes, I think that could well be the case.'

MR. SHERRARD: 'At what stage do you think you formulated the notion that Stonehouse should disappear altogether?'

MR. STONEHOUSE: 'Stonehouse should die really didn't become a reality until November 20th.'

MR. SHERRARD: 'No, that is not quite the way I put it, because I am anxious to see when the notion that Stonehouse should die first crossed your mind, if you like.'

MR. STONEHOUSE: 'Well it was always a possibility from the beginning of the fantasising.'

MR. SHERRARD: 'Yes. When did it become not just a possibility, but a probability?'

MR. STONEHOUSE: 'In July, I suppose, when I acquired the passport, it was a probability, but a doubtful one.'

MR. SHERRARD: 'To be invoked in what circumstances? Had they been formulated in whole or in part?'

MR. STONEHOUSE: 'I don't think it was formulated because this implies there was a coherence about it, it was developed. It just grew, the Markham personality grew; frankly, I enjoyed developing the attributes of this man.'

MR. SHERRARD: 'As you were already saying, he was a 'Topsy' Markham.'

MR. STONEHOUSE: 'Yes, exactly. If I acquired a credit card for Markham, this was tremendous, absolutely tremendous.'

MR. SHERRARD: 'Did you?'

MR. STONEHOUSE: 'I did indeed, and it was tremendous, because it was that new man that I wanted to be. It's just like an ordinary chap that suddenly finds that he is being accepted in a club or something, it's just a boost to him, and this became a victory out of all proportion to its significance.'

MR. SHERRARD: 'It sounds as if you rather liked Markham.'

MR. STONEHOUSE: 'I did.'

MR. SHERRARD: 'Preferred him to Stonehouse?'

MR. STONEHOUSE: 'Yes, of course. Stonehouse was a terrible person. He had produced so many problems. He was disliked, he was an embarrassment to all concerned, and you know how one can feel the miasma that has built up, and I could feel in the House of Commons and elsewhere a deep, deep feeling there somewhere of resentment against me, a deep suspicion and . . .'

MR. SHERRARD: 'Jealousy?'

MR. STONEHOUSE: 'Jealousy, envy. They were obviously unaware of what I was going through and I couldn't sit down and explain it to them because, one, they are not sympathetic anyway, you know, the more Socialist a person the less sympathetic he becomes in his personal relationships, this seems to be one of the sort of inversed proportion laws, that my own colleagues just could not have begun to understand what turmoil I was going through; but obviously they thought that I was a most successful business man, I was a tycoon, I turned my back on my Socialist ideas, and it was a terrible struggle for me, every time I went to the House of Commons I could feel that maybe it was unnecessary suspicion, but I could feel that terrible miasma there. But as I said earlier, when there was any sympathy expressed it was a terrible wound.'

It took many hours to run through the tapes; it was a unique experience in an Old Bailey trial for a Department of Trade transcript to be used in this way. The result was a graphic insight for the jury into what I was thinking and saying weeks before charges were laid against me. It was extremely valuable to the defence that my frank description of the actions of Markham together with my denials could be heard before the prosecution's case had even concluded. In addition there was an unexpected bonus. I had always assumed that the police had somehow got hold of the transcript of my interviews before they arrested me in which case that would provide some explanation – however weak – for the laying of charges. But under my cross-examination the official responsible revealed that no transcript – nor any other material from the hearings – had been given by the Inspectors to the Department of Trade (who could have passed them to the police) until after 14th April 1975. My arrest was on 21st March; so the mystery remained: why did the police prefer charges well before the inquiry had reported?

I would have some interesting questions for Chief Superintendent Etheridge, whose turn in the witness box was soon approaching.

CHAPTER NINETEEN

By the end of the ninth week, with the temperature outside reaching the nineties, the atmosphere in court Number One was even less formal. Now the jurors arrive everyday in shirt-sleeves, or thin summer dresses, giving a summer holiday look to the well of the court; they might well be sitting reading the Sunday papers on benches on Brighton's foreshore as studying papers on a fraud case. Now and then the jovial fat man in the front row points out something to his young girl neighbour (who looks no older than twenty-five) and guffaws. They all laugh dutifully when the judge makes one of his jokes – even when they do not understand. At one point, when Corkery was reading depositions, the judge turned round to the jury with a knowing look. 'Doesn't he sound like that funny man on the radio?'' Nobody knew who or what he was talking about but Corkery, keeping to the spirit of the proceedings, replied, 'It's not so entertaining.' He was certainly right.

The concessions to informality are heightened when the judge gets out of his chair to wander over to the witness box to help a witness struggling with exhibits. During the cross-examination of John McGrath, the near seventy-year-old chartered accountant and Commander of the British Empire who was my colleague in three companies, the judge got up twice making even the ushers look disconcerted. McGrath just could not find the correct page in the British Bangladesh Trust minute book and the judge, patiently exasperated, walked over to take it from him and stood for two minutes by the box leafing through the volume and reading.

The pressmen have dwindled now and sometimes the public gallery is only half-full. The seats at the back of the court are often crowded with jury members destined for duty in other cases, sitting out their time until required. The visiting lawyers from Chicago or Frankfurt also come in to watch the proceedings.

The prosecution have scored a small victory by getting the

judge to compromise a little over his legal ruling on the admissibility of the Swiss bank evidence. The computer read-out is still disallowed and so are paying-in slips without my signature of J. A. Markham. To get this concession the DPP sent Inspector Lewis back to Zurich to open his own Swiss bank account and see the workings of the system. It was a telling demonstration of the prosecution's determination not to be outdone. Tudor-Price mentioned several times that the exercise was done with Bank of England approval as though Lewis, a high priest, had been given special dispensation to do some heinous act obscene to the contemporary official religion.

At the end of the morning session Lewis was close to the dock and he leaned up to whisper to me, 'Miss Pfeifer sends her regards, she says you were the politest customer she has ever known.' Miss P. was the Swiss Banking Corporation lady who had opened my Markham account. Given the informality of the proceedings and the now – surprising – friendly relations I seem to have with the police, the incident seems not as bizarre as it really is.

Among the witnesses called by the Crown to illustrate my alleged indeptedness was Seymour Gorman, a director of a small bank called Hanover Berkeley. It turned out to be a bonus for me.

I questioned him closely about his phone calls and his attempts to get documents signed so that I would accept liability for buying shares his bank wanted to off-load. I asked whether he remembered saying on the telephone he would do to me what had been done to Jeffrey Archer (a Tory MP who had been made to resign his seat after a collapse of shares). He replied, 'Who is Jeffrey Archer?' I then said, 'I put it to you, you are nothing but a common blackmailer.' His reply was astounding. 'The trouble with you is that you regard any business pressure as blackmail.' And went on to add, 'On that definition every solicitor in this country is a blackmailer.'

I simply asked 'And you are a solicitor, Mr. Gorman?' 'Yes,' he answered. I felt I had made my point.

John McGrath had to attend the Old Bailey for three or four days for his hearings and the experience appeared to be gruelling for him as he had been terribly ill for several years. I regretted having to question him about his approval of early decisions of BBT, when overdrafts were granted to companies to enable the financing BBT shares, but establishing the facts was an essential plank to my own defence. He had been adamant that he had not signed an offer letter about facilities of £210,000 because he would not have approved it. 'It looks like my signature,' he had said, 'but I don't remember it.' Then with the minute book, obtained overnight from the Department of Trade Inspectors, I demonstrated that he had attended the meeting at which the decisions were made and that later he had signed the minutes. 'It certainly looks like my signature but I don't remember signing it,' he said. Corkery did not pursue the matter, which is always a good sign that I have scored a point.

McGrath also revealed the fascinating information that he did not meet the other director of EPACS, Michael Hayes, after 20th November, 1974, until the following 2nd January when the decision to liquidate was taken. It hardly accorded with the impression of careful evaluation of the financial position which others had tried to give. I was also able to get McGrath to prove as exhibits documents (or rather notes as he called them) produced at the time by Bingham and Gay, the Secretary, showing EPACS as having made a profit of £8,000 and £15,000 between March and November of 1974.

McGrath did not know about the consideration of the value of the leases nor, until later, that they had been sold to Limepan Ltd. As all this emerged I hoped the jury would see it as a mess of pottage from which no one person should be singled out as endowed with all the guilt, as the prosecution liked to imply. Surprisingly, despite his illnesses, McGrath turned up next day as an observer — one more spritely than he was as a witness.

The Australian policemen: John Coffey, Hugh Morris, John Sullivan and Bib Gillespie had all appeared, although only two were requested by the defence. Trips to England two years running (last year's for the committal trial) were not to be sneezed at. The change in emphasis was interesting. No longer did Coffey attempt to claim that Clive Mildoon was wearing disguises in Melbourne (at committal he had claimed that Mildoon was seen watching television wearing dark glasses and a hat). The fact that I produced *Daily Mail* reproductions of police photographs taken of me in Melbourne obviously not wearing a hat, or any disguise, helped to deflate that ploy.

I took Coffey through the significant facts of the transcript of the celebrated interview I had with the three Victoria State policemen on Christmas Eve, 1974. The tape-recorder was on even when the policemen said it was not, a revelation to the jury of police techniques. But the tape was useful to me – it showed that I did not lie about my identity although it took sometime for me to become composed and that the police gave assurances that Scotland Yard had no complaint about any crimes (apart from the passport offence).

It also showed that I explained to the policemen that I had adopted the Markham/Mildoon names to escape from pressures put on me in British business and politics. I had described to the apparently sympathetic men the horror of dealing with Aziz, newspapers and blackmailers and, at the same time, keep up appearances and a show of strength with one's colleagues. It was a similar exposition as I had given to the Department of Trade Inspectors, not so detailed but even more graphic in places. The tape also included my side of the conversation with Barbara on the telephone at 3pm in Melbourne and 4am in Andover, Hampshire. I read out the whole conversation forcing back my tears when I came to my remarks to Mathew, 'Be brave, one day you will understand what I've been through.' I had also asked Barbara to bring Sheila to Australia, which was another valuable point to establish. To make such a request on an obviously bugged telephone would hardly be consistent with the cynical conspiracy theory.

The court concluded its ninth week with the reading of more statements by overseas, witnesses not requested by the defence: Leon Howe, the Treasurer of Aeromaritime in Washington, spoke of the payments into the Victa Liechenstein company of my salary – which was important to me to prove overseas earnings. The hotel clerks in Hawaii confirmed telephone calls by Markham to a London number (where Sheila Buckley was staying) and travel agents in London and Denmark showed her journey to Copenhagen and Markham's return trip to Singapore and Melbourne via Aeroflot.

It was significant though that Harry Wetzel of Garrett (whose cheque was the subject of one charge) was not apparently coming despite 'high level' pressure put on him nor was John Mulcahy – the only bank official I had requested from Melbourne – nor the Willcocks who knew Mildoon in their Flinders Street apartments. No one, who knew me as Markham/Mildoon in Australia was being allowed to come.

We spent some time with the handwriting expert from the Police Forensic Laboratory who was able to say that the handwriting of Stonehouse, Markham and Mildoon was very similar. 'I want to be helpful to you, Mr. Stonehouse,' he said warmly, to the consternation of some other policemen in the court. It certainly is a bizarre case and will appear even more so when the defence gets under way next week. The long voyage is half-over I can already sense the delights of the haven to which, I hope, we are sailing.

Fortunately everyday, I can get some respite from the other activites at the Old Bailey which are a complete contrast (or almost). One Tuesday the court was adjourned, so that a juror could go to the funeral of her sister and I went to the House of Commons for question time for the first time for over two months; usually I arrive at the House – like the lawyers – at about four thirty. By some chance I had questions high on the list both to the Employment Secretary (on the unemployment figures) and to the Prime Minister (on when the Royal Commission on the Legal Profession was due to start its work).

The P.Q. to the P.M. could have been an interesting exchange but although it was number three it was squeezed out by supplementary questions on Government leaks.

On another day at the House I had a tea party and meeting on the terrace level for the English National Party. Thirty were expected and eighty turned up. It was an enthusiastic gathering and not a single hostile word was uttered in my direction: the venom of the previous year had evaporated showing that the tides of time can wash clean. On the following day I had the same experience speaking to the Oxford University Union at a crowded gathering in the Library, despite it being the last day of term.

I do feel the trial is an irrelevancy, wasting time on events from an unreal world long left behind, like the long cruise which has little to do with life on the mainland.

CHAPTER TWENTY

The prosecution case ended with the two policemen who had spent most time on the case being called as witnesses. First was Inspector David Townley, a stern looking tense man whose appearance was made even more menacing by what appeared to be a broken nose. He was guided by Corkery through numerous exhibits including some schedules showing money withdrawals and my liabilities and assets. Townley did not strike me as being an expert in accountancy.

In my questioning I followed up the line pursued at the committal hearing: 'Had Mr. Townley been to see Mr. Stonehouse's desk at Dover Street?' This time he said he had made inquiries about the whereabouts of the desk. 'When?' It transpired the date was after the committal in October 1975, and nearly a year after my disappearance.

Townley had made numerous visits during January and February 1975, sometimes every other day – but he had never found my desk or examined or collected the papers in it. His inquiries had, it seemed, mainly been verbal although he did collect some documents which corresponded with the ideas he had decided to pursue.

He had relied on what the people at Dover Street had told him – accepted their word. 'Would you have done,' I asked, 'if you had known they were interested parties?' His reply was understandably evasive. 'Did you know that Philip Gay was negotiating to buy the lease of 27 Dover Street under the company Limepan.'

'Ah,' he replied, as if he was making a counter-point, 'that only happened recently.'

No, he had not seen any of the notes written by Gay or Bingham before EPACS had been liquidated. No, he had not seen the list of creditors showing the credit card companies as being owed money by EPACS – that was Inspector Lewis's area. He had accepted that EPACS was hopelessly insolvent. Why? because it owed money to the banks. I pressed him on this. Had he examined the value of the assets, the leases, the shareholdings and the commissions payable? It appeared he had not done so. The fact that the bank overdrafts were £36,000 was sufficient reason to liquidate.

'Did you examine Global Imex?' No, but he had found it had overdrafts of nearly £90,000.

'Then Global Imex was hopelessly insolvent too according to your definition?'

'Yes, I suppose so,' he replied lamely.

'And the British Treasury would also be insolvent?'

'Yes,' he said and I gulped. It would hardly be true he had given me such a whopper.

'Why wasn't Global Imex liquidated then?' I asked.

'It had a director who could run it but EPACS only had an old man and a solicitor who practised in the country.'

'Did you know Mr. Charlton owed money on a loan account with EPACS?'

'Yes.'

'Why didn't you prosecute him?'

'He had not disappeared,' came the beautiful reply which later I could use with, I hoped, great advantage.

Next came the blond Chief Superintendent Kenneth Etheridge, and Corkery got him to say that it would not have been possible to interview me on his first visit to Australia in January 1975, because he did not have enough information to ask meaningful questions. At that stage he would have arrested me in England on the passport offences but had no other charges to lay; they were only formulated later. It transpired that about six weeks had elapsed between that visit and the first decision on charges. That information would be valuable to me in showing the early development of the case which was, without doubt, extremely curious.

Corkery dwelt on the need for an extradition warrant – presumably to undermine my claim that I would have been prepared to travel back voluntarily with the policeman – and Etheridge dutifully replied that his jurisdiction would not run in that case at airports where the plane had to stop. Later he acknowledged that even with an extradition warrant the authority would apply only to Australian airspace and in other countries he would rely on the co-operation of the local police. It all seemed to be splitting hairs.

When it came to my turn for cross-examination the hush in the court was quite noticeable. My first objective was to get confirmation that no one had complained to the police about my alleged criminal conduct. My question turned up an unexpected nugget: Thomas Matthews had made a formal complaint. I remembered him without difficulty, the diminutive property developer from Hampshire who had advertised in the *Financial Times* to become a director of a merchant bank and who had later bought £100,000 worth of LCG shares on a loan from the bank.

This information was no problem to me as clearly Thomas Matthews, who had nothing to do with EPACS, could not have made any complaint which led to the actual charges. I asked Etheridge the precise question (and answer 'Yes' or 'No', please) 'Did the directors of EPACS ever complain about alleged criminal activity on my part?'

'No,' came the reassuring reply, after some hesitation. And then I went through the list: the Secretary, auditor, bank managers, insurance companies, credit card companies and Somerset House. None had complained.

Etheridge became stiff when I asked him about his relationship with Harry Longmuir, the crime reporter of the *Daily Mail*. They had travelled on the same plane out to Australia on two occasions and had stayed at the same hotel for some time.

'Yes, but what were you doing in the Melbourne Hilton Hotel on the night of 18th February?' I asked.

'That sounds like the beginning of a detective story,' intervened the judge. But he did not stop the question as, obviously, his own curiosity had been aroused.

The story gradually came out that Etheridge had visited Longmuir to break the embargo and print a story on what had been a purely social occasion.

'Not at all,' he replied.

I handed him the report so as to make an exhibit and he confirmed it, 'Stonehouse blows his top — Short a pusillaminous twit — Mellish a crude bore.'

I could not resist correcting the latter to 'uncouth bully', which was the accurate version, to the slight annoyance of the judge. He might not have seen the significance of my bringing out the Etheridge connection with the *Mail* but I certainly did. It showed the police co-operation with the newspapers to get their image of a man they were after across to the public. In other words, to paint him in the worst light. In the case of the *Mail* story it had another motive: the worsening of relations between me and party leaders.

Etheridge could not say how the various police photographs had arrived in the *Daily Mail*; he was clearly a skilled performer in the box. But nevertheless I had got good value from him – particularly as I finished with a reading from my committal statement which he could not confirm. Some of it was emphatic and philosophical, parts of it ran like this:

'I am innocent of these charges. Never have I had any intention of breaking laws which as a Member of Parliament for nineteen years it was my privilege to help to make. Never have I sought to enrich myself at the expense of others. My life has largely been spent in public service, with scant financial reward. My work in the Co-operative movement earned me a pittance, as an MP my salary was modest. Had I really been that grotesque caricature of greed conjured up by the prosecution, I could long ago have lined my pockets. Millions of pounds have passed through my hands as president of the London Co-operative Society, and as a Minister of the Crown. But most of the work I have done has, at my insistence, been unpaid. The selfish pursuit of wealth is an anathema to me politically and personally. My only ambition has been to make my own modest contribution to the governance of this country, to promote its products and its ideals.

'A year ago most of my achievements and ideals lay in ruins. My life – for reasons which will emerge at my trial – had become unbearable. A man who still bore the name John Stonehouse took the bizarre and irrational actions you have heard recited in grudging half-truths in these proceedings. Those actions caused anguish to his wife and family and friends. They produced headaches for his business colleagues, embarrassment for his Parliamentary friends. The few who remained loyal were pilloried, and one was – indeed is by your ruling today – prosecuted. For all these slowly dawning consequences the man who stands before you is truly sorry. In time, when all is understood, he will make amends. My debts – of love and of friendship – will all be repaid. I will do my utmost to repay all legitimate money debts . . .

If a servant, loyal for two decades, suddenly finds himself in trouble, is it morally right for those he has served to abandon him, or even worse, to laugh at him and torture him? I needed psychiatric help, but instead I was sent two hard-faced policemen so convinced of my criminality they did not pay me the ordinary decency of asking for my explanation. I was instantly presumed to be guilty, and my public service hung like a millstone round my neck . . .

'But why was I not allowed to explain them before my guilt was assumed? The simple answer is that by this time the press had created a climate in which I was irredeemably branded an international criminal. Their campaign, as I saw to my horror in Copenhagen, commenced on my disappearance. Freed of the restraints of libel, untrammelled by any requirement of responsibility, I became fair game for the most horrible fantasies of Fleet Street. I was a Mafia front-man one day, a Czech spy the next, a CIA agent the day before. A Nigerian businessman had drowned in the Thames – Stonehouse had pushed him. Mrs. Buckley was living apart from her husband – Stonehouse had stolen her away from him. There was a Bangladesh fund. Perhaps there was money unaccounted for – I was a trustee. Stonehouse a trustee, did you say? Make it a million pounds that's missing. A man was found dead in Florida in a concrete coffin – Stonehouse had sealed his fate. It was all down to Stonehouse. All those allegations were untrue. But by the time I surfaced in Melbourne I had "International Criminal" tattooed on my forehead. I was Scotland Yard's answer to Ronald Biggs.

'So it was that on Christmas Eve and ever since, the police, the press and the establishment have treated me as a criminal although for reasons which will emerge they did not charge me for three months. They have never asked for my side of the story. No compassion was shown, no explanation requested, no courtesy extended. At first I was appalled by this seeming

157

ingratitude and in my paranoid state I made one great mistake. I identified the voice of Britain with the baying of Fleet Street, and I saw the face of my countrymen in the jaundiced eyes of the Scotland Yard officers who were stalking me with their press stool-pigeons . . .

'The timing is significant in demonstrating that this is a political trial brought for political reasons. The first charges were not brought until four months after my disappearance, three months after my re-appearance but two days after the Select Committee of the House of Commons had recommended that I could not be expelled. It is also significant that it was only four days after the first extracts of my book appeared in British newspapers, which began to give part of my side of the story. It is not coincidental that the arrest in Australia took place at that time. Having failed to get me to formally resign or to have me expelled, the establishment had to brand me as a criminal in their attempt to destroy me because they thought I was an embarrassment to them. It is also significant that Scotland Yard gave specific instructions that all the transcripts of my book should be seized. They took copies of all my book material and that material is still held in the safes at Scotland Yard. There was great anxiety to suppress or delay the book and confirmation of that can be seen in their advice to the Australian Courts to refuse bail and throw me into prison to make my position as untenable as possible. But fortunately the Australian Court acted independently of the British establishment and granted bail; I was able to carry on writing. Because of these events, the Fleet Street calumny against me and the determination of Scotland Yard to incriminate me – without seeking my explanation – I thought then that I could not get a fair trial in Britain . . .

'The problem with the prosecution is that they operate with such limited objectives and with such limited vision that they canot see the wood for the twigs, let alone the trees. The prosecution have ignored the fact that the offences with which I am charged are completely out of character. My book *Death of an Idealist* shows my background. I present it as an exhibit. Exhibit no. 663.

'You see in this court the conflict of two cultures. One is

cramped and crabbed; limited in its understanding and intent. It represents the compartmentalised society in which programmed and soulless men pursue narrow courses of action oblivious to the totality of the society in which they live . . .

'On the other hand there is the culture of the Open Society which argues for frankness and the absence of humbug and hypocrisy. It wants human actions to be judged not on a narrow basis but in their full context. I do not suggest that it is possible to grasp these philosophical problems in the course of this case. But I do promise that the attempt of the prosecution to limit the argument to a few isolated transactions that they have calculatedly torn out of their true context will be resisted with all vigour. Their intention is crystal clear: to pour the facts into a mould of criminality which is the only context they have been trained to comprehend. To follow the course they propose would be a denial of justice. In making these points I do not deny that in my recent life, under pressure, I may have done foolish things. I may indeed have allowed my idealism and my emotion to rule my actions rather than my head. In 1974, I may have been broken under the intense strain. But I state with absolute certainty I am not – repeat not – a criminal.'

CHAPTER TWENTY-ONE

It was now time for legal submissions and for this Michael O'Dell had sat up all night, preparing notes on cases which would be useful to me in arguing that certain charges should be thrown out. We decided to try on all counts, except the passport one, so as to test the judge. And we thought rashly, there might be a chance to get a fair number removed from the indictment.

But that was not to be. With the jury withdrawn, the judge's attitude was austere and impatient. He would not let me develop the points Michael had so carefully worked on, and hurried me on to the next count I had on my list. Then followed a duologue between the judge and Corkery which showed that he was leaning in the direction of excluding the two birth certificate application offences as the 'intent to defraud' was far from clear. We were preparing to adjourn for the night to face battle on the issues the next day but I feared I was not going to be allowed to get my full say. The judge, it appeared, had become decidedly tetchy. Just before he rose he suddenly said, 'As you are now going into bat I am withdrawing your bail,' and then walked out leaving me stunned in the dock with the warder behind saying, 'We weren't expecting that,' and Michael looking angry and horrified.

It was a terrible shock and completely surprising.

I was taken downstairs to the area I had not yet seen, rows and rows of cells and passages leading up to the various docks. They put me in a communal cell, hot, airless and packed with men. For two hours we sweated in the confined atmosphere. Then, handcuffed in pairs, we were escorted to a waiting bus. The experience was shattering, particularly as I had not ever been handcuffed before. It was extra difficult to manoeuvre my two heavy cases with case documents and records which I needed for my 'home-work'. At Brixton the same reception procedure ensued that I remembered from the past. At half-past eight (over four hours after I had left the dock) I reached a cell, which I was to share for the night with a pleasant enough Barbadian. Against the noise of his transistor, I settled down to try to prepare for the next crucial day – the opening of my case for the defence.

Next day the awful routine of actually getting to the court was almost as bad as the night before. I just could not understand why the number of escorting warders had to exceed the handcuffed prisoners by nearly two to one; it seemed a case of massive overmanning.

At least the judge decided that two charges (on birth certificates) were not to be proceeded with. A victory for Michael O'Dell whose ploy it had been to apply for certificates without signatures on the forms. This had forced official acknowledgement that, under statute, no applicant's name is necessary to obtain a birth certificate. However, the judge would not entertain the other submissions. 'No,' he said curtly on the conspiracy charge, which for every possible reason we had expected to dismiss. 'Now Mr. Stonehouse,' he said, 'it is for you to open your defence. You can answer questions under oath in the witness box, make a statement from where you now stand or say nothing. If you intend to call witnesses you can make an opening address and sum up at the end.'

I indicated that I would be calling witnesses and would make a statement in order to save time as I wanted to be out of Brixton just as soon as possible. Then I turned to face the jury full-on for the first time and said:

The following passages are created from notes which John Stonehouse left for the purpose. The notes formed the basis of his initial delivery of the case for the defence on Friday, July 2nd, 1976.

We have seen ten weeks of the prosecution's case, dozens of witnesses, hundreds of exhibits, and the employment of a technique designed to dredge up isolated events and transactions, and view them, as it were, through a distorting glass. There are two ways to deal with the defence. I could singly pursue every line taken by Mr. Corkery, which would keep us here until Christmas 1977, or, more appropriately, put the case as a whole into its proper perspective, commenting where necessary on the reportedly 'revealing' transactions referred to by the prosecution. . . .

I kept an open mind on how I would conduct my defence, until the end of the Crown case. Then His Lordship decided suddenly to revoke my bail and I was put in a difficulty, because quite frankly, I don't want to stay in Brixton any longer than necessary. I defend myself because it is better for the jury not to be confused by a baffle board of legal gentlemen between you and me. I want you to understand me as a human being, and not merely be dealing with the dry dust of legal cases being argued according to the professional game between barristers. You are not judging a number of crimes . . . you are judging a human being. You must, there-fore, judge that human being in the general context of his life, particularly in the context of what he was doing at the time that the prosecution alleges he was involved in criminal activity. This is a proper perspective.

The prosecution have referred to a jigsaw puzzle. I do not dispute that certain parts of the puzzle have been correctly fitted together, but many have not. Like a child who becomes impatient with a puzzle and, intent only on *completing* a picture of sorts, throws the pieces haphazardly together to form a grotesque parody of the true picture – so, the central theme of the prosecution's case is composed of contextual errors which completely mis-represent the true picture as a whole.

I have suggested that the case against me has been brought for political reasons. Indeed the apparent political overtones in this case finally decided that *I* defend myself. But in fact another background to the case begins now to emerge. I refer to the 'monumental bungling' of my case by the police. In a criminal case, there is a crime, then a complainant; then an investigation takes place. The police identify the suspect and then arrest him. In this case, John Stonehouse is identified as a criminal as this is the only explanation in the minds of the police for my conduct. Moreover the police decision is made in an atmosphere of near hysteria in the press. Indeed the 'sustained and vicious press campaign of harassment' against me leads to a period in which I must have psychiatric treatment to recover from my awful trauma. Meanwhile, political pressure is building up and a movement begins in the House of Commons to lose me my seat. I would have resigned then and there if my Australian lawyer had not told me that I would have been immediately expelled from Australia. The Select Committee set up to examine my case, decided there was no way of expelling me. I had become a 'political embarrassment'. Simultaneously in my book *Death of an Idealist*, which was being serialised in a Sunday newspaper, I was exposing the 'humbug and hypocrisy' of political life – all of which contributed to my breakdown. Politicians were becoming resentful.

It was at this stage that the police attempted to identify crimes with which I could be charged. Investigations were carried out, not into crimes, but with the purpose of finding some crimes. That is both presumptuous and ham-handed. No attempt was made to obtain all relevant documents – only selected documents were collected together to justify the charges. No attempt was made to envisage the whole picture...

There are two indications that charges were not originally contemplated. In February, 1975, the British High Commissioner in Australia gave assurances to Mr. Cameron, Minister for Immigration, that there would be no charges. Secondly, Department of Trade Inspectors who interviewed me in Australia would not have done so if charges had been imminent. . . .

I intend to keep the number of witnesses to a minimum. I will call the auditor of EPACS to deal with the prosecution's allegations about spurious minutes made of meetings. I will call a Member of Parliament to testify as to my involvement in Bangladesh, and my commitment to that cause. The former chairman of the Walsall Labour Party will be called to testify as to my work in the Labour Party. A former director of the London Co-operative Society will testify to my work in and commitment to the Co-operative movement. The chairman of the English National Party in my constituency of Walsall will testify as to my political work. A Member of Parliament, who is also a doctor, and other medical specialists will demonstrate by testimony and scientific analysis what actually happened in my breakdown. Finally, the third policeman of the Victoria State police team will give evidence about his experience on December 24, 1974. . . .

I intend to demonstrate the actual working of EPACS which in turn will show how ludicrous the suggestion is that I stole a Bank of America cheque for $12,500 drawn in favour of the company. As for obtaining a pecuniary advantage by deception (by obtaining for EPACS overdraft facilities of an increase from £10,000 to £17,500 at the Midland Bank and of £10,000 at Lloyds Bank), I will describe the background of the granting of these overdrafts and the relevance and value of personal guarantees. The theft charges will be analysed within the factual background of the operation of EPACS and I will disperse the fog of confusion and put these matters straight. I will describe my actual relationship with Sheila Buckley and will demonstrate the impossibility of conspiracy. I will describe the way credit cards were used and show the complete illogicality of the credit card charges. The full background to the life insurance policies will also be explained. All will be put in the context of one man's life and one man's breakdown . . .

Whoever heard of a man who had a breakdown being charged with credit card frauds because he didn't, on the night before his 'freak-out', send cheques to clear his outstanding accounts? Moreover the debts on these accounts are clearly *company* debts as they were incurred in the course of company business. Whoever heard of a man accused of stealing from himself? He owns the company one hundred per cent; its resources have been built up completely by his efforts. Whoever heard of a theft from his own loan account? It is a logical absurdity. If the debt exists, there should be no more than a civil claim from the liquidators. Whoever heard of a man being accused of obtaining a pecuniary advantage by falsely pretending his personal guarantee was of value? If this doctrine were generally applied there would be hundreds of thousands in the dock. In the past, personal guarantees have run into millions indeed tens of millions of pounds. Despite acknowledging in such cases that the defendants were not worth the sum guaranteed, no charges were brought. . . .

Whoever heard of a man accused of attempting to obtain property by deception on life insurance policies when no claim has ever been made? The man had only 'freaked-out' for precisely one month and three days before re-appearance. During that time there had been no attempt to fake a dead body. Bearing in mind that it is common knowledge that seven years must elapse before any claim can be entertained in the absence of a body, it is fatuous to make these charges. In fact it is against all commonsense. . . .

Why then the charges? The key can be found in the disappearance. Without the disappearance no charges can be levelled concerning theft, credit cards, the insurance policies, personal guarantees, or conspiracy. The disappearance is the pivot to the whole case and I shall explain that event in factual and scientific terms. In the prosecution's view only criminality will explain my disappearance. They have not even bothered to investigate another possibility and the 'crimes' were invented to justify their theory. . . . You might imagine by the heavy-handed way the prosecution's case has been conducted, and the sheer weight of material most of which is quite superfluous, that I was being charged with treason. Of course, to many people in the establishment my having a breakdown and then attacking humbug and hypocrisy in political and business life is worse than treason. But whatever people might think that I have been charged with, the plain fact is that there are twenty-one charges which have been strung out like a fragile daisy chain. There is not one of substance and certainly not one which justifies the extraordinary charade of extradition proceedings in Australia and all the ballyhoo that has been going on since.

The fact is that every one acknowledges that no charges would have been brought if I hadn't been a Privy Councillor, a former minister who had attracted a lot of publicity. I had my breakdown because I was trying to escape the terrible pressures suffered by John Stonehouse because he was a public figure, because he was an idealist who could no longer cope with the hypocrisy of which he had become a part. Any ordinary 'Joe Bloggs' would not have been subject to the sort of treatment the ex-minister suffered. The sick 'Joe Bloggs' would possibly have received understanding. . . .

I can understand cases in which a man with an unblemished life might suddenly commit a crime. But ask yourself, would a publically known figure destroy his whole life and make himself a fugitive for the rest of his years, destined to crawl around the backwaters of the world to avoid detection, simply to steal £30,000 and to avoid paying his credit card accounts? There must be another explanation, and I simply ask you to use your judgement on the material I will present to you together with what you have already heard from prosecution witnesses. I ask no more than that – your sincere judgement. . . .

On the question of documents, the gap in the resources between prosecution and defence is awesome. The Fraud Squad has had access over the past eighteen months to every sheet of paper they cared to examine. They have had many people examining the material. They were able to get the accounts and documents from any bank and any organisation they wanted. They have had mountains of material available. But consider my position. In Australia I had no papers – I did not even have a post card from any one of my former colleagues – I had no contact with any other person in the U.K. about company affairs. Remember how witness after witness for the prosecution asked to refer to files and diaries and even the police got dates wrong? Recovering from a breakdown, in no psychological position to cope with the renewal of pressures, I did my best for six days to answer questions from Department of Trade Inspectors.

When I came back to England I was refused bail and was taken to Brixton for six and a half weeks, completely unable to do any work for my defence. Even after my release I was not able to see any former colleagues as they had been made prosecution witnesses, and I was advised by my solicitor not to talk to them.

At the committal I was allowed under supervision to look through some files, but all the files I requested were not sent to me . . . Then while passing through Dover Street, London, I found documents piled up outside my former offices for refuse collection. I collected it with my solicitor Mr. O'Dell. It was a gold mine of material. . . .

The above paragraph concludes the substance of John Stone-house's notes. He was able to continue writing the following day in his Brixton cell.

CHAPTER TWENTY-TWO

At the end of the prosecution case it is usual for the defence to put in submissions arguing that there was no case to answer or that some of the charges were faulty on legal grounds. Michael O'Dell worked through the night preparing the argument for me, and over an early breakfast at my home in Kensington we discussed the possibilities.

It seemed that we stood most chance on the insurance charges and the birth certificates. The former had been thrown out at the committal proceedings and subsequently put back without explanation by the Crown. The latter looked extremely weak after we showed, as an exhibit, the birth certificate of Michael O'Dell himself, obtained with an application form that *was not signed*. It had transpired that, under statute, the Registry Office must supply certificates even if applicants' names are not given.

We also decided to apply to have the other charges struck out – except the passport offence on which I was most vulnerable. The theft charges involved stealing money from myself, or in one instance to Garrett where the chief witness, Harry Wetzel, had failed to turn up from Los Angeles. The credit card charges were a nonsense as the companies were clearly liable for the airline tickets to which they related. And the alleged deceit in giving personal guarantees to two banks looked ludicrous against one manager's declaration from the witness box that he *still* regarded my guarantee of value – in the long run. The conspiracy charge could be undermined in a number of ways.

But the judge gave short shrift to my arguments, based on Michael's nightwork, and apart from the withdrawal of the two birth certificate charges there were no deletions. So when the judge called on me to commence the defence there were two down and nineteen charges to go. He said I could appear in the witness box, make an unsworn statement from the dock, or say nothing. But when he revoked my bail it was like a punch in the solar plexus and did not exactly improve my morale. My appeals for the resumption of bail or even for a barrister to make an application for bail were dealt with in a cavalier fashion – as though I was merely wasting time. And when I suggested that a barrister should take over the examination of expert witnesses, the judge remarked: 'Do not play games with this court, Mr. Stonehouse.' I pointed out that it was no game; that my solicitor had advised me to make such application. He asked, 'Does Mr. O'Dell wish to address this court?' Michael did so, confirming what I had said, but it was all to no avail.

And so I launched into the longest speech of my career. First the opening address and then the statement. It spread over six days – four and a half hours per day.

I started with my early life and motivations and my ideas and drew the jury's attention to my two books *Prohibited Immigrant* written in 1959 and *Death of an Idealist*, 1975. Eleven copies of each stood on the table in the well of the court for each member of the jury. But they were not allowed to have them. Corkery drew attention to a case when a book was not allowed and the judge upheld him. It was frustrating but not that damaging as, in effect, I went on to give the essential facts which appeared in the books.

I described the operation of the companies. How EPACS had been created as an 'extension of me', and how I had obtained consultancy agreements with various companies in 1976 and 1971 which 'could well have been made payable directly to me'. The companies had wanted *me* as consultant – not EPACS – which was clear from the letters of appointment from Britten-Norman Aircraft, International Computers and Dowty.

My involvement with Bangladesh was an emotional section: how I had gone to Calcutta to see the plight of the refugees on behalf of War on Want and Oxfam, my report to the Foreign Secretary, the beginnings of aid, the squalor of the camps, the mass rape on the other side of the border as West Pakistanis crushed their Bengali kinsmen in East Pakistan. I described how ten million people had to flee for their lives from the terror; how university students and professors told me of their lucky escapes from the massacres at Dacca and Chittagong; and how the Government in exile was established to fight for independance. There could hardly have been a more telling and lurid description from a dock at the Old Bailey. It might have seemed somewhat remote from nineteen charges of theft, forgery fraud and false pretences but it was, to me, an essential basis for my defence.

I explained what idealism meant – not ambition, 'Only callow and insensitive people believe that. It is a belief in a cause to achieve good.' My activities (which had been smeared in the press, I noted in passing) in organising the production and sale of Bangladesh stamps to promote the concept of Bangladesh and raise money. I described how I had taken those stamps to Dacca two days after the cease-fire so that the Post Office could put them on sale to replace Pakistani stamps. I spoke of the Director-General who had given me an order for six months, supply of stamps, enough for the whole country. I recalled how when this was produced – at my expense – the order was repudiated by the new Director-General, who had been in a Pakistani prison for six months and wanted to undo his predecessor's decisions – 'I lost money on that.'

I described my work as a trustee of the Bangladesh Fund with Mr. Justice Abu Sayeed Choudhu as the chairman and Alderman Donald Chesworth of War on Want as another; how no money was collected by the trustees – it was paid directly by collectors into the Fund's bank accounts; and how, notwithstanding this, I had been falsely accused of stealing one million pounds from the Fund. The details by A. S. Choudhu had not been published in most of the newspapers which had printed the original story.

I explained how I had become involved in the setting up of the British Bangladesh Trust, how Bengalis had approached me saying there was widespread support for the idea of providing a service for the eighty-three Bengalis in Britain who could no longer use the Pakistani controlled banks. I had made three conditions: 1. The Bank of England should approve and support; 2. British institutions should also subscribe; and 3. If I became chairman, I should be unpaid. Then the work in setting up the bank, the negotiations with companies GKN, Plessey, Trust House Forte and others, the Crown agents and their involvement – all organised by myself. The jury were beginning to appreciate that it was certainly my baby.

Then the difficulties with Suhail Aziz. I quoted his letters claiming to support and value the concept, his offers to work for it and give help from his faction of the Awami League, and then how he demanded £5000 per year and a directorship. We had to refuse him, and his hostile retort. Then came the Aziz campaign of denigration.

The build-up came over like a thriller: How 'Mac' Choudhu at the Bangladesh High Commission had told me that Anthony Mascherenas had said he was writing an article against a Labour MP in business apparently to balance the attacks the *Sunday Times* had made on Reggie Maudling, the former Tory Chancellor of the Exchequer. How Choudhu had said, 'There is no dirt on Stonehouse,' but how Mascherenas persisted. And how K. B. Ahmed, my co-director, had learned from Dr. Basu the head of the Indian Secret Service in Britain that Mascherenas far from being the genuine friend of Bangladesh he professed to be.

I quoted from the article, particularly the damaging passage on the Bangladesh handbill which had been represented erroneously as a prospectus. That was absolute rubbish. The handbill was only a sincere endeavour to give Bengali readers equality of information with the English readers of the *Financial Times*. The complaint about the handbill was that it said that the Trust 'could' or 'would' be renamed a bank, if the Bank of England approved. In fact the *F.T.* article reproduced in the handbill had liberal references to banks.

It was necessary to describe the misrepresentation of the handbill and the activities of a Pakistani agent to undermine me as it was essential to the progression of events which followed. There was the Department of Trade and Industry Inspector who confirmed that Aziz had written to him anonymously, and then the devastating three months investigation by Detective Inspector Grant who was quite relentless in his efforts to build up the case which would give him such kudos. I described how this period had left me a worn-out man as for so long I was poised on the brink of disaster – I was threatened with prosecution for fraud which, however ridiculous in basis, would ruin my career.

I told the jury how Peter Walker, the Secretary of State, had been told nothing of the trouble. He and the Foreign Secretary, Sir Alec Douglas-Home, had both helped to stop a prosecution. The Scotland Yard team and the DPP, I said, had felt cheated, and that explained why they now had a grudge.

I described how the *Sunday Times* article had created a short fall in subscriptions and how nominee holdings were organised to make up the balance and secure the success of the launching. That scheme was subsequently rearranged as nominee holdings were transferred. All the bank officials were quite aware of it, I emphasised. Indeed they had made all the requisite entries in the books. It was intended to sell the shares as soon as the banks became established but, in the event, although the BBT survived and obtained official recognition, the rest of the secondary banking world collapsed. So our plans were thwarted.

My own trading companies had prospered through contracts I had obtained, but their strength was being sapped by the demands of the bank. It was in such circumstances that I became engaged in a frantic endeavour in 1974 to obtain big commissions on trading deals and to arrange a share exchange with foreign banks to save the British Bangladesh Trust (now renamed the London Capital Group). I went to Rumania where, with Jim Charlton, we signed a contract to take over export surplus of cement at very favourable prices. I went to Yemen to try to seal a four million pound contract for military communications from Racal which would be worth £400,000 in commissions. I explained that much of that would have to be passed on to agents acting for us so as to 'make it happen'. Do not imagine, I told the jury, that British exports are easily achieved. You do not simply send out brochures – it involves hard grind and the expenditure of expenses money which are shared with people 'on the ground'.

I told of the Beirut agents I had, how we worked on schemes for the Sudan – railway development, on petro-chemical complexes, hotels and the like, all involving vast sums and vast rewards if successful. I told of Nigeria which I had been pressed to visit where there was similarly vast potential and of how we tried to get the cement sold into that market, if not Iran. I told of our New York associates who worked with us on sugar and wheat commodity deals which could have produced large returns. The list was endless, and I could only touch on it.

But the point I wanted to demonstrate was that the so-called loan account money was in fact used as business expenditure and would have been fully accounted for at the end of the project or at the end of the financial year. Then I produced my trump card – a graph of the loan account which I had drawn up one evening in my cell at Brixton. It showed that I had owed nearly £20,000 up to the end of December 1971. Then I was in credit (in fact the loan account owed me £2000) until September 1972. From November to April 1973, I owed over £20,000, going into credit for a similar amount for one month in July. Then in August 1973, I owed £40,000 for five months, going into credit in March 1974. It was thus demonstrated that the fact that £34,000 was shown to be owing by me in November 1974, was nothing exceptional. In fact it was quite usual.

On the insurances, I pointed out that my wife had asked for them and paid for them from her own income. She had become concerned after a bomb at Heathrow in May 1974, which had blown up my car. A bomb had also been placed outside the NAAFI headquarters near our home. I had not, I emphasised, done the least thing possible to assist a claim – I had not provided a body nor had I remained in hiding long enough for a claim to be made. In saying this, I had in mind the legal definitions of the attempt with which I had been charged.

On the Swiss bank account I explained that there was no charge in that connection – in fact having a foreign account was not illegal. The money paid in had come from my own resources overseas.

And so to the creation of Markham. How the parallel personality had grown as a form of relief from the pressures that Stonehouse, the public figure, had to bear. How Markham had felt pleasure at being able to queue up at the Passport Office, and the elation he felt at getting a document which confirmed his existence. Markham really existed. He went to the Astoria Hotel where dozens of guests would have seen him, to the St. George's Hospital for an X-ray examination – again seen by many people, twice to British Airways to get a vaccination certificate, to the Management Business Services in Regent Street every other day. I wanted the jury to realise that these visits were not part of a great plan. They were too risky for that. They were attempts by me to get relief; to experience living as an ordinary person.

I described the first breakdown – buying a ticket for Australia from Pan Am in Piccadilly. The second in Miami caused a hectic flight to Mexico and on to Los Angeles the next day. Here Markham missed the connecting Qantas flight for Sydney, and slipped back into Stonehouse in L.A. Stonehouse visited Garrett there; saw Harry Wetzel and discussed the report I had prepared for him. Eventually I flew back to Miami to reconnect fully with Stonehouse once more. Then the third breakdown precipitated the hectic flight to Chicago and San Francisco and back to Miami again. All four flights across America in just two days and two nights. It came over as a nightmare, as indeed it was.

And then came the fourth breakdown which resulted in Markham taking Stonehouse over almost completely and the flight from Miami to San Francisco. The relief of it. The freedom to be liberated from the incubus was, I explained, intense. But in Hawaii I was torn again, and in distress, Markham telephoned Sheila Buckley in London and begged her not to tell. 'It was Joe Markham who phoned,' I said. 'Mrs. Buckley, a great woman, instinctively understood and did her best to help by maintaining silence.'

I described the arrival in Australia, the joy at being admitted as a migrant and the fears as doubts re-emerged. I recalled that Markham took a plane – a British Airways 747 – for Singapore and on to Copenhagen through Tashkent. The urge to go back to Europe was that great.

I wanted to get across to the jury the irrationality of it all, a far cry from a careful plan. And they listened intently – most of them – hour after hour as my story unfolded. I described how Sheila came to see me in Copenhagen and my return to

Melbourne. Still I remained in a state of confusion, with my parallel personality, the simple basic man Joe Markham, still in control. In Melbourne once again I reverted to Clive Mildoon to get further away from the pressures on Stonehouse, and wandered distractedly around the main streets of the city, even into the leading hotel – oblivious of the fact that I might be recognised by anyone.

On the final day I emphasised that I was not a fugitive. I had simply had a breakdown and after my re-appearance simply wanted somewhere to rest and recover. But I would never have run away from charges. Passports were offered to me – including an American one from the widow of a man whose age appearance and height were similar to my own. I refused them all. Now my intention was to unliquidate EPACS; pay back all legitimate debts, if I was given the chance. As far as Parliament was concerned, I had not resigned because I had had a job of work to do. A resignation could have been seen as an acknowledgement of guilt. But I announced I would resign as soon as suitable, whatever the result of the trial, 'if there is no General Election this year'.

I had told the Prime Minister that on 24th December, 1974, I had a breakdown and apologised for the trouble I had caused all concerned. I repeated the apology. 'I am truly sorry for the anguish to my family and my friends.' I acknowledged that as a result of my experience I had become a heretic. But, 'I do not want to become a scapegoat for all society's present-day sins.'

My marathon speech was finished and had lasted over a week. The jury, I was glad to note, was still with me – with perhaps one exception.

The press had come and gone, printing the bits about Sheila's 'intimate relationship' with me and the decision to resign my seat, but the bulk was ignored. The *Daily Mirror* which had, over the crucial months, printed and then repeated the report on the Czech spy story, failed to publish my denial although I branded their stories as scurrilous. I was glad that my trial was not trial by the media, but by the eleven-strong jury who had, ever so patiently, sat through my speech.

After two excellent character witnesses from two former

chairmen of constituency parties in Wednesbury and Walsall, the court adjourned at 3.30 p.m. on Thursday. The judge gave the trial participants a break for Friday. Apart from the confirmation that he was not now concerned about any delay in the proceedings I was glad to have an extra break – although it was to be 'enjoyed' in a Brixton cell where the sun is never seen.

CHAPTER TWENTY-THREE

There are two aspects to defence tactics in calling witnesses. The first is to undermine the allegations made in the prosecution case, and the second to provide alternative explanations for actions which are suggested as pointing to criminality.

Most of the attempts made to pin the label of outrageous conduct on me had been deflated. It had been made clear by the superintendant in charge of the case that no one had actually made a complaint that an offence had been committed by me. The charges themselves were, therefore, postulated by the police. But a number of potentially dangerous points had been made not directly connected with charges, and these had to be dealt with.

For example, it had been emphasised by Corkery that I had been responsible for 'spurious, utterly dishonest minutes', and that the last year's salary of £10,000 from EPACS had been voted in very suspicious circumstances. Almost as an afterthought, it was added that I had failed to have the proper tax deduction made from this salary. I had to kill these vicious canards and doing so was relatively easy.

The meetings, about which complaints had been made, were shown as taking place at Devonshire House, W1 – the offices of the auditors of the company. The police, although they had carefully visited every possible witness, had significantly failed to see the auditors of EPACS. It was a condemning omission. Who better to objectively inform the police of EPACS' affairs? A lot of time had been spent in taking statements from Dixon Wilson, auditors of the British Bangladesh Trust, although it was not named in the charges. I guessed that the decision not to see Citroen Wells, auditors of EPACS, was quite deliberate.

Accordingly, one of my first witnesses was Jack Marks, the chartered accountant who is the senior partner in Citroen Wells. He was excellent. Precise, straightforward, he provided ample repudiations. According to him, the annual minutes and returns of small companies, especially those with single or family owners, are normally prepared in his offices and sent to the company concerned with a 'consent to short notice' which indicates, when signed, that the shareholders and directors' consent to the meeting. The address of the auditors is shown as a matter of course, although the actual meeting is normally never held there.

Marks then produced the 'consent for short notice' for the particular meeting Corkery had complained about. It was signed by all the directors, including John McGrath himself, who had been persuaded by the police to make such a song and dance about the £10,000. Then I produced my income tax returns for the past three years showing a nil liability for tax, and Marks confirmed that all tax due on the £10,000 had indeed been paid and he had been my adviser on tax affairs.

Corkery asked for Marks' files to examine overnight to assist his cross-examination, but on the following morning had little of value to pursue. My daughter Jane's arrangement to take over some shares and a loan from Global Imex to me, which was never taken up, were the points he laboured in a very tedious way.

For some reason, ostensibly the heat in court Number One, we all moved down to court Seven in the new block for one day. Its design was not nearly so impressive although the air-conditioning was superior. At least it gave the judge the chance to exercise his wit, which he has done from time to time. 'If you feel too cold, members of the jury, just tell me and I can move this switch here to change the temperature. It's one of the marvels of modern science. They can stand downstairs in the boiler room and tell which judge is in which court by reading the temperature gauge.'

The battle on the admissability of medical evidence was the next hurdle I had to face. Barristers had believed that most of it would not be allowed because it was *post-facto* the events. The examinations by psychiatrists were conducted after my first apprehension in Australia and, in England, after I had been extradited.

The first medical witness, Dr. Gerard Gibney, had been waiting patiently for a week since his arrival from Melbourne and the first argument took place over his appearance. It went easier than I expected. Corkery had produced a list of cases which all appeared to deal with insanity pleas but which had no relevance to the present case. I pointed out that the evidence would not concern the charges directly, which Corkery was apparently worried about, but would provide an alternative explanation for the disappearance. It became difficult for objections to be sustained and without the jury present, Gibney was heard.

He gave a clear account as to how he interviewed and treated me early in 1975, and how he had concluded that I had committed the equivalent of suicide – a psychiatric suicide – repeating much of his evidence given at the extradition proceedings in Australia. As the judge was satisfied he was then allowed to repeat the evidence in front of the jury.

The next witnesses, Dr. Lionel Haward, a psychologist who had conducted tests after my return to England, and psychiatrists who had seen me even later – were more difficult to admit. I had a clash with the judge when he pressed me to provide an explanation for calling them and I explained briefly what they would do. Sarcastically he said, 'You are being your usual revealing self, to which I replied, 'I'm at a great disadvantage in this dock. When I give a long answer, you criticise. There is an implication in your remarks which I don't like.'

'I'd say it to counsel,' said the judge.

I then suggested the medical witnesses be heard without the jury so that their evidence could be evaluated directly; I guessed the judge was trying to trick me into saying something which would enable him to strike the evidence out altogether. If in answer to his remarks I had said, 'I want them to show that I could not have committed criminal acts,' he certainly would not have allowed them anywhere near the witness box. It was that feeling which prompted me to burst out, 'I'm a layman. I'm not qualified. You're asking me to talk about my own symptoms. You've shown such prejudice in this case; it's most displeasing. If only you'd try to get at the truth it would help enormously.'

That night returning in handcuffs, as usual, to Brixton prison I felt strangely better; it must have been the satisfaction of putting behind me the humbug of pretending that the judge was fair. Normally, as soon as I arrive, I am locked in my solitary cell and left for twelve hours until the following morning. But this evening a friendly warder gave me a game of chess – as well as confiding to me that he used to be active in the Young Conservatives. It seems that most of the warders support the National Front, so he must be an exception.

Later I heard that the friendly warder had been reported by one of his colleagues for fraternising with me and had to appear on reprimand before the governor.

Something of interest happened during the chess game which is worth recalling. Dr. Blythe, the doctor in charge of the prison hospital, came to see me exuding a charm which immediately made me suspicious. '*Mr*. Stonehouse, I'm sorry I didn't see you when you first came in; you only saw a part-time doctor. Are you sure you are alright? Sure there is nothing we can do for you?' Gradually he worked his way round to the real point of the interview. 'You know you could plead diminished responsibility don't you. Are you calling medical evidence to do that?' The doctor was quite wrong but I did not enter into that. I simply said, 'Not at all. The medical evidence is simply to explain my disappearance – it was due to a breakdown – and to rebut the prosecution's suggestion that it shows criminality.'

'You saw Dr. Scott in court today did you?' said Dr. Blythe. Indeed I had: Peter Scott the consultant psychiatrist at Maudsley Hospital had been advising Corkery all day. The doctor, having completed his errand, withdrew, and I returned to my cell confident that the prosecution were now in a very difficult position in that they had failed to find reasons to contest the medical evidence.

On the next morning this proved to be the position, with Corkery conceding but the judge still trying to exclude the other doctors. 'Well, if the prosecution don't object, how can I continue to do so?' seemed to be his final resigned attitude.

So we had dummy runs – without the jury – and this gave Corkery his opportunity to test the defences of my witnesses; one was found to be exceedingly weak but the others stood up to the combined attack from counsel and judge.

Dr. Maurice Miller, the Labour M.P. for a Glasgow constituency confirmed he had noticed a deterioration in my condition in 1973 and 1974 and had advised me to see a psychiatrist. His diagnosis had been that I was in an anxious and depressed state. His evidence was valuable in that it pre-dated the alleged offences.

Dr. Lionel Haward was marvellous, clear and firm. But when it came to Professor J. B. Watson the head of Guy's Hospital Psychiatric Department I noticed his perky and confident manner deflate under the scathing remarks – particularly from the judge. 'Do you mean to say you *never* obtained Mr. Stonehouse's medical history from his own medical practitioner? Wasn't that rather essential to a proper diagnosis?' The professor looked (and probably felt) like a naughty schoolboy caught out by the headmaster. He was also made to disgorge his confidential file which put him ill-at-ease.

Dr. Ronald Laing, the author of *Divided Self* and nine other leading books on psychiatric subjects, also took part in the dummy run and was obviously much stronger in his personality and views.

After some delay while the judge considered the authorities and precedents, he ruled that the evidence could be heard before the jury. Dr. Miller, although he had been up half the night voting in the House of Commons, was on form. He only drew two questions from Corkery. 'Is Mr. Stonehouse highly intelligent, and highly adaptive?' 'Yes,' said Miller with Corkery beaming at the jury as though something quite extraordinary had been conceded.

Dr. Haward told of his psychometric tests which showed a hysteroid personality, as there were quite significant discrepancies in the results, and there were symptoms of depression and severe anxiety. And this he diagnosed had been caused by acute stress. Because the illness was chronic he had formed the opinion that it had been present for some time, possibly one year or two before the tests were first conducted in August 1975. In a hysteroid, he said, it is possible for parts of the nervous system to be cut off and one of the characteristics could be a change of identity in order to effect an escape. He differentiated between a hysterical patient, who changes internally, and someone who merely fakes an alias to escape. The latter tends to change appearance as well as name.

He produced his graphs to demonstrate how he analysed the changes in identity between Stonehouse, Markham and Mildoon, showing the last two as providing an approximate to the ideal self. I asked if the need for relief in a parallel personality could explain the disappearance in 1974 without any ulterior motive and Dr. Haward confirmed it could. He went on to say that it would be usual to come back when pressure had been reduced. As an example of a similar case he referred to *Three Faces of Eve*, a book written about an hysteric with three personalities which had been made into a film shown on TV. Dr. Haward then examined paintings I had completed before 1974 and said he had seen them first at my home in October 1975 and had volunteered an interest in them. The colours indicated great stress, particularly in the last large one showing dark reds and ominous blacks. 'If that had been painted by a patient in my Greylingwell hospital I would be very concerned.' The patient would be considered to be ill.

The witness concluded that in the present case the individual was not fully aware of his reasons for acting in the way he did.

'Would that apply to the disappearance in November 1974?'

'Yes,' he replied.

'And to the earlier events – the "clothing" of Markham?'

'Yes, because the hysteroid personality has a continuous existence.'

In his cross-examination Corkery decided to attack without respite. He was quite vicious. After comparing my disappearance with that of the Great Train Robbers, Wilson and Biggs, he took a test card from Dr. Haward's own file and proceeded to throw scorn at the questions. 'That is confidential,' said the witness, 'and if the details are revealed, the value of the tests would be invalidated.' 'I have no power to stop publication of these proceedings,' said the judge, 'but the press would have heard you.' Corkery proceeded to answer the questions in a mocking way to ensure he obtained a low score as a hysteric.

'How does that make me?'

'Quite normal,' said the psychologist.

'That doesn't prove he is,' said the judge.

'Now let's take it another way,' said Corkery. 'Supposing I like antiques and deep sea diving and a large manor house ... What is my score now?' he paused, having carefully chosen answers to ensure a high score.

'You would be psychotic,' said the psychologist and the public gallery laughed.

As the witness failed to be dislodged from his scientific opinion Corkery resorted to abuse. 'Can't you answer that question with a simple, No?' he snapped at one point. But the doctor's equanimity and firmness were not budged. Following him Professor Watson showed a complete change in demeanour, although he confirmed the points written in his report. He did not think I was lying when I said I had suffered a breakdown and he believed it went back before 1974, possibly to 1970 or 1971.

My problem was one of finding a true identity, as in my life my identity had been expressed in causes outside myself. The Markham and Mildoon period were attempts to find the basic self and it was his opinion that I half wanted to be discovered.

Corkery started with all sweetness and light. 'Thank you, Professor, for talking in terms we all understand, not like yesterday.' (referring to Haward) 'You would agree your opinion is based on some information and if you had more information about the case your opinion could be amended.'

'Yes,' the rot was already setting in.

'May I put a hypothetical question?' said Corkery cunningly. 'Supposing Mr. Stonehouse had chosen another identity to take money, escape from his responsibilities and set up a new life with his lover, would that influence your view.'

'Yes.' (How could he reply otherwise, but he should have added a qualification, as Haward, a firmer character, would have done.)

Gradually, Corkery persuaded Watson to undermine his own evidence even to the point of agreeing that his earlier statement, that I had 'half wanted to be discovered,' was too categorical.

Significantly, neither the judge nor Corkery referred to the absence of consultation with the private medical practitioner (which had been their bull point in the dummy run). As the witness had become malleable to the prosecution's points it was no longer necessary for that ploy to be played.

I felt thoroughly dejected by the game that goes under the name of justice.

CHAPTER TWENTY-FOUR

I am learning more about the intrigues of the law the longer this trial goes on. It is most certainly a game of wits in which the participants have to be alert at all times to the tricks of the other side. Michael O'Dell suspected that the Director of Public Prosecutions was not providing him with the full list of witnesses interviewed by the police. We kept coming across people who had given statements and whose names had been kept quiet. My barber, Harry Leigh, who had visited me on the night before I had left on that fateful journey to Miami, was one such name, and Lesek Nowicki, an architect who had become a nominee to hold BBT shares, was another. Michael bombarded the DPP with letters to try to prise the details from them. It is the well recognised convention that they should be provided to the defence and their reluctance was suspicious.

Finally on 10th June, only a couple of weeks before the defence case was to begin, Michael received a long list of names which had been omitted from the list provided in January. It was very revealing. On it appeared Miss Susan Benjamin, a ticket agent for National Airlines who had said that on November 14th, 1974, I had made a booking for a flight from Miami via Los Angeles to London for 22nd November. As this booking was arranged only a week before I disappeared, it could have significance as to my actual conscious intentions at the time. Another name was Steve Erdos, the manager of the Regal Hotel in St. Kilda, Melbourne, who said that I had made bookings in the names of *both* Markham and Mildoon, which would throw doubt on the allegation that I used the name of Mildoon merely as an alias to avoid detection. It was especially significant as I had been apprehended by the Victoria State police just after leaving the Regal Hotel. The prosecution agreed that both statements could be read.

They were less co-operative on another matter of even greater importance. One of the names given reluctantly by the

DPP turned out to be that of an Australian customs' official who had examined the Markham trunk before it was collected for customs' purposes. But when a Melbourne solicitor eventually tracked him down he refused to talk before he had permission from superiors and a copy of his police statement. On the very day I was finishing my defence I heard that finally he had spoken to the effect that he had seen no women's clothing in the trunk. This was dynamite, as the prosecution were relying heavily on Ward's evidence that I had told him Mrs. Buckley's clothes were in it.

After a long exchange with the judge, during which both Michael and I described the difficulties of contacting this witness (the judge did not believe me at first), and with Corkery making no concession whatsoever, the judge came very near to approving an adjournment so that the official – Robert Hill – could come from Australia to give his evidence. At this point Corkery relented and said he would agree to work out a compromise. This turned out to be a statement, which Hill agreed on the telephone, confirming everything we wanted. If the witness had in fact appeared in person he might have been shifted; as it was we had played poker and won. The prosecution's case on conspiracy was clearly collapsing.

Dr. Ronald Laing, author of *The Divided Self* and nine other books on psychiatry and a practising psychiatrist for twenty-four years, gave evidence on my mental condition. Through him I read into the record several extracts from my book *Death of an Idealist*, which the judge had refused to let the jury see on the grounds that it was a self-serving statement. He confirmed that my description of my experience indicated intense irrational emotions of persecution and feelings of guilt, although believing I was innocent; and showed a partial psychiatric breakdown with partial disassociation of personality. He confirmed that in his report he had called it psychotic and the splitting of the personality into two or multiple pieces. He went on: 'The conflict is dealt with by this splitting instead of dealing with it openly. The mind is compartmentalised, so in one compartment the pain is not felt.'

He said that his experience with malingerers was considerable – particularly when he was a captain in the Army. In my situation, he said, psychiatric diagnosis must include assessment as to whether I was malingering; and his diagnosis did take that into account. It was 'partial reactive psychosis. For some time he became irrational and confused under emotional and other pressures.'

In cross-examination Corkery tried to undermine Laing by questioning his qualifications – why had he described himself as Fellow of the Royal College of Medicine when it was the Royal Society of Medicine? Later Laing reciprocated when Corkery made a mistake in a name. Laing said, 'I'm glad you can make a slip of the tongue as well as me.'

Jane, my daughter, gave evidence on her reactions to me, my change in personality from 1971 and my feelings of persecution in 1974. She recalled the awful scenes of breakdown which she had observed when she stayed with me in Melbourne in early 1975. 'I was frightened he'd gone over the top,' she said. 'He lost complete control of his body, screaming around banging his head against the floor. I was terrified because I had never seen anything like it before; to see it in my father was a great shock. I thought it was a manifestation of his recovery from a breakdown; he was picking up the pieces.'

Corkery asked about Mrs. Susan Hill: 'Did you take her and other young friends to be nominees for BBT shares?'

'Yes, nothing wrong in that.'

And on the silly business of Susan Hill calling herself a dress designer, Jane emphatically said she had advised her to say this because, in fact, she had designed dresses and did not want just to put 'housewife'. It occurred to me how ridiculous the trial had become when such matters were considered either relevant or important. Corkery's attempt to undermine Jane's testimony came with – 'Did you not cash in on the publicity by having an exhibition of your paintings in Sydney?' (A question which was apparently handed up by Etheridge.) In fact, as came out, she had had several exhibitions in London before the visit and the Sydney one had not made money.

For about a week Michael had been trying to get Edward Short, MP, to throw light on the political aspects of the case and on the medical evidence he had been given. But Mr. Short avoided having any subpoena served on him and would only talk to people on the telephone even when they went to the House of Commons to see him. His solicitors – Lord Goodman's firm – threatened to get an injunction to prevent him being called. I gave up trying and closed my defence.

The prosecution had taken about ten weeks and my defence a little under three weeks; Sheila Buckley's, which followed, took an hour. It just about put the case against her into perspective. In a quiet soft voice Sheila read a statement from the dock. Lord Wigoder, who wears a hearing aid and obviously has difficulty in hearing, jumped up at the beginning and asked her to speak up but, with thunder and lightning off stage, it did not do much good. Her words were all the more effective for being delivered in such a cool, unforceful way. On the following morning the jury were allowed to take the statement to read for themselves.

She said her marriage to Roger Buckley was in August 1969.

Because of the sex angle the press next day gave Sheila's statement the full treatment but with some significant omissions. The *Sun* put the story in a front-page spread pushing the first ever landing on Mars into the back pages. Most papers failed to print the point that she had divorced her husband on the grounds of his adultery, including the *Daily Mirror* which – in earlier days – had used its full front page for an inaccurate story: 'Stonehouse stole my wife' by Roger Buckley.

The trial by media can never be fair.

'I was divorced from him in March 1973, following my petition on the grounds of his adultery, which he did not contest, and also in view of the many other facts which I found out about him. There were no children of the marriage. I left him in June 1971.' And she went on:

'At that very difficult and emotionally disastrous time, Mr. Stonehouse's friendship and practical help to me were second to none which had a most stabilising effect, for which I shall always be grateful to him. Sometime after I had parted from my husband and at a time when my marriage was being dissolved, my friendship with Mr. Stonehouse grew, and eventually I developed a very personal and intimate relationship with him.

'At no time prior to my going to Copenhagen in December

1974 did I know of the characters or names of Mildoon or Markham which it is alleged were created by Mr. Stonehouse. I have heard and read the evidence in relation to the emergence of these characters, including the bank accounts and the cheque cards, etc., but I had no knowledge of these matters until long after Mr. Stonehouse disappeared.

'It is alleged that Mr. Stonehouse was transferring some money from EPACS to himself, and thereafter transferring some of these monies to bank accounts in the names of Markham and Mildoon. I know nothing of this allegation. It follows from this that I have never spoken to anyone and referred to myself as Mr. Markham's (or Mildoon's) secretary . . .

'I am charged together with Mr. Stonehouse with theft in respect of certain specific cheques issued from EPACS' bank accounts. My only recollection of these cheques is that I have seen from the exhibits that I in fact signed them, which certainly does not surprise me, for I signed many hundreds of cheques during my employment, and did so as part of my regular duties, originally at the request of Mr. Stonehouse. In practically every case the accountant, Mr. Le Fort, would ask me to sign a batch of cheques which he had prepared, I suppose to save the time of Mr. Stonehouse who was always incredibly busy. Mr. Le Fort would then invariably hand some of the cheques to Mr. Stonehouse, retaining and dealing with the remainder himself. It follows therefore that although the cheques may have borne my signature, I would have nothing to do with the actual handling of them . . .

'To this day I have never seen any of the books of any of the companies and frankly, I do not think I would have understood them if I had seen them. I have absolutely no knowledge whatsoever of book-keeping and it remains a complete mystery to me. I therefore was never aware of the condition of the loan account – whether it was in credit or in debit . . .

'I first became a director of EPACS and of two of the other companies in the group in 1970. This was at the request of Mr. Stonehouse. I was regarded in the administration of the company as having no real "say" in the running of the companies. As a director and secretary I, on occasions, signed letters which were drafted by others, and I was also frequently asked to sign forms which were sent to Companies House. Mr. Le Fort would invariably compile the forms or sometimes, I think, the auditors would have done so. The same procedure was adopted for Inland Revenue and Value Added Tax documents – they all bore my signature as secretary, but I was totally reliant on the professionals for the accuracy of the documents . . .

'I regarded Mr. Stonehouse as being dynamic, hardworking and a brilliant politician and businessman; I trusted him absolutely. He was extremely active and led a very full business and political life. I have no doubt at all that the initial success, after the formation of the companies and the London Capital Group, was due to the work of Mr. Stonehouse . . .

'In 1974 I noticed that without any doubt Mr. Stonehouse was suffering from considerable strain which had become more intense and his health, in my opinion, had greatly deteriorated. I saw him resting frequently which I had never seen him do before. Much of his zest and enthusiasm had left him – he gave the impression of being a very, very tired man. I felt that he was suffering greatly as a result of the considerable pressures he was under at that time . . .'

Then she came to the events of November 1974 and my visit to Miami.

'He telephoned me from there, I think from the Miami bank where the meetings took place, and asked me about letters and telephone calls I had received at the office. One of the things I had to tell him was that I had only just managed to ascertain that he had been chosen to lead the Commonwealth Parliamentary Association delegation of MPs to Tanzania. The delegation was due to leave in mid-December of that year, and it was quite an achievement to have been chosen to go at all, let alone to lead it. I was delighted by this accomplishment.

'At about midnight on 21st November, 1974, I received a telephone call from Mr. McGrath asking whether I had heard the news that Mr. Stonehouse was dead. I said that I had not and that it must be a mistake. He told me that he had heard the news on the BBC. I returned to my room stunned and shocked at the news. A few minutes later the telephone rang again. It was my sister saying she had received a telephone call from Philip Gay who had told her the news and asked her to inform me. Although I had no reason to disbelieve the news I found it difficult to accept and I had a sixth sense that Mr. Stonehouse might still be alive. Fleetingly, suicide entered my head as a possibility, but the thought was too grotesque to think about and anyway I felt his presence. I felt sure that I would *know* if he had been taken from me – if he were dead. I had no evidence or knowledge at that time to back this feeling. It was simply my intuition.

'On I think Friday, 22nd November, 1974, I was in my room when I was completely bowled over to receive a telephone call from Mr. Stonehouse. I asked him where he was but he did not reply to this question. He sounded completely distraught and it was very difficult to make any sense of what he was saying. He was incoherent and I thought he sounded suicidal. He said things like: "Help me, Sheila." I asked him whether he was physically well and he answered yes. I asked him whether I should let his family know that he was alive and he said emphatically that I should not. I asked him whether this was wise but he simply repeated that I should not. He asked me to give my word that I would not tell anyone that he was alive until he gave me permission to do so. He sounded so desperate I had no option but to give him my word. I tried several times to get him to say where he was but he would or could not say. I assumed he was still in America because I recalled the reports that he had left his passport in his room in Miami. The telephone call lasted for about four minutes and Mr. Stonehouse weakly said that he would call me again.

'Because of my promise to Mr. Stonehouse I did not tell anyone of my knowledge that he was alive, and in any case I considered it would be dangerous to do so in view of a possible suicide attempt by him. Above all, the only thing that mattered to me was the safety of Mr. Stonehouse.

'On the evening of Monday, 25th November, 1974, I received another call from Mr. Stonehouse. I did not know that he was going to telephone me but I prayed that he would. When speaking to Mr. Stonehouse on this second occasion, he was still very distraught. He told me that he was in America and kept repeating that he was so sorry for asking me not to tell anyone he was alive; he was putting me in a very difficult situation. The telephone calls were extremely confusing since at all times Mr. Stonehouse spoke in the third person. For instance, he referred to "John" as another person and said that he had to die to get away from the pressures in England. He said that he was moving on. It was not clear to me and I do not think it was clear to him either where exactly he was going, but he might have mentioned Australia at this time. He told me that he would try to contact me some time in the future. He still sounded very ill and all I could do was to speak to him in a comforting manner, assuring him of my support. It seemed unwise for me to place further stress on him by asking too many questions and the ones I did ask of him he seemed unable to comprehend. He again repeated that I was not to tell his family or anyone that he had been in touch. At no time did he use the first person – "I" – it was always "he" or "him". He sounded very confused as to who he actually *was*. This call lasted for about five minutes.

'I do not think that Mr. Stonehouse telephoned me again until the early morning of 4th December, 1974, by which time I was becoming frantic with worry about his safety and also about the many problems I was having. I believed at the time that I might be pregnant, wrongly as it turned out, and that Mr. Stonehouse was the father. He still sounded very distraught and spoke still in the third person. He repeatedly said: "They won't let him die, why won't they let him die?" He said he wanted to see me which filled me with delight since I took it that perhaps he was beginning to recover from whatever he was suffering from. He explained that he was in Copenhagen and my mind boggled to know how he got there – that is without a passport. I told him that it would be impossible for me to see him there without the possibility of bringing with me half the English press corps. In a frantic voice he said that if I did not go he would have to come to see me. He sounded far too ill to return to England at this time to face the deluge of the media and perhaps recriminations from his family. Rightly or, with hindsight, wrongly, I told Mr. Stonehouse that I would try to get to Copenhagen on 6th

December, 1974, and he said he would telephone me later that evening to confirm that I had arranged a booking.

'Mr. Stonehouse rang me again on the evening of 4th December and I confirmed that I would be with him on the 6th; he sounded so relieved and said he would meet me at the airport. He still sounded very confused and rather incoherent – the call lasted only a couple of minutes.

'On the afternoon of 6th December I went to see my doctor for the purpose of obtaining some tranquillisers, as by this time I was feeling under a very great strain, and I knew that I had to be strong for when I met Mr. Stonehouse. When I entered his surgery I broke down. The strain of my ordeal was making my head split and my tears, although embarrassing for all concerned, seemed to help. As I tried to pull myself together the pain in my head ceased a little – up until that time I had been completely unable to cry and it seemed to be just the thing I needed. The doctor commiserated with me but, unfortunately, I could not tell him of my dilemma. He gave me some sedatives and warned me about the dangers of taking an overdose.

'I was aware that I was being constantly followed, presumably by the press at that time and I did not expect to get to Copenhagen without them knowing. I quite expected my trip to result in it being known that Mr. Stonehouse was alive, but at least I had the comfort of knowing that I would be there with him when this happened and that I could take care of him. I was, however, fairly satisfied that by the time I had reached the airport, I had lost my followers in the traffic. When I arrived at the airport in Copenhagen I found Mr. Stonehouse sitting right in the middle of the foyer, his head resting in his cupped hands, looking pale and much thinner than when I had last seen him. He was completely distraught, nervous and drawn. He was not wearing any form of disguise and I could not understand why he had not been recognised as he sat there, with many British people all around, having arrived on the same plane as I had. Mr. Stonehouse's photograph had been on the front pages of newspapers for weeks and the chances of his being recognised were enormous. I stayed with him in Copenhagen until 8th December when I returned to London.

'While I was with Mr. Stonehouse he explained to me that he had become Mr. Markham and that he had a passport in that name. He did not explain how he had acquired it and I did not ask him too many questions for fear of making his condition worse. He told me that he had been in Hawaii and that he had flown to Melbourne but had left again the next day. He asked me on several occasions why I thought they would not let John Stonehouse die. I did not reply. He had read the English newspapers and he was very distressed to see the disgusting allegations being made against him in the press. He said that he was going to Australia where he hoped to be left alone, emphasising that he just had to have peace. My aim was to get him back to England when his condition had settled, but I felt sure that if he went back at that time, the strain of the return would prove of great detriment to his mental health. To me, that was of prime importance. Before I left he asked me to write to him in Melbourne in the name of Mildoon. It was then that he told me that he was also Mr. Mildoon, which had the result of leaving me totally confused, but my own confusion was the least of my worries.

'On my return from Copenhagen, I still did not tell anyone of my knowledge that Mr. Stonehouse was alive. At this time I was being hounded by the press who wanted me to make a statement to them in regard to my relationship with Mr. Stonehouse, which I considered was none of their business, and they were also over-anxious to acquire a photograph of me. It was around this time that I met Mr. Stonehouse's wife, who was also being questioned by the press as to any knowledge she may have of Mr. Stonehouse's relationship with me. In anger she told me of the other affairs she believed that Mr. Stonehouse had had with other women. I was very upset and I felt very lonely and isolated. I was the only one who knew that Mr. Stonehouse was alive and I was hearing terrible things about him that challenged the whole basis of our relationship. Having escaped from my parents' home by climbing over a high wall and travelling to Wiltshire where I was met by Michael Hayes, staying with friends of his for a few days, it was with these awful thoughts in my mind and this feeling of complete loneliness and desperation, that I wrote the first of four letters which, much to my distress, have been read out in this court on two occasions. The "code" used was, of course, not a pre-arranged one. I merely wanted to make the letters a little difficult for a nosey bank clerk to interpret. I wrote the letters in the third person since he always spoke of John Stonehouse in the third person and I therefore thought that perhaps he could comprehend the situation more objectively. My one hope was that as a result of my letters and the dilemmas I outlined in them, the real John Stonehouse would once again emerge, whereupon I had no doubt that he would come home to rescue me, for above all else, he is a gentleman and a very loyal and true friend.

'On Monday, 23rd December, I was interviewed by Woman Detective Chief Inspector Tilley in the presence of Detective Sergeant Crook. They were conducting a missing persons inquiry into the disappearance of Mr. Stonehouse, and it was probably one of the most difficult moments I have yet had to experience, being unable to enlighten them. By this time the burden of my secret had become unbearable and I longed to communicate with somebody, to share the strain, but I just felt I could not seriously contemplate that − I could not trust anybody at all. I had no way of knowing how such an action would result. I felt intuitively that with peace and rest Mr. Stonehouse would be back, with his pride and dignity intact. It was so very important to me.

'At 4 a.m. on Christmas Eve, I received a call from Mrs. Stonehouse who told me that Mr. Stonehouse was alive and was being held in a Detention Centre in Melbourne. She said Mr. Stonehouse had asked her to arrange for me to be sent out to see him but Mrs. Stonehouse had refused. She told me that she was immediately going to Australia and she made me give my word that I would not travel there in the immediate future. I readily gave this assurance. Later that morning the press arrived in force with many offers to escort me at their expense to Australia. The very first offer I received was from the *Daily Telegraph* reporter.

'Immediately after the New Year I went to stay with my aunt in Cornwall to get away from the press but mainly for my parents' peace of mind. After a couple of weeks I had to return to London to deal with the House of Commons mail addressed to Mr. Stonehouse. I met up with my sister who handed me a letter from Mr. Stonehouse, which had arrived at her home in Howitt Road on 6th January, 1975. In the letter Mr. Stonehouse said he would be coming home and planned to get the BOAC flight out of Melbourne on 6th January. He said that he felt a little better and that he was very concerned about me and my welfare. The letter was dated 23rd December, 1974. I destroyed this letter as it contained expressions of personal feelings which I did not want the press to get hold of . . .

'At about the beginning of February Mr. Stonehouse telephoned and, learning of my being surrounded by press, asked me to go out to Australia. He was at this time living in Melbourne with friends. I initially said no, but on reflection it seemed a pretty good idea as I had long outstanding invitations from friends in Sydney to go to see them, one of whom had been asking me to visit for ten years. Also, the thought of my being able to see how Mr. Stonehouse was, eventually convinced me that a short stay there would be an excellent idea. Anything would be better than staying in England as I was fast running out of addresses which were not known to the press; the pressure had become intolerable.

'Shortly afterwards, on February 6th, I went with Ian Ward's friend, Lionel Blake, to Amsterdam, and then on to Singapore where I was met by and stayed with Mr. Ward's friend, Miss Yeo. I stayed with her for a few days and discussed many things, amongst them my visit to Copenhagen. Eventually I flew on to Perth where I was met by Mr. Stonehouse and I think the scene at the airport where Mr. Ward and his photographer also materialised, has been quite adequately described. I travelled with Mr. Stonehouse by car to Sydney, whereupon I joined up with my friends whilst Mr. and Mrs. Stonehouse returned to Melbourne. I did not see Mr. Stonehouse again for some weeks, but he telephoned me when he could, especially when the Department of Trade Inspectors were interviewing him for six days. He sounded on those occasions as though he could not go on, such was his apparent utter exhaustion . . .'

She then described her arrest and said in conclusion which she delivered in a very firm voice:

'I would just like to add that although I have been much criticised in the press for my silence when I knew Mr. Stonehouse was alive, after his telephone call to me, I can only say that I considered my actions at the time to be the only possible way of dealing with the situation. Even though I find myself in this dock as a result of those actions, I cannot change my mind, even now. If I had the same decisions to make all over again tomorrow, I feel certain that those decisions would remain the same. My ordeal has been, to say the very least, painful, but the safety of a man or a woman is of far greater importance than pain and humiliation. I have no regrets.'

CHAPTER TWENTY-FIVE

The closing speeches are always taken in the order: prosecution, defence and then the judge with the last word, ostensibly on the law but also with a summing-up of the case as he sees it. It had become cruelly apparent to me that the judge had often followed Corkery's own cross-examination of my witnesses with questions which Corkery had simply forgotten or made a mess of. It was therefore vital for me to make the best opportunity of my closing remarks which were to be sandwiched between Corkery and Lord Wigoder, for Sheila Buckley. I would have to undermine the prosecution, as best I could, and then develop the positive points for the defence.

Fortunately, Corkery played into my hands. His three-day speech was full of minor inaccuracies and illogicalities, was inconsistent in major respects to his opening speech fourteen weeks before, and culminated in a completely new and unsubstantiated allegation against my wife. He attempted to defuse the medical evidence by saying sarcastically, 'My own mental stamina has not done so well. Dr. Haward called me psychotic or mentally deranged on 17th July. Good reason for you to pay particular care and apply commonsense.' It was no defence, he went on, to argue diminished responsibility; that only could apply in murder cases where there was abnormality of mind. It was no defence to say irresistible impulse, nor to say one is emotionally disturbed. So, 'Why', he asked, with a flourish of his half-moon spectacles, 'the doctors and psychiatrists? No doctor can assist you on the charges in this case; their evidence is based on hearsay and they haven't sat here for fifty-six days as you have.'

On the point that the police had not bothered to see me on their first visit to Australia when their inquiries were starting he said it was because of the 'judges' rules'. Later when I tried to read out a section of the so-called rules, which are in fact only guide-lines, the judge ruled me out by saying they only apply when the police *intend* to interview someone. It effectively exploded Corkery's point for there is nothing in the judges' rules which would prevent a policeman seeing a suspect, even in Australia.

'No one can doubt his abilities,' said Corkery – and I waited for the dagger thrust. 'He had worked hard in the Co-op, had high ambitions, was brilliant according to Mr. McGrath, and was well-versed in commercial matters.' Then the thrust came – 'He had tremendous energy and was a tremendous gambler.' He developed the theme of gambler for some time but I noticed it was hardly consistent with his other favourite allegation that I was a devious and cunning planner.

Corkery spent a long time going through the letters Sheila wrote to me in Melbourne in December 1974, when I was living there as Clive Mildoon. As this was the umpteenth time it seemed tedious, until he started reading between the lines and jumping to the conclusion that my wife Barbara, and possibly my daughter Jane, had known I was alive at the time.

When my turn came I attacked him bitterly on this. Why hadn't he, I asked, questioned Chief Superintendent Etheridge about this aspect, so that the allegation could have been exposed earlier, or at least raised it in his own opening speech? Then Mrs. Stonehouse could have come as a witness to deny it. Why hadn't he asked Jane who had been a witness? And I added, 'It was a last minute smear, typical of the way Corkery has conducted the prosecution.'

I set the scene for my closing speech by explaining why I had decided to defend myself. So much depends on the verbal game played by professionals and I wanted none of that:

'Members of the jury,' I said, 'for the sake of my own health I wanted to bring out the whole story – warts and all – and to be frank with you about the activities I was committed to as a businessman trying to keep an organisation I helped form, in existence. The verbal game in this court has been worse than I ever expected with lies, deceit and trickery and as bad as the House of Commons, but the humbug is worse, as dressed up in all this decorum, you are not supposed to notice.'

The withdrawal of the first two charges – on the birth certificate applications – had been represented as an attempt not to overload the charge-sheet. In fact they were not proceeded with because of the difficulties of proving an attempt to defraud after the defence had demonstrated that forms do not even *have* to be signed or even have a name and address of applicant. 'It is obvious from the charge sheet that the prosecution have scraped the barrel to throw everything at me, including putting back charges the stipendiary magistrate threw out, and *now* he has the cheek to say he doesn't want to overload it.'

I went on: 'We must not rely on the verbal gymnastics of Mr. Corkery but take the evidence before the court. I am going to ask you to use more than your commonsense, your intelligence as well, as it is needed to get beneath the surface Corkery has skated over so as to get at the merits or demerits of this case. Fifteen weeks ago you may have thought this the case of the year – if not the decade – so much ballyhoo. While we have been here, murder cases and fraud cases involving hundreds of thousands have started and finished and a bank robbery involving millions has started just down the corridor. What is the main burden of this case? A loan account. When I first heard of the charge in Australia, I said something which stands the test of time: "How can a man steal from himself?" Once transferred, it belongs to that person and is his responsibility and might be the subject of a civil claim. If the prosecution had been able to show forgery of cheques, *that* would be clothing for the allegations. But no one has suggested the loan account was not properly conducted in the sense that cheques were not properly drawn. No one has suggested the cheques were forged or signed by persons not entitled to. The prosecution say that as I disappeared on 20th November, 1974, somehow or other this shows that when I took money out I was acting dishonestly. This is an inference based on an innuendo which in turn is based on smears.

'When you look at the charges you can see how hollow and trivial they are. The loan account charges involve £29,000 – that is the sort of money Mr. Stonehouse could have made in one year without any bother: the consultancy fees, which I could have taken personally, amounted to that. It would be ludicrous for a man to engage in this sinister, calculated plan, which is a figment of Mr. Corkery's imagination, simply to steal £29,000.

'As far as the personal guarantees to the banks are concerned these were, in the context of my business, for a comparatively small sum of £17,500. One of the deals I was negotiating could more than make up such a liability. It is common knowledge that personal guarantees have been given by others: William Stern, the property developer, for £50 million, Shaeftel, the film producer, for £2 million, and last week we read about Mrs. Ann Godfrey for £16½ million. But none of these people are in the dock at the Old Bailey and I have been unable to find one case of charges for personal guarantees – yet they've done it to me for £17,500.

'Yet it is clear from the evidence that Midland Bank slipped up in not registering their mortgage on the leases at Dover Street with the superior landlords. If they hadn't slipped up they would have been able to get their full value on the overdraft to EPACS instead of allowing Philip Gay and Charlton to buy the lease for a mere £5,000.'

I could sense I was carrying some jury members with me on this point, because neither of these witnesses had to my mind been frank about their involvement. As to the Lloyds Bank, I reminded them that Mr. Gundry, the manager, had said he regarded my personal guarantee as of value 'in the long run'.

On the insurance charges I pointed out that my wife had taken them out and she had paid the premiums. There was no claim and would be no claim. I had not committed the 'last act' in the so-called attempt, as I had not fabricated the evidence, i.e. faked a mangled or burnt body, nor stayed away long enough in a remote place like Brazil until a claim could be made. What was important in relation to all the charges was the *intention* in my mind at the time and, as an ex-insurance underwriter, I knew no claim could be considered, without a body, for seven years.

As far as conspiracy was concerned, I said there was a general feeling that as a charge it should be dispensed with. It had been dragged up in recent years to get people for something extra and to get in evidence which would otherwise be irrelevant to the specific charges – it was a wonderful umbrella for any prosecution. Conspiracy was already on the chopping block of the Law Commission considering reforms, and might be scrapped altogether in five or ten years' time.

I was a bit worried at this stage that the judge, who was watching me closely, would stop me as I was straying on to matters of law but, surprisingly, he did not, and I was able to keep up my flow, gaining strength and vigour all the time. It was marvellous to have that court as my captive audience – it was so attentive – and to know that my time was not limited as it would have been in any other forum. My shoes were pinching my toes – I had been wearing the same pair for five weeks – and I eased them off as I spoke, continuing, more comfortably, on my stockinged feet without anyone knowing, except possibly the prison officer who sat just behind.

I emphasised that the onus of proof is on the prosecution. 'I could stand here mute and you could find me innocent. It doesn't matter what I say. If they don't prove their case, I'm innocent.' Then I added that Corkery had reminded me that I had written to Sir Harold Walter in Mauritius, saying I would be mute throughout the hearings. 'That shows my state of mind early in 1975 when I was so sick. I am very glad I've had time to recover and to regain my strength.'

On the genesis of the case I recalled that on 24th December, 1974, I had told the Prime Minister, Harold Wilson, that I had suffered a breakdown; it was obvious something strange had happened but instead of sending a psychiatrist or a friend the establishment had decided to let Scotland Yard have their run. Yet it took them over six weeks to think about a charge and three months to make one. At that time you would have thought, 'That a man with two decades of public service would be entitled to some consideration. The establishment decided to act like it has in its peculiar way – it is not a single conscious person sitting down and deciding, it is amorphous and moves mysteriously and it will be a long time before we know fully why they took the actions they did. Despite it all I have recovered to some extent and I am not sarcastic when I say the judge helped by withdrawing my bail four weeks ago. There is nothing better than being dragged away handcuffed night after night, and shut up in a small cell for twenty-three hours a day at weekends, for coming to terms with oneself and losing false pride. As Professor Watson said, I did not know my real identity – I was immersed in causes and did not find myself until recently.'

I felt much better in getting that off my chest and turned to the essential first step of my closing speech, namely the undermining of any credibility Corkery had. Is he consistent? I asked and, Is he unnecessarily repetitious? If the answer to the first is 'No' and to the second 'Yes' then he has not done a very good job. Very haughtily I took as a 'hypothetical example' of inconsistency a case of a bank snatch, with two boy witnesses who identified the suspect but with a third boy not called by the Crown because he held the opposite view. I described how counsel had changed his line as the hearing proceeded thus demonstrating the weakness of the brief. As I spoke, I watched Corkery's face as he realised what I was actually referring to. It was the Peter Hain case which he had unsuccessfully prosecuted. To my amazement the judge even let me get the name out.

I then showed the relevance to my case. The witness they had tried to keep out was Jack Marks, the auditor of EPACS, although they called three witnesses from Dixon, Wilson the auditors of the British Bangladesh Trust which was not even mentioned in the charges. They had also tried to keep out Hill, the Australian customs' officer, who had seen the trunk without any women's clothes in it. 'It shows the devious ways of the prosecution,' I said. 'The object of their game is to get a conviction by fair means or foul, including cheating and deceit.

'And on the disappearance the Crown says the motive was criminality. In the Hain case it was mistaken identity, in this case it is mistaken motive.'

Then I launched into my real attack, gathering power and energy. 'There are five examples I give of inconsistencies – no doubt you can think of others.

1) The biggest non-story of the case.
2) the damp squib, with acknowledgements to the judge (who had himself used the expression).
3) the hyperbole-extraordinary.
4) the red herring.
5) the poppycock story.

The first was Ian Ward's story of Sheila Buckley's clothing in the trunk, which we now know was based on a vague conversation Ward had not followed up. It was not collaborated and it appeared as a story in the *Daily Telegraph* a week later, after being telephoned from a public phone at Perth airport by a tired reporter who had no sleep, at three or four in the morning. 'What manner of man is this Ian Ward?' I asked. He was a star witness brought from Singapore, a journalist who could get his stories terribly wrong on Vietnam – as had two American Presidents. He had befriended me over a period of weeks, then provided his friends in London and Singapore to help Sheila Buckley to travel to Australia to escape press harassment in England just to get an exclusive story. Ward had condemned his own colleague Kenneth Clarke for printing an article without cross-checking it with me and then had done the same thing.

The affidavit from Griffin Bartlett, the old school friend with whom my wife and I had stayed in Yellingbo, confirmed that she had been there before the trunk arrived. Yet, and I rubbed it in deliberately, Mr. Corkery had said in his opening statement that Ward had seen the trunk 'before Mrs. Stonehouse had ever arrived in Australia'. He must have known different if he had read the evidence of Inspector Sullivan, the Australian policeman who had referred to my wife being with me early in January 1975, before I had met Ward.

And I capped the point by again quoting Robert Hill, the customs' official who had not seen 'a black slip, blouses and women's shoes' although Ward claimed they were 'on top' of the contents of the trunk. His story in the *Daily Telegraph* had stated: 'A trunk full of Mrs. Sheila Buckley's clothing' was sent by me from London or Miami and this was clearly nonsense. And yet it was on the basis of this ridiculous story that the prosecution relied largely for their conspiracy theory. But Corkery had dropped most of it in his closing speech.

The damp squib was the vain attempt to show Mrs. Buckley had made telephone calls saying, 'Mr. Markham's secretary.' Five witnesses – all girls employed at the bureau in Regent Street – had been lined up to say they would never say 'Mr. so-and-so's secretary'. In fact, Edward Cox the former manager at the bureau had said under cross-examination that some of them did so; the witnesses were all stood down and the point collapsed.

The hyperbole-extraordinary was Corkery's reference in his opening, which was not repeated in his closing, that some minutes of EPACS were 'bogus, false, spurious, dishonest', but they had not bothered to see the person who had typed the minutes in the office of the auditors, Citroen Wells. If so they would have got an explanation.

They had tried to suppress the existence of the 'consent to short notice' which had been signed by all the directors, including McGrath and Haynes, and that showed the draft minutes and the place where the meeting was going to be held. Furthermore, McGrath had signed the balance sheet and annual accounts which included the £10,000 remuneration which Corkery had said he had not approved.

We reached the lunch break and I went downstairs to eat the plastic food produced by the convicts who work in the prison kitchens and to sip the thick tea which only army chefs and prisons can brew. I should not really complain. The food in the public cafeteria on the third floor is even worse.

Then in the afternoon I described the red herring: the ludicrous allegation that tax had not been paid on the £10,000 income from EPACS whereas the tax returns for three years put in evidence by Jack Marks, who had also been my tax advisor, showed a nil liability today and tax of over £9,000 paid over the period.

The poppycock story was the nonsense that I was planning to set up a new life with Sheila Buckley. There was no evidence for it whatsoever; she had no pre-knowledge of Markham and had never been seen in the same place as him. The telephone calls from Hawaii which I had made to her and the erratic meeting in Copenhagen would indicate the absence of a great plan. If so, why did Markham go to Europe immediately after arriving safely in Australia?

'If there had been a conspiracy between us would I, emerging from an awful traumatic experience and having spent hours with the Victoria State police, telephone my wife on 24th December, 1974, and say, "Can you bring Sheila out to

Australia?" Is this the cunning, devious calculating man, Corkery keeps talking about? And with the telephone call being monitored?'

Corkery had referred to cheques for $1,000 which Sheila Buckley received from Victa in Liechtenstein as evidence of funding by me. In fact, I pointed out that the transfer of funds into England invalidated the other theory of Corkery's that sterling was being transferred out of England to Switzerland in cash. 'Why not fund Mrs. Buckley with the cash and leave the dollars overseas, if that were the case?' I asked.

She had gone to Australia in February 1975, but if there had been an earlier frustrated plan, intelligent people might argue that it would be very unlikely she would go to Australia at all.

I criticised Corkery for his repetitions – a weakness of an advocate with a weak brief. He had talked about the 'plundering and thieving of the funds of EPACS' without any evidence whatsoever, hoping that with the verbal juggling and repetition you might pick it up as from a hypnotist. But this is no substitute for argument or proof, I added. The conspiracy charge I dismissed, by re-emphasising that in business matters Mrs. Buckley acted under instructions just like Alan Le Fort or Philip Bingham. Supposing it had been suggested that I had a homosexual relationship with either of these young men, then they would be in the dock because the prosecution were not after facts but smears.

On the problems of the bank, I reminded the jury that although Corkery had made reference to the 'unscrupulous' Aziz he had not referred to Anthony Mascerenhas. He had used his position as a freelance writer with the *Sunday Times* to place an article which would destroy the reputation of the Englishman who had done more than any other to establish Bangladesh and who had been made a citizen of that country. It may sound fanciful, I added, but it was common knowledge – and Harold Wilson had confirmed it – the South African agents had been acting against Jeremy Thorpe; and the Shah of Iran had agents acting against certain left-wing MPs. 'So is it fanciful that Pakistani agents were working against me?'

Describing the nominee holdings of shares that were arranged to avert the collapse of the British Bangladesh Trust after the damaging *Sunday Times* article, I asked why were the other participants not called: Keith White, the Fellow of the Institute of Bankers, who had been approved as general manager by the Bank of England and K. B. Ahmed, the originator of the bank. Why am I being singled out when obviously other people were involved?

I finished the first day of my speech and returned to Brixton, after two hours in the Old Bailey cells, handcuffed to Rafi Ameer, a smart young Indian accused of drug dealing. As usual the bit players in the Bank of America case who were in the prison van were in good humour. 'How's it going, John?' they inquired. 'Fine,' I said and meant it.

The following day was my birthday and I started, rather facetiously, by referring to a present which I had just received from Mr. Eichenberger of the First National City Bank of New York. He had written to confirm that his bank, which had acted as nominees holding £10,000 worth of shares of EPACS, had never had a communication after 20th November, 1974, about EPACS affairs. This showed that the proper procedures for the winding up of EPACS had not been adhered to, as such a major shareholder had not been advised of the winding-up proposal. The letter was accepted as evidence and was to prove very useful.

The day was also celebrated during the afternoon break when Michael O'Dell cut the birthday cake in the well of the court and handed out slices to Jane, Dan Awdry, the Conservative MP who had come to see me, Dr. Frank Hansford-Miller, the chairman of the E.N.P., and others. It was all much too informal for the court usher who literally shook with worry about the incident.

I spent a little time on the Finsec Holdings account which was the Stock Exchange investment taken out for BBT and subsequently transferred to Sheila as nominee when the share values collapsed, to avoid the bank showing a loss. I demonstrated that £40,000 had been paid into the account by EPACS up to October 1974, to enable the bank to meet the shortfall and emphasised that this transaction was hardly consistent with the prosecution's allegations that Sheila Buckley and I were taking out all the money we could.

On the Swiss bank account opened by Markham, I criticised Corkery's lack of logic in suggesting the payments-in came in cash from England. In fact, I said, they came from monies controlled by me in the Victa account in Liechtenstein which had acted as my agent, receiving payments from overseas over many years. It would be just as foolish to say that as Henry Smith was in Barking last Sunday when a sub-postmaster was murdered, then Henry Smith must have done it. Putting two isolated facts together does not entitle the drawing of such a conclusion.

Dealing with the schedules showing my liabilities to various banks, I explained that most of them were covered by the security they held in the form of shares and property. The prosecution had failed to bring forward all the details of my assets so it would not be fair to draw the conclusion that, in late 1974, I knew I was hopelessly in debt and therefore not able to sign personal guarantees. I was thinking of the value of EPACS and the knowledge that in the long run I could honour the guarantees, as indeed Gundry, the bank manager, was still saying.

On the loan account charges, I produced for the jury the schedule I had written out in Brixton with a graph clearly showing a pattern of drawings over the years. This document made an impression on the jury, most of whom followed me closely as I went through the various transactions. And, I emphasised, it had all been approved by the auditor who Corkery had declined to cross-examine on the matter. Unfortunately the loan account had become a ragbag into which went all sorts of withdrawals which might well have gone into other more appropriate accounts. The 'overseas' agents' account had been used up to 1973 but had lapsed as the loan account became the vehicle for all such transactions.

I took up what Michael Sherrard, Q.C., the Department of Trade Inspector, who, during the six days inquiring in Melbourne, had asked, 'Why didn't you ensure that all the books were in apple-pie order?' That is the way their minds work. If there had been a conscious plan to disappear then that is exactly what would have happened. The accounts would have been in 'apple-pie' order and no questions could have been asked. I pointed out that my requests to the Inspectors for the receipts and documents in my desk and the safe had not been granted. The papers had probably been thrown away in the rubbish.

The discrepancy between what Detective Inspector Townley had said about not knowing which was my desk, until after the committal proceedings, and Bingham's evidence that Townley had gone through the desk 'fairly thoroughly' on his early visit, was curious. Someone was lying and we do not know which one. 'They both can't be telling the truth.' Furthermore the evidence is clear: nobody looked in the safe.

I went on to say, 'The Garrett cheque for $12,500 would not have been paid into an English bank unless the money was needed to be used for expenses in England.' If the intention was theft and getting cash overseas it would have been paid directly into the Victa account in Liechtenstein avoiding sterling altogether.

With regard to the credit card charges, I reiterated that the alleged frauds concerned company business – travellers' cheques on *Barclaycard*, some of which were actually left in the Miami hotel and airline tickets for James Charlton, my co-director and myself. None of the companies suggested criminal proceedings. 'They were started by those people there,' I said, pointing to the police at the table in the well of the court, 'in an emotional atmosphere against me, fanned by the press. Never did I intend to defraud those credit card companies, and the offices of EPACS accepted liability for those expenses. I ask you to reject out of hand these charges.'

It was five minutes past four and I had to finish my birthday oration. When I eventually returned to my cell in Brixton, I was so tired I cleaned my teeth with shaving soap. When I realised the funny taste I washed it out, but it was still there early next morning when the jangling of the warders' keys woke me up.

On the next day I asked the jury for one favour. Usually the assumption is that the person in the dock is guilty. 'Why would they go to all that trouble?' can easily be in anyone's mind. 'But, please, for a time assume innocence and see how the story fits together. You've got a man in public service for twenty-five years or more – Uganda, Co-op and politics – would he throw all that away with all the immense ability he is supposed to have, according to Mr. Corkery, when he is trying to score a point? Would he do that for £29,000 to go round the world as a demented person?' I also asked them to assess the effect on the witnesses of the layers of consciousness and experiences. 'I am not suggesting anyone is lying. That is for you to decide. The Department of Trade Inquiry is still to see many of them; naturally they're going to take a line which protects them as best as possible.'

I touched on examples of witnesses who had particular interests to protect: Philip Gay and James Charlton, for instance, who formed Limepan to buy the Dover Street lease for £5,000 and who still ran Global Imex which owes EPACS £13,000. The five witnesses from Walsall had shown that the press stories indicating that everyone in the constituency was against me, were incorrect.

Then I came to the disappearance, the pivot of the case as Inspector Townley had acknowledged. It is no offence to disappear. Thousands do it every year, I am told by the Salvation Army: many are not known so it is not publicised. People in public fields do it, for example the managing editor of the *Daily Mail*, John Golding, has disappeared and not been seen. If I could have disappeared quietly and had my breakdown quietly and then come back, we would not have had all this bother. The disappearance, far from being a cunning plan, was the most clumsily executed operation in the history of disappearances. There was exposure at all times like a man taking down his trousers in St. James's Park. I then detailed the places Markham had been: Astoria Hotel, openly talking to Mrs. Reilly and Mr. Irani and lapping it up.

I could sense that a few members of the jury were not taking my point so I emphasised: 'I know it is difficult to understand if you've never had a breakdown, but one in nine of people have psychiatric treatment during their working lives. That's the fact. I know it's like leprosy and you react against it. In particular it is very difficult to accept a person in public life because your faith in this society begins to flake a bit.'

All that going to the Astoria Hotel, to the bureau on Regent Street – every other day from the beginning of September to the end of October, according to Mr. Cox – was completely unnecessary to any plan to disappear. So there must be another explanation. I set out the other places: banks, British Airways for vaccinations, St. George's Hospital for the X-ray, the Lebanese and US Embassies, Thos. Cook and the Post Offices. At these places there were over forty people with whom Markham was in direct confrontation, any one of whom might have recognised Stonehouse. There were between two and three hundred people in these places who also might have known him. If not, then they could have remembered after seeing photographs of the missing Stonehouse in the papers.

'You must ask the questions: Would an intelligent, rational man do any of these things and take such extraordinary risks if engaged in Corkery's suggested plan? Of course not, for it is not necessary to any plan to disappear. Any person doing so could simply go to the USA or Brazil, which has no extradition treaty with Britain, and buy a passport or identity there. If I had been a Czech spy, denied by the Prime Minister but still reported in the *Daily Mirror*, I could have stayed in Russia during my two stops in Tashkent and Moscow. I could have told a story to the Russians and had a life of ease for evermore in the USSR.'

I went on to the breakdowns – in plural. It was not just one; there were several before the break came. I had not intended to, but nevertheless found myself once again describing the terrible 'lost weekends' when I was criss-crossing the United States and Mexico changing into Markham, almost completely, and then back again. I got carried away with the whole court being so quiet. One could, I suppose, have heard the proverbial pin drop except that my voice was booming away.

'If you have not suffered that sort of thing,' I said, 'you don't know what it is. It's real suffering but dismissed by these people' – waving my arm in the direction of the prosecution – 'whose only interest is to get a conviction because they are not interested in the totality of human beings. Is it possible that this highly intelligent person makes it all up just to have a defence at the Old Bailey? Worked it all out before just in case he was charged? They are blinkered. Once they start a prosecution even they can't stop it. Under all that clothing is humbug for they are not allowed to say even if they think he's innocent.

'Convict me of every damned charge – send me to prison for the rest of my life,' I said in desperation. 'I don't mind because I *know* I am innocent.'

There must be some explanation for this irrational behaviour such as slipping into the Mildoon identity, but staying in the same area of Melbourne and actually booking into an hotel for 23rd December, 1974, where he had been booked under the two names Markham *and* Mildoon. 'This man is disoriented. It is rubbish to suggest that Mildoon is an alias to hide away. If so he would not have remained in Melbourne, he would have gone to Queensland or Alice Springs.'

Corkery's overkill exceeds all overkills, I said, when he compares me to the Great Train Robbers, Charlie Wilson and Ronald Biggs. 'Do you think he honestly thinks there's a comparison? They had nearly killed a man and were running away from a crime which had been detected. I hadn't committed any crime and there would be no charges without the disappearance.'

And the final answer is that I was coming back, as I recovered. 'I wrote to Mrs. Buckley that I was and the police probably intercepted it.'

The breakdown was not due simply to a failure to cope with business pressures – that is far too simplistic an attitude, for I had dealt with far worse than that in 1974. My problem was the breakdown of the John Stonehouse personality – a man who, over the years, had become an image man. Professor Watson described how he thought I had these problems of identity. Throughout my life I projected myself as an idealist, into Uganda, the Co-op, Labour politics and then Bangladesh; and then the ideals broke one-by-one putting a lot of pressure on the image man.

I quoted what Jo Grimond had said in reviewing my first book *Prohibited Immigrant*, written in 1959 on my experiences in Uganda and Rhodesia. 'Mr. Stonehouse emerges as one who has made practical efforts to build a better Africa.' And compare it with my disillusionment. 'Where is there worse despair today than in Uganda under General Amin?' And on Bangladesh, the hopes turned to tears with Sheikh Mujibur Rahman brutally murdered and a military dictatorship in his place. 'It was not just business and blackmail. I could no longer cope with being John Stonehouse, the idealist, and that's why the freak-out came.'

Dealing with the evidence for the breakdown I explained it was not brought forward as a defence to the theft and such charges, for there were no crimes or offences. It shows the explanation for the disappearance. Even if I was the sanest man in Britain in 1974 and the disappearance was calculated, I am still innocent. During the dramatic passages while I was describing aspects of my breakdown, the prison officer sitting in the dock behind me was reading my book *Death of an Idealist*, which he had borrowed. Apparently he was so absorbed in both the speech and the passages of the book which corresponded that he inadvertently switched on the alarm bell. I realised something was wrong when I heard shouts and scuffles from below the dock and saw a flustered warder running up the stairs. He was waved away. I heard later that forty warders had rushed to the scene.

I took the jump through passages from the Department of Trade Inquiry in February 1975, during which I had experienced my breakdown at a time before charges had been laid and assurances were being given that none were and that extradition was not being contemplated. Then on to the medical evidence from Dr. Haward, the scientist with his objective tests, Dr. Maurice Miller, MP, and the three psychiatrists Doctors Gibney and Laing and Professor Watson who were all agreed that I was not lying about the breakdown and that I had suffered a psychiatric illness in 1974. Their combined experience is over one hundred years, I added, rather unnecessarily.

On the afternoon of the third day of my speech, I turned to the business matters especially the winding up of EPACS which would easily have been avoided. Notes made by Philip

Gay on 16th December, 1974, showing the debts and assets of the company had fallen into my hands, through the rubbish. They showed that apart from the corporation tax due and the bank overdrafts whose repayment could have been phased over a period as the rents came in, the other debts were minor amounting to about £5,000. Mr. Charlton's debt of £500 on his loan account would have repaid those if Gay had really wanted to keep EPACS going.

'The proof of the pudding is in the eating,' I said. 'The leases were not taken over by the superior landlord, so EPACS should have enjoyed the profit rental for the past eighteen months.' In the last full financial year the profits on rents were £28,000. Gay had estimated a total value of £128,000 on the leases in October, even if only with £64,000 would still be enough to maintain solvency. But they were not considering the facts; they were determined to liquidate in the emotional atmosphere of January 1975, and damn my interests. EPACS was to be the waste bin for all the problems.

As I finished for the day I felt I had most of the jury with me, although one cannot be sure. Jury members tend to sit sphinx-like and inscrutable but, at least, I did not sense the sort of hostility I had from the judge.

Next day, Friday, I knew would have to be my last and there were several important points still to emphasise: the influence of the press stories on the bringing of charges, the function of the judge and the independence of the jury and the essential need for the prosecution to prove their case 'beyond reasonable doubt'. The first I achieved by showing some press cuttings and describing some of the outrageous articles – the second by quoting Lord Justice Devlin. It was a stroke of luck that Michael O'Dell had found his Hamlyn Lecture for me. It was a gold mine. The judge looked uncomfortable and quizzical as I read:

'In short, there cannot be in law a perverse verdict of acquittal. In a case in 1935 Lord Chancellor Sankey said that for the judge to say that a jury must in law find the prisoner guilty would be to make him "decide the case and not the jury, which is not the common law". As the Lord Chief Justice said recently, in a debate in the House of Lords, no one has ever yet been able to find a way of depriving a British jury of its privilege of returning a perverse verdict.'

I read that, I said, with my eye half on Mr. Justice Eveleigh, as meaning that *you*, members of the jury, are absolutely independent. And I went on with quotations about the jury being 'the warders of their own obedience and are answerable only to their own conscience, so that no man can be convicted against the conscience of the jury', and 'the obvious fact that judges and juries do not always agree in their conclusions. . . . When there is a difference of opinion the explanation is that the jury has given weight to factors that impress the lay mind more strongly than the legal.' . . . and, still more, 'Our history has shown it much easier to find judges who will do what it wants than it has to find amenable juries. . . . The malady that sooner or later affects most men of a profession is that they tend to construct a mystique that cuts them off from the common man. Judges, as much as any other professional, need constantly to remind themselves of that. For more than seven out of the eight centuries during which the judges of the Common Law have administered justice in this country, trial by jury ensured that Englishmen got the sort of justice they liked and not the sort of justice that the government or the lawyers or any body of experts thought was good for them.'

Mr. Justice Eveleigh allowed me to say it all without interruption but I felt sure that if I had attempted to make the points as my own opinion I would have been quickly stopped. Fortunately Lord Justice Devlin put it so much better.

On the matter of 'beyond reasonable doubt', I asked the jury to imagine an iron curtain with the prosecution trying to get me over to the side where freedom was denied. But to get me across the barbed wire and avoid the obstacles and landmines of the 'reasonable doubts'. And the doubts were sticking all over the place.

During the break Michael O'Dell came over to talk to me in the dock. 'Geoffrey has won his case,' he said beaming. 'We're winning.' Geoffrey Robertson, my brilliant counsel in the committal proceedings, had secured the balance of Ameer on the drug charges in the other court after a legal argument.

I finished my speech early in the afternoon of the fourth day saying, 'You are judging not just a charge sheet but a man's life. You have a real responsibility, each vote really counts. I ask you to ask your own conscience as Lord Justice Devlin advises. If I am found guilty then the flood-gates could open for all sorts of prosecutions: of gamblers on the Stock Exchange, of businessmen giving personal guarantees. Of course I have offended people in the establishment but that doesn't mean I'm necessarily a criminal. Clearly some would like me to be a scapegoat. The word comes from the Middle East: a goat is chosen into which all the sins of the village are put as a symbol; then it is thrown into the desert to expire.

'Some people, conscious of the evils in our society and the need for things to be cleaned up, would like me to be a scapegoat, but you are judging the precise charges on the charge sheet not the general charges. Please do not make me the scapegoat, that's the easy thing to do and it won't solve society's problems.'

I thanked Michael Grieve the barrister who had taken a long note, and Michael O'Dell, my lawyer and friend throughout, and the members of the jury 'for your patience and close consideration of what I have had to say'.

I sat down, relieved it was all over. I could now say nothing more in the hearing. My fate was in other hands.

CHAPTER TWENTY-SIX

Lord Wigoder, in defence of Sheila Buckley, made the shortest speech in summing-up, about two and a half hours spread over part of a Friday afternoon and then on Monday morning of what was expected to be the last week of the trial. Brevity was, in fact, a telling commentary on the weakness of the case against her; there was little, if anything, to answer. In a nutshell he dismissed the attempts to bring in extraneous matters by simply saying, 'It is not an offence for a pretty girl to fall for a married man otherwise the courts would be full of cases.' There were also no charges, he said, of agreeing to my disappearance. 'It is not a charge and it is not an offence.' He went on to emphasise that she had no such knowledge and that there was not a shred of evidence in that direction.

The cheque charges he dismissed by showing she had signed hundreds of them, and the amounts withdrawn on the loan account during 1974 were half the value of drawings in 1973. She had no reason to doubt the validity of requests she received from me any more than had Philip Bingham or Alan Le Fort. Lord Wigoder spoke softly and relied on quiet courtesy more than fireworks to impress the jury; they followed him closely so it was probably effective.

Mr. Justice Eveleigh launched directly into his advice on legal points and his summing-up, as though he was extra-keen to get it all over with. He spoke from carefully written notes as though he was very anxious to avoid errors. 'Your verdict in this case has to be unanimous, each of you must be agreed to either Guilty or Not Guilty on each of the charges. The time has not yet come when I can speak of a majority.'

He then explained the law as he interpreted it. On theft: 'A person is guilty if he dishonestly appropriates property belonging to another with the intention of permanently depriving the other of it.' And it is not dishonest, 'if he believes in law he has a right to it.'

On the personal guarantees: The pecuniary advantage is the

overdraft facility, he said, and the deception in 'falsely pretending his guarantee was of value and in good faith' does not
have to be the only reason but it must be a material reason in
causing the banks to grant overdrafts. The insurance charges
produced an interesting comment on something I was supposed
to have said to the effect, there can be no attempt if no claim
is made.

'I have to tell you,' he emphasised, 'in the circumstances of
this case that Mr. Stonehouse's contention is not in law correct.
There is an attempt in law if he falsely staged his death by
drowning, dishonestly intending a claim to be made and the
money obtained in due course.' He added, ominously and with
a vigour I had learnt to recognise, 'If I am wrong, there's a
higher court can put me right.'

On the passport application form charge his initial interpretation of 'intent to defraud' was limited to 'intention to
obtain something to which he was not entitled' which seemed,
on the face of it, extremely narrow. He quoted me as saying
that a criminal offence requires proof of guilty mind and that
I contended I had none. 'I have to tell you,' he said with a
manner that perfectly conveyed the description 'laying down
the law', 'I have to tell you, it's not a feeling of guilt, meant
like someone can rob a bank without being weighed down by
guilt. All it means in the context of this case is that he had an
intention to get a passport to which he was not entitled. The
use to which he intended to put it is immaterial. Mr. Stonehouse told you he did not at that stage intend to use it to
disappear – it gave him a feeling of increased identity. That is
immaterial.'

The judge went on to try to stress the matter of Robert Hill,
the Australian customs' official whose name was kept secret
until 10th June, although the police had interviewed him in the
previous year. 'The police,' said the judge, 'take a great number
of statements from people who might not be called.' Then he
gave an example concerning a referee shot at a Cup Final with
thousands of witnesses: 'Would not expect them all to troop
into the witness box – must be a selection.' He seemed to have
missed the point that there was only one Mr. Hill and he *had*
seen the trunk before Ward.

218

In an excursion into company affairs he suggested that if a concern of one million pounds financed half its shares by buying them itself, 'the value of shares bought by a shareholder has gone down overnight. He's got a share in a company with £500,000 instead of one million.' I sat in sheer amazement. The result, as I would see from his example, was that the £1 share would still be worth £1 as, although the company's capital would be half a million instead of one million pounds, the half million of self-generated capital would simply cancel itself out. Just to get it right for my own satisfaction, I imagined one hundred men putting £1 each in a company but ninety-nine of them actually 'borrowing' his £1 from the concern itself. The man who actually put in £1 would still have it there if the other £99 are unscrambled. In other words the actual value of the real investment is not affected.

I feared that the jury's opinion was being swayed by the impression, in my view misleading, which the judge was giving about the nominee holdings in the British Bangladesh Trust. I realised how very damaging this could be. It was also not a little annoying that he constantly referred to it as the 'Bank of Bangladesh' which it never had been, nor ever aspired to be.

At the end of the first day of the judge's summing-up, I could well understand the force of the comment made to me by a score of people who had more experience of the 'processes of justice' than me; it's the last word that counts. I am now finding myself objectively fascinated in observing the inter-action of influences on the jury leading up to the climax; it even overshadows my apprehension.

On Tuesday of the last week the Old Bailey is very quiet, most of the courts having risen for the summer recess. The bank defendants are off because a juror has food poisoning so there are only four prisoners, including me, on the handcuff run from Brixton.

With Sheila, I wait on the stairs leading to the dock from the cells as the court usher intones the usual 'greeting': 'All those who have anything to do before Their Lords, the Queen's Justices in the Central Criminal Court, draw near and give their attendance. God Save the Queen.' And I wonder how many more times we will hear these words.

The judge continued his summing-up and expanded further on the prosecution's case. On the value of the leases he brought up the possible cost of delapidations of the buildings as though it would be a new and vital point affecting the valuation.

The solvency of EPACS he dismissed after reading out details from the liquidator's list of *unagreed* creditors as though the list constituted proof. At this stage Tudor-Price, who had been left in charge of the prosecution in Corkery's temporary absence, jumped up to point out that the total of debts the judge was reading out only concerned *unagreed* creditors. In the figure was the debt of £188,000 which only came about as a result of the reversal of entries by the bank and which I had indicated I was contesting.

When it came to summarising the case for the defence Mr. Justice Eveleigh adopted a different tone of voice. Before it had been vigorous and emphatic. My points he delivered in a softer voice. He dealt fairly with my account of the Markham parallel personality and the relief it gave me. It was uncanny sitting listening to a synopsis of my breakdowns and as the account unfolded I felt again the terrible anguish that it had all been. In dismissing the medical evidence, he said, 'Apart from Dr. Miller, the MP, the doctors did not examine him in 1974.' What they say, he added, is simply what could have happened – a possible explanation, 'it is for you to decide.'

His attack on Dr. Haward was less severe than I expected. 'He is not a medical doctor; his degree is in psychology,' he said dismissively. But he could not get away from the fact that Dr. Haward's tests were objective and did not rely on what the patient said to him. In the cases of the psychiatrists, he said, they can only work on the basis that what they are being told by the patient is true. This observation, I thought, should rather emphasise the value of what the psychologist said came from *tests*.

The the judge returned to the question of payments in and out of EPACS' account with, as he irritatingly put it, the 'Bank of Bangladesh'. Look, he said, at the bank account. Mr. Le Fort said the money transfers were for the benefit of the bank but there you see £150,000 coming in and going right out again to three of Mr. Stonehouse's companies. And he paused as copies of that page of the bank account, which the jury had never seen, were passed around to them. I waited a moment for the point to be made that there was no evidence that the £150,000 had actually been removed from the bank. It was most likely that the transfers had been an internal operation within London Capital Securities, which it had by this time been renamed. Indeed, I much doubted whether the liquidity of the bank would have allowed £150,000 to be transferred *out*. The judge had not grasped that the loan into EPACS was only part of a triangular transaction, with LCS providing the other side of the triangle – namely £150,000 to the lending bank.

As the judge did not clarify the point I rose to make the observation that the evidence of the bank account did not 'necessarily mean the money went out of the bank' but he cut me short with: 'You've already addressed the jury.' The judge then turned to the jury and said, 'You may think this was a very important page in the story.'

By this time I was angry. The judge was dealing with evidence only incidental to the case for it had nothing directly to do with the charges. The transactions of the bank were immensely complicated and if any specific charges had been laid on them then they could have been examined exhaustively. But to look at only one part of the money transfers, that Alan Le Fort wrote up, and draw firm conclusions, seemed to me to be obviously missing the point. Moreover, it was raised after the defence had completed its arguments. The jury were being asked to come to conclusions about me on matters which I could not comment on.

Worse was to follow for in dealing with the case against Mrs. Buckley the judge produced a whole bunch of letters written by banks concerning overdraft facilities. He was endeavouring to demonstrate that Mrs. Buckley 'must have known' about the financial affairs because she probably opened the letters even when marked 'Strictly personal and Confidential'. The bundle was passed to the jury having been prepared by the prosecution, at the judge's request. The jury had not seen them before and they would, of course, be the last exhibits in their hands. I was astounded, as the defence had no idea this was going to happen.

Then the judge read through them at length, stressing the bank manager's tough turn of phrase. 'And why was the overdraft only for three months?' he asked knowingly, not pausing to explain that most banks give short term loans which are extended. As he read, I realised that most, if not all of the overdrafts, concerned companies other than EPACS.

The most apparently damning correspondence was about the overdraft for Global Imex which was not named in the charges and continues in business. The judge did not point this out probably because he did not know, as the letters did not identify the company concerned.

I sat in the dock powerless and not knowing how much the jury would be influenced by what I felt only indirectly concerned the case against Mrs. Buckley or myself.

The judge then turned to the letters Sheila had written to me in Melbourne in December 1974 – the very same letters which Sergeant Coffey had intercepted, and copied without authority and which had been raked over interminably. Mr. Justice Eveleigh was not to be out-done for he found even more interpretations to read between the lines of those much-interpreted missives.

Some observers had predicted that the judge would 'go soft' on Sheila in order to show me up as the villain of the piece; but his attack on her was strong. I came away from the Old Bailey feeling sick that the system allows such last-minute influence on the ostensibly independent jury.

The judge asked the jury to come in half an hour early for the closing stages of his summing-up, no doubt to leave an impression in their minds of the importance of finding a verdict within the day.

He touched on points in Sheila Buckley's statement and in Lord Wigoder's arguments, taking about thirty minutes to dispose of them. Then came his summary which expanded even further on points for the prosecution. Referring to me: 'He would not give the name of any foreign agent or transactions when interviewed by the Department of Trade Inspectors even though he had taken them to lunch (meaning the agents!). Prosecution now say he has latched on to any foreign name in correspondence and claimed it was an agent.'

However, the exhibits, particularly the Annual Report and handbill of Global Imex, showed they were agents; furthermore a score of witnesses had demonstrated their difficulties in remembering names and details without access to their files. I was, again, singled out for censure. A comment such as, 'You will of course bear in mind that, between November 1974 and late February 1975, when he saw the Inspectors, Mr. Stonehouse had suffered a number of traumatic experiences and you will remember he was under psychiatric treatment at the time,' would have put the situation into perspective, but no such remark passed the judge's lips.

Having taken the jury at length through transactions and bank letters which had nothing to do directly with the charges, the judge then advised them, 'You'll find, I'm sure, your task much simplified if you keep your eye on the ball. Look at the matters in the indictment and decide those. You must look at the charge and ask yourself if the prosecution has satisfied you as to every element of the charge so that you can feel sure. Will you now please consider your verdicts.'

He then asked for Exhibit 861 to be handed to the jury. I therefore asked it to be made clear that the correspondence related to Global Imex and not EPACS.

The jury went out after a court usher had sworn not to allow anyone to speak to them – and not to speak to them herself.

I returned to the cells to reflect that it is very important for anyone about to have a breakdown to ensure before he does so that his company affairs are 'in apple-pie order' – to adopt Mr. Sherrard's phrase – that his credit cards are completely paid up, and his milk bill, and to ensure that he has a psychiatrist handcuffed to him at all times so that the evidence of trauma is irrefutable. And, of course he must cancel all life insurances, especially those taken out by other people, and write a circular letter to all bank managers explaining that he is about to flip, otherwise they might think he was deceiving them.

The Verdict

The jury were out for nine and a half hours. There were several false alarms about them coming back, especially at seven o'clock when the whole court, except the judge, convened, only to be told that the jury had just sent out for food.

It was not until 8.15, as I stood on the stairs with Sheila, that I heard the jury roster called. Beryl Darbyshire, the intelligent-looking woman on the front row, had become the forewoman, or should it be foreperson? After her name the others were called, one by one, and answered their names.

This time, after we were called up, both of us had to stand facing the front of the court as the clerk asked the forewoman, 'Have you reached a unanimous verdict in respect of John Thomson Stonehouse on count three?'

'Yes,' was the soft reply and I knew immediately it could only be Guilty, as a unanimous verdict of Not Guilty was so highly unlikely.

'Do you find Guilty or Not Guilty?' asked the clerk.

'Yes,' and then as an afterthought, 'Guilty,' said Beryl Darbyshire.

And so through the list with the judge making sure the clerk put the question clearly on Sheila Buckley regarding a unanimous verdict and in her case the answer came back surprisingly, 'No.' I was amazed to hear not a single Not Guilty in her case but I was glad, at least, that she still stood a chance of a favourable majority verdict.

I listened in sheer amazement to the Guilty verdict on count four – the Garrett cheque – he consultancy which I could easily have had in my own name. Guilty, too, on the forgery of the Markham application for a credit card and, shock of all shocks, the Guilty verdict on count twenty-one – the Royal Insurance policy although no claim had been made. As I watched the crowded court – Chief Superintendent Etheridge being congratulated by the man from the D.P.P.; and the row of Scotland Yard officers obviously highly pleased,

— I felt more interested in the extraordinary motivations which caused the result than in my own fate.

The jury were told they were going to a hotel and would be brought back at ten o'clock next morning. Then the clery said, 'Take Stonehouse down; Sheila Buckley continues on bail.' I returned to the cells. Back I went to Brixton with the prison officers in the van saying, 'If you were just Harry Smith of Tooting Bec there wouldn't be all this carry-on. It's the MP after your name that does it. The press tried you and you were pre-judged.'

I said it was all so unjust because, apart from the passport offence which I had virtually acknowledged, although there were special circumstances for it, I *was* innocent. But, in my heart, I felt that if the people of England really needed to express their orchestrated venom on me then perhaps I could still perform some service in accepting the role of the sacrificial lamb.

THE FINAL DAY

After sixteen hours and seventeen minutes, the jury's deliberations came to an end and precisely one minute after four o'clock in the afternoon on Friday, August 6th, the members of the jury filed back into the court. I had spent the day looking through some of the morning papers and playing chess and backgammon with Michael O'Dell and now I steeled myself for final judgement.

As the charges were read to her, the forewoman answered haltingly. On fourteen of the remaining fifteen charges against me (two had already been dismissed and four others had the day earlier attracted verdicts of Guilty), majority verdicts of Guilty were recorded against me (the jury having failed to reach a unanimous verdict on Thursday). Of the charges against Sheila Buckley, five attracted verdicts of Guilty (a majority verdict in each case except on the fourth count which was unanimous). On the twelfth count, the conspiracy charge, both Sheila and I were found unanimously Not Guilty.

That the jury had taken so long to reach their conclusions and the fact that the judge had had to demand majority verdicts because the jury could not unanimously agree on most of the charges, had all combined to heighten the inevitable tension in the hours leading up to the verdict call. Now, feelings of bewilderment and disbelief among many who had followed closely the necessarily complex case, were naturally and sadly evinced in those closest to me in private life.

Following Mr. Justice Eveleigh's sortie into the possibility of funds still being available in Swiss bank accounts, I began my final address to the court:

'I would like to thank judge and jury for their patience in this case, the jury in particular for the very careful way in which they have considered the material available to them. I do appreciate it and realise it has not been an easy case. For the purposes of this statement I accept the verdict – you know my view, but your view as eleven jurors is superior in the event. Thank you for coming to what is for you a sincere and honest verdict. I realise that due to my inexperience of law it has been trying for you. For my part there has been no intent to waste time . . .

'You (the judge) have allowed me a long time to make my statement to the jury and make my summing-up speech. May I ask you to bear in mind, when sentencing, the suffering caused by the whole traumatic affair – suffering largely of my family, close friends and of course myself. I have already been the loser from so many points of view. My career is in shatters and cannot now be recommenced. My position in the public eye is destroyed, and indeed I have now precious little private life left to me. I have at least had the consolation of being able to recover from the breakdown I suffered in the years after 1971, and the terrible experiences of 1974 which gave rise to my aberrant behaviour in that year.

'I ask you to bear in mind my lifetime of work for people here and abroad – long years of altruistic work on their behalf. I ask you to bear in mind also my service to the State, during which I gave of my best, particularly from 1964 to 1970.

'In considering a sentence in any case, you have to consider the deterrent value and the reformation the sentence might bring about for the person convicted. Will you allow me to comment on these two aspects. As far as the deterrent effect is concerned I have lost practically everything I possess, and I think you will accept that the aberrant behaviour of 1974 is most unlikely, if not impossible, to be repeated. I am now shattered politically and in my personal life, and there is hardly anything else I can give up for whatever suffering I may have caused. It is worth noting that no individuals have suffered except family and close friends, and no one has suffered financially from the crimes for which I have been convicted. Your Lordship might also wish to bear in mind that, as I am now stronger and largely recovered from the breakdown I suffered two years ago, I am in a better position to be able to perform some service and this might weigh in your mind . . .'

Lord Wigoder next spoke on behalf of Sheila Buckley, saying that she had not been in trouble before and that it is possible to state quite confidently that she will not appear before a court again. Her entanglement in the case quite clearly has arisen out of emotional involvement. Pressures have been brought on her which must have been apparent during the trial, he said.

Mr. Justice Eveleigh then turned to me. If I had faced up to the situation from the beginning, he said, he may well have been led to accept an explanation that business cares had led to my downfall. 'It may well be that in defending this case every inch of the way as you have done, you had others in mind. I strongly suspect that is the case. But, having done so, as you were entitled to do, a different picture has emerged from that which otherwise might have been presented in this court.' I had, he continued, falsely accused others of cant, hypocrisy and humbug when I must have known my defence embodied all three . . . I had pretended to the jury, when I chose not to give evidence in the witness box, that the withdrawal of bail was a decisive factor when it was 'plain as a pikestaff to any lawyer' that I had made up my mind from the beginning to make a statement 'from the safety' of the dock . . .

'You were not an unlucky businessman escaping from undeserved financial problems,' he said. 'It all arose from your initial devious behaviour, whatever its object may be.' He added: 'I don't think any penalty I can impose will make the slightest difference to the way in which you personally will behave in the future. But I have no reason to think there will be any repetition of these offences.' A deterrent sentence, although the public may be ill-informed, is very rarely expected to achieve much for the individual. The object is to inform others that they cannot profit from this or any similar behaviour, Mr. Eveleigh added before sentencing.

The Sentence

Five years in prison on counts 5 and 8;
Six years on counts 4, 6, 7, 9, 10, and 11;
Six years on counts 14, 15, and 16;
Six years on counts 17 to 21;
Six months on count 13.

The judge ordered that all these be served concurrently, but added a further year for applying for a passport in the name of Markham. Sheila Buckley was sentenced to two years' imprisonment on each of the five charges for which she was convicted, each concurrent, but suspended for two years. Were it not for the fact that he recognised the position she had got into, the judge had said: 'You would be sentenced to imprisonment which you would be called upon to serve here and now . . . One had only to see the manner in which he sought to mesmerise the jury in this court to know he could have told you anything, and while it is clear that you knew the situation, he no doubt persuaded you your duty was to go along with him.'

The speech by the judge in giving sentence was, in view of the way he had come across to me during the whole trial, exactly as I had anticipated. It seemed that not only had I committed certain offences, I had also committed the cardinal sin of defending myself. In taking the course – which is open to any defendant – of making a statement from the dock, instead of going into the witness box, I had also damned myself.

While hoping that some important points that I have made over the past weeks might register among my readers, I realise in truth that now I can only wait for time to heal the wounds.

APPENDIX

On March 21, 1975 I was charged with fifteen alleged offences; some time later the number was increased by a further six. The full list is as follows:

Two counts of uttering forged applications for birth certificates in the names of D. C. Mildoon and J. A. Markham.

Uttering a forced application for a passport for J. A. Markham.

Stealing a Bank of America cheque for $12,500 drawn in favour of Export Promotion and Consultancy Services Ltd.

Two counts of obtaining a pecuniary advantage by deception by obtaining for EPACS overdraft facilities of an increase from £10,000 to £17,500 at Midland Bank and of £10,000 at Lloyds Bank by falsely pretending that his personal guarantee was a guarantee of value and that the facilities were required for the purposes and benefit of the Company.

Five counts of stealing EPACS cheques for amounts of £7,500, £6,981.25, £2,112.10, £3,029.87 and £3,188 totalling £22,811.22.

Conspiracy to defraud the Creditors of EPACS, with Sheila Elizabeth Buckley, on divers days between 30th day of April and 25th day of December 1974, by enabling J. T. Stonehouse unlawfully to receive payments from the said Company in the knowledge that the Company would thereby become insolvent and be unable to pay its lawful debts to its Creditors.

Obtaining an American Express Credit Card in the name of J. A. Markham with intent to defraud by virtue of a forged application and a forged letter of reference.

Obtaining from Barclays Bank travellers cheques to the total value of $870 by deception namely by falsely pretending that he held the Barclaycard, which he then presented in good faith and that he intended to pay for the goods and services which he obtained by use of it.

Two counts of obtaining from National Airlines tickets

value £355.95 and British Airways two airline tickets value £422.65 by deception by falsely pretending that the Diners Club and the American Express cards which he presented were held in good faith and that he intended to pay for the goods and services he obtained by the use of them.

Five counts of attempts to obtain money by deception: on 20th day of November 1974 attempted to enable Barbara Joan Stonehouse to obtain cheques for

    £25,000 from the Canada Life Assurance Company

    £25,000 from the Norwich Union Life Insurance Company

    £25,000 from the Phoenix Assurance Company

    £20,000 from the Yorkshire General Life Assurance Company

    £30,000 from the Royal Insurance Company

by deception, by falsely pretending that he had drowned so that the benefit payable on his death under life insurance policies had become payable by the said Insurers.

Note:

The total of the amounts alleged to have been obtained illegally came to approximately £29,000 and the total of the alleged 'attempts' under life insurance policies came to £125,000.

J.T.S.